Region of the Dead Sea

(FOR DETAIL MAP OF JERUSALEM IN 1948
SEE BACK END PAPER)

170   180   190   191   196   200   150

WADI ED-DALIYEH

MUGHARET 'ABU SHINJEH

KHIRBET MAFJIR

TELL-ES-SULTAN (ANCIENT JERICHO)

JERICHO

ALLENBY BRIDGE

140

WADI QILT

WADI 'ABU GHARABA

ANCIENT ROAD

NEW TESTAMENT JERICHO

SYRIAN MONASTERY AND TRADITIONAL SITE OF BAPTISM OF JESUS

MOUNT SCOPUS

MOUNT OF OLIVES

NEBI MUSA

132½

SAWAHIRA BEDOUINS

Jerusalem

KALLIA

130

CAVE II   CAVE I

El BUQEIA

KHIRBET QUMRAN

KHIRBET MIRD (HYRCANIA)

QUMRAN FARM

AIN FESHKHA

SHEPHERDS FIELDS   IBN 'UBEID BEDOUINS

RAS FESHKHA

124

Bethlehem

Qumran Cave Area

120

HERODIUM

TA'AMIREH BEDOUINS

Dead Sea

Wilderness of Judea

110

MURABBA'AT CAVES

1285 FT. BELOW SEA LEVEL

100

EN GEDI

Jordan

NAHAL HEBER CAVE

1 2 3 4 5 6 7
MILES

90

DRAWN AFTER SURVEY OF PALESTINE MAPS

Israel

After July 19, 1948)

NAHAL TSE'ELIM

80

MASADA

John C. Trever

THE UNTOLD STORY of QUMRAN

FLEMING H. REVELL COMPANY • WESTWOOD • NEW JERSEY

Scripture quotations are from the *Revised Standard Version of the Bible,* copyrighted 1946 and 1952 by the Division of Christian Education, National Council of Churches.

End paper maps suggested by map drawn by Dr. Frank M. Cross, Jr., in *The Ancient Library of Qumran and Modern Biblical Studies,* published by Doubleday & Co., Inc.

TO THREE—
Elizabeth, my wife,
John Paul and James Edgar, our sons—
from whom
the Dead Sea Scrolls have required
incalculable sacrifice and infinite patience

Contents

Preface

DURING the winter of 1946-1947 three Bedouin shepherds happened upon a cave secluded among the rocky crags overlooking the northwest shore of the Dead Sea in Palestine. From a bowl-covered jar the youngest shepherd withdrew three leather scrolls which were destined to create a new era of Biblical studies in the Western world. Through all these many years the story of how those and other scrolls reached the hands of Biblical scholars has remained obscure and confused. As the first American to examine, study, and photograph the documents about twelve months after their accidental discovery, I labored to bring them to the attention of the world. Thus I have maintained an intimate interest in uncovering the details of the drama which surrounded their discovery.

One evening many years ago I was enthralled by the words of the late Dr. Edgar J. Goodspeed, who recounted his experiences with ancient Greek papyrus manuscripts in a lecture entitled "Adventures With Manuscripts." Not long after I became involved in the story of the Dead Sea Scrolls, the full meaning of his title dawned forcefully upon me. These ancient leather manuscripts have produced an adventure as exciting as any mystery story.

When so often during the past dozen years I have been asked, "Why do you not write the full story about the Dead Sea Scrolls?" my stock answer has been, "How can you write a mystery story when the mystery is not solved?" The answer was not entirely facetious. As long as I felt any uncertainties about key points in the story, I hesitated to add to the confusion which already existed from the many conflicting accounts. The knowledge that I had been partly responsible for some of that confusion has further restrained me from publishing anything until the facts could be established.

Several persons who were involved in the original discovery have died; others have chosen to remain silent, while still others have offered information which proved to be distorted or confused, probably from failure of memory. A few have been objectively helpful. Gradually, through the years, I have sifted all the evidence from correspondence, personal interviews, and publications, until now I feel the story can be recorded with a considerable degree of certainty. Sincere and determined effort has been exerted to keep any new errors from creeping into the account. New evidence, of course, will continue to be welcome.

In view of the nature of the story, I have followed the advice of many friends and tried to address this book to as many readers as possible. Since it contains a considerable amount of new information never before published, however, I have felt it necessary to keep the Biblical scholar also in mind. The popularity of the story of the scrolls leads me to believe that the layman will be understanding at those points where some tedious details are included for the sake of accuracy of the record. I shall hope too that the scholar will be patient about the local color and other details which have been included in the interest of the lay reader.

It would be difficult to name all those institutions and persons who have in one way or another contributed to the adventures recounted here, though a few to whom I am especially indebted should certainly be singled out: the American Schools of Oriental Research, which awarded me the fellowship for study at their Jerusalem school in 1947, and which again in 1950 provided additional assistance for manuscript study in England; St. Mark's Syrian Orthodox Monastery and its former Metropolitan, Athanasius Yeshue Samuel, whose telephone inquiry opened the door to my adventures; the International Council of Religious Education (now a division of the National Council of Churches), which generously granted me a six-month leave, with salary, to pursue paleographic research during 1950-1951; the American Philosophical Society, which contributed a stipend to enable me to spend three months of that leave in England and later awarded me their John F. Lewis Prize (1955); Drs. Millar Burrows and William H. Brownlee, who adventured with me in Jerusalem and gave generously of their assistance then and since; Mr. Anton D. Kiraz of Bethlehem, who, through many hours of personal interview and copious correspondence, has patiently endured my incessant questioning and intensive cross-examination to help uncover the facts; the Palestine Archaeological Museum and especially its gracious curators, Mr. Harry Iliffe and Mr. Yusif Saad, who granted me many privileges and generous services during three trips to Jerusalem; Drs. W. F. Albright, Herbert G. May, and Luther A. Weigle, who read the manuscript in an early draft and offered many helpful suggestions.

To my colleagues in the Department of Religion at Baldwin-Wallace College, who have relieved me of extra duties—especially Dr. Ernest Knautz, who voluntarily assumed some of my teaching load during one quarter—I am most grateful; and to the administration of the College, which has provided skilled secretarial assistance in the person of Mrs. Robert Carroll, who has labored over this manuscript without the benefit of adventure.

To one who has patiently endured many repercussions from this adventure, and yet has labored long hours at typing, editing, and research toward improvement of this manuscript, a special measure of appreciation is due—my faithful wife, Elizabeth.

Berea, Ohio

JOHN C. TREVER

List of Illustrations

Color Plates

THE UNTOLD STORY OF QUMRAN

American School of Oriental Research, Saladin R...

February was the sixth month since I had arrived ...
American Schools of Oriental Research[3] for a much ...
archeological study. After three years of teaching Old T...
Bible at Drake University, I had determined that to be a ...
must have a year of study in the lands of the Bible ...
A.S.O.R. fellowship, I was one of the fortunate thr...
1947-1948 academic year in Jerusalem.

With the increased tempo of Arab-Jewish strife ...
during 1947, there was much concern and trepidation a...
over my leaving a wife with two small children and ver...
for ten months. Mrs. Trever and I felt, however, th...
opportunity for an experience so basic to my professio...
had already been frustrated once before in plans for a ...
awarded the Two Brothers Fellowship upon graduating ...
1940. It would be better to proceed on faith, despite t...
concluded.

A Telephone Call
in Troubled Jerusalem

THE books, papers, and filing notes piled around my desk left little room to work, but they were all necessary for studying the trees of the Bible. My interest in this subject had been quickened on that beautiful Wednesday, February 18, 1948, a day that seemed to presage an end to the chill winter which had brought much-needed rain, but great discomfort to the drought-plagued Holy Land. It was a day that also marked the beginning of a great adventure.

The part of Jerusalem that could be scanned from my second-floor window had been washed clean by the torrential rains. Lofty Aleppo pines bordering the School property, gray with dust most of the year, were sparkling green, their uplifted branches etched sharply against the azure sky with its tufts of fleecy clouds. The dense foliage, darkened by the lengthening shadows of the late-afternoon sun, screened from sight all but a few red-tiled roof tops of this newer part of Jerusalem. For purposes of study, this obstruction of the view was beneficial.

The previous October, when I had accepted the assignment to study the flora of the Bible for a class in "Biblical Backgrounds in Palestine," little had I dreamed how complex was the problem of just the trees of the Bible. Was Abraham's camp near

Hebron among oaks or terebinths (Genesis 13
Hebrew *tappuach* refer—an apple, an apricot,
was the sycamore tree that Amos "dressed" (Ar
similar questions, had unduly prolonged my
occupied my attention on that particular afte
proved to be the last day on which much atten
many months.

I could not have been at my desk for mo
tapping on the door disturbed the unusual per
(that is what we all called him, for it was hard to
Jibril), hesitatingly opened the door and asked i
look at his glum, serious face, usually smiling
"Someone wants to know about some ancient
added. When he repeated the word "Hebrew,
conspiracy with the Jews. During those tense day
self-appointed detective to watch for pro-Jewish
visitors. I reminded Omar that in a school of
about Hebrew manuscripts was normal. Were n
concern, I argued? Descending the stairway, I w
hallway just off the dining room, where the te
Omar, apparently still unconvinced, followed cl
that followed, I noticed him hovering within ears

As I lifted the receiver of the old-fashioned t
voice. The speaker said he was Father Butrus So
dox[1] Monastery of St. Mark's in the Old City of Je
he continued, he had been organizing their co
catalogue of them. Among the books he had fou
which had been in the Monastery for about forty
tion about them. He was inquiring, therefore, i
some data for the catalogue.

His reference to "ancient Hebrew" prompte
Hebrew?" Yes, he seemed to think it was. This was
How could the monks have scrolls in archaic Hebrew i
be incredible. Surely he must be mistaken. I qu
obvious that little more could be gained over the
ments—but how?

A vision of embattled Jerusalem flashed throu
City were surrounded by barbed-wire entangleme
lenged everyone who sought entrance. If not obvi
Jew. Even though still somewhat tanned from thr
Egypt the month before, I was obviously not an Ar
areas, received that very morning, would not adi
under another jurisdiction. How could I get throu

After taking my family to stay with my mother in Pasadena, California, I started on August 5, 1947, for New York by train. There I boarded the American Export Lines converted troopship, S.S. *Marine Carp*. Although a "first-class" passenger, I found sixteen men assigned to my cabin! Dr. William Brownlee, another of the Fellows, chose "tourist class" on the same ship; he was quartered with 125 men, navy style, in a large dormitory in what seemed like the hold of the ship. The only virtue the ship could claim was that it provided cheap transportation to the Near East. Needless to say, we both spent most of our waking hours out on deck during the two-week voyage.

At dawn on August 30, I joined the cluster of early risers on deck, intense with excitement over the first glimpse of the Holy Land. A dramatic scene greeted us. In the distance, still shrouded in the residue of the night's darkness and a thin mist, the Plain of Acre spread out like a vast stage whose curtain was being drawn slowly aside. The sun, a red ball of flame, was just breaking through the thin layer of clouds which hovered close to the hills of Galilee. Great shafts of tinted hues darted skyward, as though heralding the adventure that was about to unfold.

Slowly the ship drifted into the broad, sweeping Bay of Acre toward the modern city of Haifa, which splashes over the steep slope of Mt. Carmel. It stands like a sentinel guarding the entrance to what was then the only harbor of Palestine for seagoing ships. The spell was soon broken as the frenzy of docking operations on boat and shore began, punctuated by the shouts of officers, seamen, and longshoremen.

For the next three months, classes and field trips proceeded normally at our School in Jerusalem. We were quite free to move about and managed to visit every major part of Palestine, drinking in each sight and scene with avid delight. The Bible literally came alive all about us. One of the incredible features of the Bible lands that we soon noted was the amazing degree to which their antiquity had been preserved in contemporary scenes. Village life seemed unaltered by the advance of modern civilization. Apart from the few major tourist centers—Jerusalem, Bethlehem, Nazareth—and the bustling modern cities of Tel Aviv and Haifa, the ancient Biblical stories unfolded as if they had happened yesterday. We were soon seized by a deep empathy with the Bible, and each new excursion quickened our appreciation for the privilege that was ours.

Occasionally bombings, snipings, skirmishes, and other evidences of strife among the Jews, Arabs, and Mandate authorities marred the joy of our excursions; but these disturbances only served to emphasize the reality of the Biblical story, which was born in strife and hardship. We soon became used to the sirens around Jerusalem, which sounded almost daily alerts.

When, in early October, the United States pronounced in favor of the *Ad Hoc* Committee's report to partition Palestine, it was answered in Jerusalem with the bombing of the American Consulate. Our movements became greatly restricted. Then, late during the night of November 29, 1947, came the announcement of the United Nations' decision to partition the country. It electrified the tiny land, and the fury of conflict mounted daily. Battles raged almost nightly, particularly in the quarters to the north of our school. Concentration on Biblical research became increasingly difficult.

Located on Saladin Road about half a mile north of Herod's Gate to the Old City, the American School was in the Arab Hussein Quarter, a relatively new part of Jerusalem. Nearby, to the west and northwest, lay the Mea Shearim Orthodox Jewish Quarter. Directly to the north, lying in a valley at the foot of Mount Scopus, was the Sheikh Jarrah Arab Sector. The Nablus Road, which joined Saladin Road in a sharp V at St. George's Cathedral a block north of our school, separated the two hostile quarters. At a vulnerable point a block beyond the Cathedral stood the American Colony Hotel. Many an evening we stood in darkness at the window of the dining-room wing of the School to watch tracer bullets flashing between these two newer sections of Jerusalem and outlining the Cathedral and the American Colony.

During December the tempo of hostilities mounted. On the thirteenth the frightful bombing of loaded buses awaiting departure from the market place at the Damascus Gate numbed us with shock. I shudder to think how narrowly I missed being one of thirty-two injured and thirteen killed when, on the twenty-ninth, the attack was repeated at the same spot. Only five minutes earlier I had strolled leisurely by, stopping to watch a troop of Scottish soldiers parading with their bagpipes past the picturesque Gate.

The strain began to tell on the members of our School. Dr. William Beling, the other of the three Fellows, sent his wife to Geneva, Switzerland, on December 18. Dr. Millar Burrows, the Director of the School, said little but showed obvious signs of growing concern. Notes of reassurance repeatedly punctuated my letters to my wife, written perhaps as much to convince myself as to ease her mind.

For three weeks during January, 1948, four of us students made a "flight to Egypt," where we rejoiced in the peace and freedom of travel. Dr. Beling decided not to return to Jerusalem, but joined his wife in Geneva; the rest of us found our way back with some difficulty. Meanwhile, Dr. Sherman Johnson, Annual Professor at the School, had left with his family for Turkey. By early February, therefore, only three students and the Director and his wife remained at the School in Jerusalem.

The heat of strife increased. On the evening of February 15 we saw bright flares over the Sheikh Jarrah Quarter at nine thirty, introductory to another battle. Although I avoided alarming my wife by relating stories about the troubles all around us, I commented briefly about the situation in a letter dated that same evening:

The situation here is about the same—Jewish attacks, Arab reprisals, or vice versa. . . . Either it [partition] will be enforced by the U.N. with a perpetual state of strife existing, or there will have to be a reversal of policy. . . . The new part of Jerusalem is gradually being reduced to a shambles, and is a tragic sight to behold.

Certainly conditions were far from normal, a factor frequently forgotten by some people who may have known Jerusalem under circumstances other than those of the winter of 1947-48.

It was early that same Sunday, February 15, that Dr. Burrows, his wife, and Miss Ann Putcamp, a student, left the Jerusalem School for a two-week trip to Baghdad. We students had urged the Director and his wife to get away for a respite from the tensions of Jerusalem, for January had been a particularly difficult month there while we had been enjoying Egypt.

Shortly before leaving, Dr. Burrows handed me a letter in which he appointed me Acting Director *pro tem.* Dr. Brownlee and I thus were left alone at the School with the servants. Both of us settled down to the academic projects on which we had been working for some months, hopeful that nothing serious would befall our School during the Director's absence.

My first responsibility as Acting Director appeared the following Wednesday. Omar complained at breakfast that he was unable to get bread under the old ration; a new ration permit would have to be secured. The better part of the morning was therefore occupied in chasing about to various British and Arab officials, seeking the renewal of the ration. Discouraged by the evidences of rising anarchy, I returned to the School and told Omar to use his own ingenuity to get bread. I had failed in my first assignment! But the bread we had on the table the next day was especially good. (I never asked Omar where he purchased it, or how much he paid for it.)

Taking advantage of the trip to the military zone "A" on the southwest side of Jerusalem that morning, I continued on to the German Colony to the office of my friend, Abdullah Ramawi. He had promised to obtain special passes for us from the Arab High Committee. The pass he gave me was to prove of inestimable value in the weeks ahead. On returning I stopped at the American Consulate, near the Y.M.C.A. in zone "B," to visit the consul general and report what was happening at our School.

Because it was such a beautiful day, quite in contrast to the several previous stormy days, the desire to take pictures once again possessed me. There was still an hour until lunch. Returning to the School, I hastily grabbed my cameras and drove to the Palestine Archaeological Museum, where a beautiful wildflower garden provided some excellent subjects.

At the entrance to the Museum one of the guards said that Mr. Harry Iliffe, the curator, had asked to see me. Upon being ushered into his office, I learned that Mr. Iliffe wished me to accompany him the next Monday to the excavation at Khirbet Mafjir near Jericho to take color pictures of an Arabic mosaic recently uncovered. Eager for the opportunity to render such a service to the Department of Antiquities, but totally unaware of the complications my promise would bring the next Monday, I readily agreed.

Returning to the garden, I set my camera for close-ups of the brilliant scarlet anemones. Hardly had the first picture been snapped when a burst of gunfire shattered the silence of the Old City, just across Suleiman Road from the Museum. Being shielded by the Old City wall, I continued to work, stooping low behind the garden wall for double protection. The skirmish did not continue long, so I was able to return to the School only a little late for lunch.

Shortly after lunch Dr. Brownlee and I set out on foot for the Garden Tomb, not far from the School, to take further advantage of the fine day for flower pictures. As we turned on to Nablus Road, I remembered a scene I wanted to capture from the grounds of the École Biblique, the French Dominican school of archeology. A huge mound of earth lay toward the northeast part of their property, from which some ideal photographs of our School and parts of Jerusalem could be taken. We entered the first gate, and a servant at the French school greeted us at the door and led us to the mound. There we were not disappointed, for the view was perfect; besides, the mound was studded with a carpet of bright yellow daisies.

We continued on to the Garden Tomb, a lovely spot carefully tended by a British Christian and his wife, who believed with deep sincerity that the double-tomb chamber in a rock cliff which forms the north boundary of their property was indeed the "new tomb" of Joseph of Arimathea in which Jesus had been laid and from which He arose (John 19:41; see p. 95). We lingered in the Garden, photographing clumps of cyclamen and other early spring flowers which had successfully withstood the buffeting of the late winter storms. On emerging from the Garden we parted, Dr. Brownlee continuing on toward the Old City, where he sought some packing materials for things he would soon be carrying home. I returned to the School and my desk.

It must have been about four thirty in the afternoon when Omar came to my room and asked if I would answer the telephone. As the conversation with Father Sowmy continued, I remembered the distinctive garb of the Orthodox Christian clergy, which enabled them to move freely about Jerusalem. I asked him if he could come to our School. He assured me that he could. "If you will bring those manuscripts here to the School and let me study them," I proposed, "I will promise to give you the information you seek." Then, realizing what a hasty statement it was, I added, "Of course, it may take some time to get the information." He readily agreed to come at my convenience, and I suggested two thirty the next afternoon.

Returning to my room, I pondered the call briefly. Probably the Syrians had a relatively modern Torah scroll or an Esther scroll, I reasoned. On several occasions such documents had been shown to me by friends who thought them highly valuable. I discharged the matter from my mind and returned to the study of trees of the Bible.[4]

2

"Let Your Evidence Lead You..."

THURSDAY dawned dark and cold. I had planned to continue photographing objects in the Palestine Archaeological Museum, but a bright day was essential for good color balance. Remaining at the School, therefore, I took care of some miscellaneous duties and continued the flora studies. A dental appointment, scheduled for ten thirty that morning, had been postponed by the dentist until Friday. We were becoming accustomed to such uncertainties in troubled Jerusalem.

The strenuous activities of the previous day began to tell on me, for after lunch I lay down to rest and fell fast asleep. At 2:25 I awoke with a start, as though prompted by a subconscious reminder of the promised appointment with the Syrian monk from St. Mark's Monastery. Hardly had I straightened the bed a little and combed my hair when, from the window, I saw a taxi arriving at the School gate. Hastening down the stairs, I arrived at the front door as Omar was opening the heavy steel gates, which were now kept locked. I greeted the smiling Butrus Sowmy, whose flowing black robe, the habit of the Syrian Orthodox monastic order, billowed as he walked. With him was a man in a khaki-colored uniform, and wearing a *keffiyeh*[1] draped over his head and shoulders. I took him at first for a British police officer, but soon learned that he was

Father Sowmy's brother, Ibrahim,[2] a customs official for the Mandate government at Allenby Bridge.[3]

I was genuinely happy to greet them, for regardless of what came of the appointment, I had looked forward to the opportunity to get acquainted with another branch of the Eastern Orthodox Church.

Jerusalem, at 2,600 feet above sea level, can get very cold in February. The buildings are stone, and the stone floors retain the cold. How grateful I was for the heavy woolen socks my sister had insisted I pack the previous summer! Only a part of the School could be heated, for oil was very scarce, and electricity, necessary to operate the furnace, was lacking much of the time. The wires into the School were repeatedly severed during the Arab-Jewish skirmishes north of us. Frequently we were obliged to study with only the light from kerosene lamps.

On that particular day, however, we had electricity; and I had warmed my room a little by means of a small electric hot-plate that had been purchased for heating water to control temperature while developing color films in the cold basement laboratory. It may have been as high as 65° Fahrenheit in my room by the time the Syrians arrived. Thinking that it would be more comfortable to discuss the documents there, I invited them to follow me upstairs. When we entered the room, they complained almost at once that the room seemed stuffy, and the monk proceeded to fling wide the window. Out went my precious bit of heat! The Syrians, of course, in their unheated Monastery, were quite accustomed to the chilling cold of Jerusalem's winters. Another lesson in the ways of the East had been learned.

The loss of heat was soon forgotten, however, as I focused my attention on the small leather satchel Father Sowmy was carrying. Laying it on my desk, he lifted the cover and withdrew what looked like a roll of Arabic newspapers. Removing the paper, he handed me a very brittle, tightly rolled scroll of cream-colored leather, less than two inches in diameter. Very gently I pulled back the end of the scroll and saw that it was written in a clear, square Hebrew script, not at all like archaic Hebrew.[4]

Before I had a chance to note more than the somewhat strange character of the script, they lifted from the satchel a large scroll, about 10½″ long and 6″ in diameter, and handed it to me. Removing the Arabic newspaper, I saw that this scroll was made of thinner, softer leather and was much more pliable. It was about the same color as the first one, but with a darkened center, evidence of much handling. It unrolled easily.

Laying the heavy document on my bed, slowly I began to open it. A sheet of leather, containing two columns of text, had become detached from the rest of the document. The linen thread used to bind the sheets together had disintegrated. On the left edge the text was badly blurred by someone who had attempted to re-ink many letters which had been worn away by handling. Obviously this was the end of the scroll. It had been rolled backwards, with the last column on the outside. I continued to unroll another six to eight columns.

Here was not what I had expected! The script was puzzling to eyes more accustomed to Kittel's *Biblia Hebraica* in modern printed Hebrew and a few relatively modern Torah and Esther scrolls. I had expected the identification to be easy, but this scroll was different. It fired my imagination. Suddenly there flashed through my mind the words Dr. Burrows had spoken to me several times as I worked on my doctoral dissertation at Yale University six years before: "Let your evidence lead you where it will." My promise to the Syrians, I realized, would take time to fulfill; the evidence must be studied carefully.

The form of the script intrigued me, for I knew it was the only clue for dating the document before me. Obviously there was no colophon[5] on the last column of the scroll. Remembering that my wife had recently sent me a box of 2″ × 2″ color slides on the history of the Bible text,[6] I took it from the desk drawer and began to thumb through the section on the Hebrew text. The British Museum Torah Codex,[7] I

British Museum Torah Codex (by author, courtesy of the Trustees of the British Museum)

recalled, had been considered one of the oldest extant Hebrew Bible manuscripts. I sought its illustration first. A mere glance at the photograph in my magnifier was convincing enough that the manuscript on my bed belonged to a different category and age.[8]

The next older Hebrew document illustrated was a papyrus fragment (measuring about 3″ × 5″) called the "Nash Papyrus,"[9] inscribed with the Ten Commandments and the Shema' (Deuteronomy 6:4). I recalled that Dr. W. F. Albright had published an analysis of it in which a date in the first or second century B.C. seemed indicated.[10] In the magnifier only a few of the characteristic forms of letters were clear, but the

Nash Papyrus (courtesy of the Cambridge University Library)

enlarged final *mem* (M) and the elongated *kaph* (K) first caught my eye. These forms were very similar to those in the manuscript lying before me. The greater irregularity of the bottoms of the lines on the Nash fragment, as well as on the Syrians' manuscript, was also suggestive of a similar date, I thought.

My heart began to pound. Could this manuscript, so beautifully preserved, be as old as the Nash Papyrus? Such a thought appeared too incredible, but the similarity to the Nash Papyrus was strong evidence leading in that direction.

Suddenly the story of Constantine Tischendorf's experience at St. Catherine's Monastery in Sinai flashed through my mind. In 1844 that great Greek scholar had found in a wastebasket there some forty-three leaves from a Greek manuscript of the Bible, older than any other previously known. In his excitement he revealed to the monks their tremendous importance and worth. It was fifteen years before he was able to see the rest of that now-famed "Codex Sinaiticus," which since 1933 has been the prized possession of the British Museum. *I must not hazard the chance of duplicating Tischendorf's error,* I thought.

Restraining my enthusiasm, I calmly asked the Syrians if they would permit me to take a picture of a column of the larger scroll. They agreed, but then I recalled that the camera I needed was at the Museum, where I had left it the day before, intending to return that morning. All I could do was to copy by hand a few lines from a well-preserved section. The obvious beginning of a paragraph, three lines from the bottom of the fourth column from the end (Column 51), seemed ideally suited for the purpose. Trying to reproduce the form of each letter as carefully as possible, I found my hand unsteady from the mounting excitement. The strangeness of the script to my inexperienced eyes made me especially cautious.

As I copied, the two Syrian visitors began to relate their story of the origin of the manuscripts. It was a former Metropolitan, they said, who had purchased the documents for the Monastery about forty years earlier. Some Bedouins, it seems, had found the scrolls in a cave near 'Ain Feshkha, which is on the northwest shore of the Dead Sea; they were in a jar sealed with potsherds. One of the scrolls, Sowmy said, was thought to contain Isaiah, but he seemed vague about it.[11]

Ibrahim remarked that while working at Allenby Bridge he had studied about the history of Jericho and the Dead Sea area. From his studies he had learned about the Essenes who lived in that region during the lifetime of Jesus. As a result he had become very interested in the Essenes. He had suggested to the Syrians at the Monastery that these documents might have belonged to that ancient sect of Jews and been deposited by them in the cave during a period of persecution, perhaps when the Romans attacked Jerusalem in A.D. 70. Since the scrolls had been "wrapped like mummies" originally, he added, they must be very ancient, for mummification had long since become a lost art. (Some of his facts were wrong, but his inferences were certainly to prove valid.)

Except for these few strong impressions, much of what the Syrians told me that day was lost in my concentration on the copying. I vividly recall, however, how Ibrahim leaned against the window sill as he related his part of the story, and how Sowmy wandered nervously about the room, constantly fingering the string of beads he carried.[12]

With the copying finished, I was bursting with curiosity. I longed for solitude in which to pursue the study of these strange lines of Hebrew. I took time, however, to unwrap the three other scrolls in the satchel to examine them. One was about the same size, color, and texture as the first one.[13] Another was much narrower and on a dark brown leather, inscribed with beautifully clear and large characters. Its entire lower edge had disintegrated or been eaten away.[14] The last scroll they had was too brittle to open. Its advanced state of decomposition on one side gave every indication of great antiquity; it was as dark as the previous one, but much larger. No script could be seen, but a small fragment which the Syrians claimed belonged with it revealed a somewhat different script that was badly disintegrated.[15]

As we rewrapped the scrolls and returned them to the satchel, I assured the Syrians, with as much composure as I could muster, that what they had was of great interest to me. I re-emphasized, however, that it might take considerable time to gather the necessary information they requested. Primarily what they sought, it seemed evident, was confirmation of their belief in the antiquity of the documents. The evidence for dating such manuscripts would demand a most careful analysis, I explained, and would ultimately require consultation with many scholars. They must be patient, I repeated.

Since they needed a taxi to return to the Old City, I ushered them downstairs to the telephone. Father Sowmy made the call, after which we lingered in the garden for a short time as I explained something about the work of the American School.

As soon as the men left, I wasted no time getting back to the slip of paper with its precious lines of Hebrew. As I passed Brownlee's room, I noticed his door was ajar. Seizing the slip of paper from my desk, I rushed to his room to unfold the story.[16]

Brownlee followed me into my room, as I impatiently sought to decipher the passage. As he copied the lines, we noted the double occurrence of the unusual form *llw'*. Literally, it would mean "by not," which seemed senseless at the moment. It was the kind of evidence, however, which could lead to quick identification if the document were Biblical, I decided.

Having borrowed the large Hebrew dictionary from the School library for my flora studies, I turned in it to the common word *lô'*, "not." There were five columns of discussion about it. Quickly I scanned them for the strange form. At the very end was a paragraph which included all occurrences of this form in the Old Testament. A check in my Hebrew Bible on two references in Chronicles revealed no similarity to the context copied from the manuscript. Another reference to Amos 6:13 proved equally futile. The next reference showed *two* occurrences in Isaiah 65:1. With growing expectancy, I hastily turned to it. There, word for word, and almost letter for letter, was exactly what I had copied from the manuscript! It was a scroll of Isaiah, without a doubt! I lost little time communicating the discovery to Brownlee, who was avidly at work on the passage in his room.

Almost immediately my thoughts turned to the task of getting the scrolls photographed. Only by publication and free scholarly discussion could their antiquity be established, I reasoned. What two young scholars thought about manuscripts with such a mysterious origin would not be very convincing to the world of Biblical scholarship, we well knew.

That evening at dinner, our friend Abdullah Ramawi happened to be a guest of Miss Basimah Faris.[17] I told him of the importance of getting into the Old City to visit the Syrian Monastery to see the manuscripts again. He said he would be glad to take me to the Jaffa Gate of the Old City the next morning. There he would arrange to have the pass he had given me two days before stamped by the Old City military official. Then I could get to the Monastery freely.

That evening was spent laying plans for photographing the scrolls, studying the detailed map of the Old City to be sure of the way through the maze of narrow passageways to the Monastery entrance, and recording the details of that eventful day. The certainty concerning the antiquity of the scrolls was growing in my mind, as the words in a letter written that evening to my wife indicate:

I cannot see how it [the Isaiah Scroll] can very well be a fake, however. It would take an artist of extremely skillful ability to produce such a manuscript in modern times. If it is genuine, it may prove to be a sensational discovery. Thus I can't afford to take a chance on it.[18]

Where would the evidence lead me?

The frustration of that night was described in my first published account:

Sleep was almost impossible that night. Numerous questions flooded my mind. How long was the large scroll? How much of Isaiah was there? Could it be authentic? Those few evidences of a corrector's hand on the last twelve columns seemed a certain argument for authenticity. But how could such a perfect manuscript be as old as the Nash Papyrus? Out of sheer exhaustion I fell asleep, still arguing with myself![19]

Events moved so rapidly after my first view of the scrolls that it was several months before I noticed the meaning of the whole passage which had led to the identification of the Isaiah Scroll. Thumbing through a Gideon Bible one evening in a hotel room, I turned to Isaiah 65:1 and was startled to read the ironic words:

I am sought of them that asked not for me; I am found of them that sought me not . . . .

Brownlee in his account, however, remarks, "But, to me, in retrospect, the scroll has said something different:

I was ready to be sought by those who did not ask for me;
I was ready to be found by those who did not seek me! (RSV)

The scroll had been seeking me, but I had successfully escaped it."[20]

3

Convictions Confirmed

DEIR Mar Markos, as its members call it, or the Monastery of St. Mark, is located in the Old City of Jerusalem south of King David Street in the Armenian Quarter. It is not far from the Church of St. James (Acts 12:1-2). This Quarter occupies the southwestern hill of Jerusalem, mistakenly referred to as "Zion's Hill."

The Syrian Monastery surrounds a small, nicely appointed chapel believed by its communicants to be built on the site of the home of John Mark's mother, where, according to Acts 12:12-17, Peter went after his escape from prison. Visitors to the Monastery are shown an early Syriac inscription beside the entrance to the chapel which links the site with the passage in Acts. Exactly how old this inscription is, however, is not easy to determine. Another tradition associates the church with the "upper room" in which Jesus shared the Last Supper with His disciples.

The Monastery is best known for its small but valuable collection of old Syriac manuscripts. It was to this library that I was determined to go on the morning of February 20, 1948.

Breakfast was served at the American School from seven to eight in the morning. As in most schools, the students usually arrived nearer to eight than seven. That morning, however, I entered the dining room at seven sharp and began breakfast alone. Eagerly I awaited the arrival of Abdullah Ramawi, who was to conduct me into the Old City. No one from the School had been there for several months, and the very idea now seemed like a new adventure, to say nothing of the anticipation of seeing the scrolls once again. At eight o'clock Mr. Ramawi had not yet appeared. Miss Faris, sensing my disappointment, offered to help me get to the Syrian Monastery.

It was another beautiful day and I much preferred to walk to the Old City, as usual. Miss Faris suggested we take the bus, which would carry us directly to the Jaffa Gate. At Herod's Gate just south of our School we boarded one of the dilapidated buses. Its ancient engine rattled and groaned, and its body creaked under the load of Arabs on their way to market.

Near the Damascus Gate huge conical cement blocks had been strategically placed in the road on either side of the approaches to the broad market place to keep traffic at a snail's pace for careful scrutiny by armed guards. Our patient driver skillfully zigzagged the bus between the obstacles. A few passengers waited to board the bus; otherwise the great square north of the Gate was deserted. The market place had been moved farther east. At the very place where the two frightful bombings had occurred the previous December our bus paused briefly. The vivid memory of my narrow escape there sent a wave of chills up and down my spine.

Jaffa Road, where the bus line ended, sloped gently from Allenby Square down to the Jaffa Gate through a line of small shops just outside the Old City. Most of the shops that day had their heavy corrugated-steel shutters drawn tight and locked. Several torn shutters, gaping holes in shattered windows, and charred timbers dramatically justified the owners' fears to continue business. Except for the ever-present uniformed Arab soldiers and barbed-wire barricades, the scenes around the Jaffa Gate appeared almost normal. Fridays always brought many fellahin (farmers) and villagers to Jerusalem, for it was the Muslim holy day. Many thousands came to worship at the El-Aksa Mosque in the Old City and to trade in the bazaars.

At the Jaffa Gate we left the bus and were soon lost in the crowd of Arabs pressing toward the heavily barricaded Gate. Armed guards queried everyone who sought entrance. As we stood waiting our turn, I recalled with some amusement the predicament I had encountered at this same spot the previous September. As part of a test for an international driver's permit, a British police officer had asked me to drive into the Old City. At several points the School station wagon was barely able to maneuver the narrow passageways of the Armenian Quarter. On the way out, the jam of people and animals by the Jaffa Gate was so great that the officer left the car and used his authority to force a passageway to the Gate. At that time I had waited patiently, amused at the discomfiture of the officer, who was much annoyed by the delay. Now, however, I was the impatient one, anxious to get to the Syrian Monastery on quite a different mission.

Our turn finally came. Miss Faris spoke rapidly in Arabic to the guard. I sensed that he was reluctant to let me pass with her. He seemed to be arguing with her, as he cast critical glances toward me. I felt helpless, but continued to hope that her powers of persuasion would get us through. Our immediate objective was the Arab Emergency Committee office a short distance inside the Gate. Presently the guard motioned us

Entrance to St. Mark's Monastery

forward, as another guard took me by the arm and guided me through the Gate toward the office. Miss Faris pressed ahead of us, working her way through the crowd and into the doorway of the old building. Once inside, we saw a long line of Arabs, perhaps twenty-five or more, waiting their turns (I learned later) to report their complaints against the Jews. I had visions of a long wait, but apparently the sight of a woman and an armed guard with a Westerner in tow interrupted the proceedings. At the far end of the room the official at the desk motioned to us to come forward.

More rapid Arabic followed, and I recognized words that indicated the discussion was centering around our School and the possibility of its harboring Jews. When the officer motioned to me, I stepped forward and, with a greeting in crude Arabic, handed him the pass which Mr. Ramawi had given me two days before. He studied it carefully, then talked further with Miss Faris who, I am sure, gave me as fine an introduction as I have ever received. Presently the officer stamped the pass, added his signature, and handed it back with a cordial gesture. Thanking him, I clutched the pass with elation. Now I was free to enter the Old City any time.

Once out in the market square, my thoughts returned quickly to the mission ahead. I thanked Miss Faris profusely for what had obviously been a difficult task; from what she told me about the conversation with the Emergency Committee official, she had rendered a service not only to me but also to the American School.

We were soon lost in the crowd of shoppers, merchants, goats, sheep, and donkeys, as we squirmed our way down narrow, shop-lined King David Street toward the small passageway that turned sharply to the right at Christian Street. My study of the route into the Armenian Quarter the night before served me well, for we made each turn correctly in the maze of passageways among the closely-packed stone buildings. Soon we came upon the large gray metal doorway to St. Mark's Assyrian Orthodox Monastery. As I pulled the iron bar to ring the Monastery bell, Miss Faris wished me success and went about her business.

Slowly the heavy door swung inward, and a small boy peered from behind it. I merely said, "Butrus Salmi" (it was not until sometime later that I learned his correct name, Sowmy), and he motioned me into a small courtyard within. Then he closed and barred the cumbersome door. He said nothing, probably assuming correctly that this stranger from the West could not understand Arabic. He motioned to me to follow him up a stairway that led to a second-floor balcony. On the upper level he disappeared through a doorway, and I waited at the head of the stairs with a vague feeling of uncertainty.

Silently I prayed for guidance, that it might be possible to win the friendship and trust of these people about whom I knew so little. Something within me seemed to answer, "Just be yourself." There was not much time for meditation, however, for within a few seconds the black-robed and bearded Butrus Sowmy appeared at the doorway which led into what he called their "office." His greetings were most cordial, though he expressed surprise to see me so soon again. I apologized for coming at such an hour but said that I had found the passage copied from the large scroll to be from Isaiah. He seemed surprised and delighted.[1] I hastened to add that many questions had arisen to make it imperative that I see the documents again. Inviting me into the room from which he had come, he said he wanted me to meet the Metropolitan.[2]

Inside the entrance to the room, I noticed an elderly gray-bearded man, also robed in black, seated on a long couch. (He may have been Father Yusif, though my memory is hazy.) A vision of the Biblical patriarchs flashed across my mind. Behind a small desk in the far right corner of the small room stood the Metropolitan, a dominating, portly figure, his black eyes set deep in a round, jovial face draped with a heavy black beard. I stepped forward to shake his outstretched hand, as Sowmy introduced him as His Grace, Athanasius Yeshue Samuel. His handclasp was warm and friendly, and I immediately felt at ease. He invited me to be seated at the other end of the couch on which the elderly priest sat.

The usual formalities in such a meeting in the Near East involved talk about incidentals until demitasse cups of thick, sweet Turkish coffee had been served all around. While the coffee was being prepared, therefore, I took advantage of the opportunity to inquire about the historic background of their church. Perhaps such a display of interest would help win their friendship, I thought.

In answer to my question about their origin, they emphasized that theirs was the oldest continuously existing Christian church. They mentioned the name "Assyrian" as

32 /

the usual means of identifying themselves. Did that mean they were Nestorians? Their reply was an emphatic "No!" They belonged, they said, to the Eastern Syriac-speaking church which developed in the area of ancient Assyria, and long before Nestorius. Then I asked if they were Jacobites, feeling sure that would identify them. To my amazement the Metropolitan again said, "No!" Their church, he explained, was much older than the Jacobites. It had begun in Edessa (modern Urfa, which is today in southern Turkey, a little east of the upper Euphrates River) very shortly after the resurrection of Jesus. Theirs was the only church which still used the language of Jesus in worship. Now I *was* confused, for all their descriptions indicated the Jacobite Syrian Christians, with whose Bible, the Syriac Peshitta,[3] I was familiar.

Fearing that further questions on this subject might defeat my purpose, I conceded that their explanation had clarified the matter for me, though inwardly I resolved to find some other way to satisfy my curiosity.[4]

Language seemed to be no barrier, though frequently the Metropolitan and Father Sowmy would converse in Arabic. Many times Sowmy seemed to act as interpreter for the Metropolitan. The quality of Sowmy's English had already so impressed me that I frequently found myself forgetting the language situation, occasionally to my regret.

The coffee having been duly served, it seemed a good time to turn the conversation toward the documents I was impatiently waiting to see again. I addressed some questions to the Metropolitan about the story Sowmy had related over the telephone and again in my presence. What was the name of the Metropolitan who had purchased the documents from some Bedouins? There was no immediate answer, as the Metropolitan and Sowmy conversed in Arabic. The name which was finally given—Bishop Phalaxinos Yacob—meant nothing to me, but I jotted it down. A new point was added, however: the Bedouins had first tried to sell the scrolls in Bethlehem.[5]

Their reference to the fact that the scrolls had been found in a jar prompted me to suggest that it would be a great asset to the problem of dating if the jar could be found. It was their understanding, they said, that the Bedouins had taken two jars from the cave to use for water. "Could you contact the Bedouins to see if those jars are still in use?" I inquired. They promised to try.

I inquired about the library catalogue which Sowmy had originally mentioned as the basis of his telephone call. They showed me a book in which were handwritten entries listing the documents in their library. Sowmy turned to the page on which the scrolls were listed and pointed out the need for additional information. In all of this discussion I apparently detected no discrepancies, for early the next morning I wrote in a letter:

I began to pour out questions to the Bishop about the manuscripts. I also wanted to re-check their story. It all fitted together perfectly, with obviously no attempts to conceal anything or make anything up. The Bishop has only been here fourteen months, so doesn't know any more than the rest about the documents.[6]

Then their key question was addressed to me. Had I determined the age of the manuscripts yet? Fortunately, the questions that had flooded my mind the night before were still unanswered. It was easy to be perfectly honest as I pointed out that it would be some time before any statement could be made regarding the age of the documents. With some elaboration I emphasized the difficulties in determining the age of undated manuscripts. One person's opinion would not carry much weight with scholars, especially the opinion of a young (I was then thirty-two) and unknown student. Many scholars would have to be convinced through personal study and discussion.

Here was my cue! Only as the manuscripts were photographed and published could their antiquity be established, I argued. Scholars must debate the evidence before agreement could be reached. I had to restrain myself, for fear of overplaying the point. As casually as possible, I assured them that I would be very glad to invest the necessary time and materials to photograph all the scrolls, adding some comments to the effect that although the materials might prove to be wasted, I was willing to take the chance.[7] Breathlessly I waited while some more conversation in Arabic ensued. Soberly the Metropolitan stated that only very rarely had anyone been allowed to photograph anything in their library. He went on to relate some unfortunate experiences they had suffered as a result of some previous requests.

My heart sank, but a new approach suggested itself. Did they know the story of Tischendorf's discovery of the famed Codex Sinaiticus at St. Catherine's Monastery? Yes, they knew it well, but mostly from the standpoint of that Monastery's dislike for Tischendorf, who, they felt, had cheated them! Quickly I shifted the story to its outcome. Did they know what happened after that manuscript had been published in full facsimile form? Britain paid Russia $500,000 for it in 1933! They appeared not to have known this fact but were obviously impressed,[8] for they asked how the photographing of the scrolls could be done. Would I bring my photographic equipment to the Monastery? It was hard to help them see that such a procedure would be most difficult. I tried to describe some of the equipment that would be needed, and urged that the photographing be done in the laboratory of the American School. At first they demurred, but finally were persuaded to take the scrolls to the American School at nine-thirty the next morning.

Having taken this important step, I was emboldened to ask if I might see the documents again. The Metropolitan pulled a large bunch of keys from beneath his robes and proceeded to unlock several locks on a door almost adjacent to his desk. He entered the room which he called their library (actually an oversized closet), and soon emerged with the small leather satchel which Sowmy had carried the day before. I suggested that we concentrate on the largest scroll.

Sowmy moved a small mahogany table before me and placed the scroll on it. With the loose end-sheet of the scroll removed, I proceeded to unroll it slowly, watching particularly for evidence of corrections which I then believed might give a clue to authenticity, if written by another hand. There were very few insertions in the first twenty columns examined; several of those were obviously corrections by the original scribe. Only three or four single-word insertions indicated corrections by others. Curious symbols appeared from time to time in the margins, but they offered no clue.

Section from Column 33 of Isaiah "A" Scroll, showing later corrections

Almost at the middle of the scroll, three large insertions by different hands suddenly appeared (on Columns 32 and 33), two of them projecting vertically into the left margins. I paused to ponder these carefully. They were not made by the same hand. The one at the upper left was by a less skilled hand. The others were in much darker ink, by a highly trained hand with a beautiful stroke (even better than that of the original scribe). The darker ink immediately suggested a much later addition. But the differences between the hands struck me as incontrovertible proof of authenticity! There were indications of later forms of letters, approaching the traditional Hebrew forms. No modern forger could possibly make such corrections on a forged manuscript and design such developmental differences in density of inks and in forms of letters. No modern forger could know that much about ancient Hebrew writing, I reasoned. *There was no doubt that this was a genuine manuscript.* My excitement rose as the thoughts raced through my mind, but the need for caution steadied me. I continued to unroll the rest of the scroll to see if the beginning could be identified.

Section from Column 28 of Isaiah "A" Scroll, showing later insertion

Column by column the amazing document unfolded before me. More insertions appeared. One large one in a very fine but again much darker ink, by an obviously later hand (Column 28), further strengthened my conviction. A new kind of evidence began to appear, with signs of ancient repairs to the document. A deep tear in the upper left corner of a column (18) had been repaired by gluing a piece of leather behind it. Two columns further, a break in the middle had been sewn together. Another four columns and a huge tear appeared; it had been repaired with both sewing and leather backing (Column 12). *What forger would bother to make this kind of repair?* I argued with myself. The work was obviously too old to have been done by the Syrians, and they assured me they had not repaired the documents.

The last eight columns were badly broken, and I realized there was a repair job ahead before these could be photographed. The darker brown leather was much more brittle than that of the first part of the scroll; the cracks and breaks were numerous. Carefully I worked through the tattered columns, keeping each separated piece where it was, but looking for what might be the beginning column. Finally it appeared, quite badly broken; but the upper righthand corner of it was among the broken fragments, clearly indicated by the upper margin reinforced by a strip of leather backing. Sewing marks at the righthand edge indicated that a cover had been attached. Fragments of it were present when first purchased, the Metropolitan said. The writing was not as well preserved, but I began to copy what was on the fragment, not yet quite certain of the words. My mind was too excited by the accumulated evidence to ferret out the words, anyway.

Suddenly I noticed by my watch that it was almost 10:25, and I remembered the appointment at the dentist that had been postponed to 10:30 that day! The time jerked me back to reality, and I hastily rolled up the scroll and put it back in the satchel as I apologized to the Syrians for having to leave so unceremoniously. They seemed very understanding, and I literally dashed out of the Monastery, and through the narrow maze of passageways out to King David Street. With great strides I leaped from one broad step to the next up toward the Jaffa Gate. I felt as though I were walking on air, but I wondered if my inner joy had been noticed by the Syrians. Had I stayed longer, I am sure I would have burst with excitement.

The dentist was a little behind schedule, so that my tardiness made little difference. The temporary filling he had put in a broken tooth the previous Tuesday was soon replaced. By eleven o'clock I was walking rapidly toward our School, stopping only for a brief chat with the Reverend Walter C. Klein, American Chaplain at St. George's Cathedral, as we chanced to meet near the New Gate. I shared with him a little of my excitement about the scrolls.

Knowing that all my photographic equipment would be needed at the School the next day, I drove the station wagon to the Museum to get it. On arrival at the Museum I discovered that one of the officials was just removing the Jerash[9] artifacts from the exhibit cases to return them to Amman, Trans-Jordan. Here was too good an opportunity to miss, and I appreciated his permission to take color pictures of a few of the objects in his office, where he was packing them. As he came periodically to the office with more objects, I shared snatches of conversation about the scrolls which so dominated my mind. By 12:25 P.M. my supply of film was exhausted. Quickly I packed the equipment into the car to return to the School.

Having promised to pick up Brownlee at twelve thirty for a luncheon engagement at the Y.M.C.A., there was still no time to examine the passage copied from the manuscript. During lunch I did more talking than eating as I shared with our American friends some of the mysteries in which we were becoming involved.

Once back at the American School, I lost little time in examining the words copied from the Isaiah Scroll, with the help of a Hebrew Bible. There, word for word, appeared the very first verse of the Book of Isaiah. There was no heading to the book and no indentation, for the first word began at the margin. The entire book with its sixty-six chapters was included in the scroll! This, too, seemed incredible, for seldom is an ancient manuscript found to be complete.

The afternoon passed swiftly as I made arrangements for the visit of the Syrians the next day and readied the basement laboratory for the photographic work. Brownlee meanwhile searched the School library for resources on Hebrew paleography. A battle raged to the north of the School, and the electric wires were severed once again, leaving us in darkness that night.

After dinner Brownlee brought his kerosene lantern to my room and placed it near mine to provide enough light to study the two fragments of script we now had. Huddled over the two small tables under the pale yellow light, we examined the retouched photograph of the Nash Papyrus in the frontispiece of a book on the history of the English Bible.[10]

Brownlee had succeeded in finding Albright's analysis of the tiny papyrus in the *Journal of Biblical Literature*.[11] The chart of comparative forms of key Hebrew letters from the fifth century B.C. to the third century A.D., including those from the Nash Papyrus, provided our best clues.

My first impression about the relation of the Isaiah Scroll to the Nash Papyrus was gradually confirmed as form after form of these key Hebrew letters seemed to check with those carefully drawn in Albright's chart. Before long both Brownlee and I became convinced that the Isaiah Scroll clearly belonged in the same paleographic period as that small fragmentary document. In his article Albright had concluded that the Nash Papyrus probably belonged to the second half of the second century B.C., and he felt certain that it must be dated in the Maccabean Age (165-37 B.C.).[12]

With the evidence gathered that morning for the authenticity of the scroll, and now the additional evidence to confirm my initial impression that the script belonged to the same period as the Nash Papyrus, we felt completely overwhelmed. Sleep was almost impossible that night as the full impact of our confirmed convictions sent wild dreams racing through my mind.

4

A Day of Days

THE kerosene lantern on my desk cast an eerie yellow light about the room as I sat writing a letter to my wife at dawn the next morning. I began with the words:

I haven't been able to sleep since 3:30 this morning, so at the first streak of dawn I got up and am now going to continue with this letter for a little while, anyway. Unfortunately, we have no electricity, so I am using a kerosene lamp. But soon it will be light, for the sky is clear as a bell. From my window I can see streaks of yellow on the horizon to the southeast. Our wires into the property apparently have been damaged by a recent battle to the north of us. The Saudi Arabia Consulate is also without lights for the same reason. The electricians worked all afternoon yesterday on them, yet had no luck. It is most tragic, since I am counting on light to photograph the manuscripts this morning. Perhaps they will have them fixed by the time I need them.

Carefully I outlined plans for the big day. Successful photographing of the scrolls demanded steady, diffused light. Would we have it by the time the Syrians arrived with the scrolls? That was now a major concern. The day was going to be clear. I could use the light from a basement window, if necessary, but incandescent light would be so much better. Besides, we would have to work fast and accurately to finish in the length of time the Syrians had agreed to allow.

A count of my film supply revealed only thirty-six sheets of 9×12 centimeter "Panatomic-X"[1] cut film and one sheet of "Commercial Ortho." That was not enough to put each column on a sheet, as it should be done. We would have to check the exact number of columns to determine how best to use the limited film. But we should first check the measurements of the documents.

Everything was in readiness in the basement laboratory at the School. A large drawing-board, resting on four color-developer containers and covered with a piece of red corduroy cloth, served as a place to lay the precious documents. Tripod and camera straddled the copy-board, and a floodlight in a diffusion reflector was angled down toward the platform from each side. Such an arrangement was awkward and hard on the photographer's back, but it was the most convenient under the circumstances. A special transformer was necessary to reduce the 220-volt Jerusalem current to 115 volts for use with the American-made photoflood lamps, but fortunately one had been brought by a member of the School for his radio. Its capacity was insufficient to carry the high wattage of such lamps; thus, they could be turned on only long enough to take each picture—if there would be any electricity to turn on!

Since the age of twelve my favorite hobby had been photography. How thankful I now was that W. Ellis Pickett, beloved teacher and Scoutmaster, back in 1928 had suggested my doing an exhibit of beginning photography for a local Scout-a-rama. I was truly a beginner, learning only from instruction books and nightly experiments in the family bathroom. The exhibit did not win any prizes, but it inspired an interest which played a crucial part in my getting through college, seminary, and graduate school. During those later years I had to learn every kind of photographic technique, and particularly copy work, both in color and in black-and-white media. While I was in seminary, the Yale Gallery of Fine Arts provided me a job which involved copying every manner of picture and graph for lantern slides which professors requested for their lectures. Every week end our New Haven attic apartment was turned into a photo laboratory to meet the demand for a dozen or more slides. The discipline of experience had been my inestimable teacher.

Promptly at nine thirty that morning a taxi arrived with our distinguished guests. Dr. Brownlee stood at the door of the School to take a movie as I greeted them at the gate. Father Sowmy, firmly grasping the leather satchel with its priceless contents, was overshadowed by the Metropolitan, who strolled forward, his silver-topped staff of office pacing each step. His jet-black robe parted in the breeze to reveal a gray woolen, full-length gown with a row of bright red buttons from top to bottom. A broad silk vermilion sash divided him across the middle, and a jewel-studded gold cross swayed from a heavy gold chain around his neck. His black, silken, onion-shaped miter glistened in the sun. The two men presented a striking picture of Eastern Orthodox religious habits.

With typical American lack of ceremony we ushered them down the stairs to the basement, apologizing for the lack of comforts and hospitality. After all, it was just a laboratory. They seemed to enter into the spirit of the occasion with alacrity, though a little later Sowmy gently reminded us of the Near Eastern coffee custom. We had forgotten! Brownlee quickly responded with a dash to the kitchen to see if Helen could supply some. She was most obliging.

Formalities were forgotten in our eagerness to get on with the exciting task. We set to work at once to unroll and measure the Isaiah Scroll. Where could it be done? The basement floor, we felt, was not a proper place to lay so important a document. Suddenly Brownlee remembered the roll of wrapping paper he was buying in town for packing when the Syrian call had come on Wednesday. He fetched it from his room, and we cut a strip long enough to accomodate the whole Isaiah Scroll. Each scroll was thus interlined with strips of Brownlee's paper.

We counted fifty-four columns of text on seventeen sheets of leather sewn together with linen thread. It measured 23 feet 9 inches, as far as we could determine, with the broken columns at the beginning.[2] It was immediately apparent that two, and sometimes three columns would have to be put on each sheet of film. Such a procedure offended my photographic sensitivities, but there was no other solution.

The electricians had arrived about eight o'clock that morning, promising to have the current restored by the nine-thirty appointment. Selecting the same column from which I had copied two lines two days earlier (Column 51), I laid the scroll on the prepared platform and focused the camera. The lights flashed on, and we almost cheered—they flickered, and went out again! The electricians seemed to share our disappointment, for one came to explain the difficulty. Quickly we moved the platform, tripod, and camera over near a window, where the sun made a rectangular patch of intense light on the bare floor. It meant readjusting, refocusing, checking for light intensity and exposure. I clicked the shutter for a test exposure. Just then the lights flashed on again. This time they held steady. Back to the original place between the floodlights we moved the equipment again. One more test shot with the precious film had to be taken. Two would have been better, but I was counting each piece.

I dashed to the darkroom, adjacent to the laboratory, where developer, short-stop, and hypo were already waiting in trays to develop the test shots. Since speed was essential, I used a fast developer on the tests, holding my limited supply of fine-grain slow developer for the final negatives. Within five minutes the test shots were ready to examine—both were usable; one was excellent. Now we could proceed with the major task, only being certain that the conditions at the copy-board remained the same.

Meanwhile Brownlee had begun to examine and measure the small scroll to see what problems were involved in photographing it. We knew already the repair work which lay ahead with the first eight columns of the Isaiah Scroll. The smaller scroll measured a few inches short of 5 feet (1.42 meters), made up of two narrow strips (about 5 inches wide) of a coarse, dark-brown leather, sewn together. The beginning was badly disintegrated, with only half of the first column remaining (see p. 94). The lower part over the entire length had been eaten away to large scallops by insects or worms during its long hibernation in the cave. The text on each column was therefore broken along the lower edge. How many columns were lost and how many lines of the beautifully preserved script were missing could only be conjectured. The document would have to be carefully translated and analyzed to determine that.

It was apparent from our check of the Isaiah Scroll that only two places in the manuscript could be photographed by allowing three columns on a single sheet of film. The rest would allow only two columns each. The fifty-four columns would therefore require twenty-six sheets of film, *if no errors were made.*

Since the tests were made on Column 51, I decided to use the extra sheet of "Commercial Ortho" film on another single column. One of my first thoughts on seeing the scrolls had been to get several prints to Dr. W. F. Albright at Johns Hopkins University to see whether he agreed with my conclusion about their chronological relation to the Nash Papyrus. Thus we rolled the scroll to Column 50 and took one more shot. Returning then to the end of the scroll, we proceeded to photograph two columns on each sheet of film.

The process soon became routine; we worked as a team, even employing Sowmy. Brownlee helped move the scroll to each new position and pressed those points which would not lie flat when I was ready to take the picture. Sowmy sat in a chair by the electric outlet to control the floodlights. I adjusted the scroll, centered and checked the focus of the camera, inserted the plate-holder, called for the lights (checking the intensity periodically with an exposure meter), set the shutter and snapped it. When he was not pacing the room, the Metropolitan sat on a tall stool, hands cupped over his staff, watching the whole process with obvious amusement. With only a dozen plate-holders, my periodic trips to the darkroom to replace the exposed film gave the others a few moments to relax.

By noon it was obvious that not even the Isaiah Scroll could be finished before lunch time. We begged the Syrians to remain for lunch. Brownlee hastened to the kitchen to see if Helen could prepare for two guests. As usual, she complied most graciously. When she called lunch about one o'clock, forty-one columns of the great scroll had been recorded. Only one sheet of film had been lost through error, but it was noticed in time to permit a duplicate exposure without delay.

Lunch was a welcome respite from the intense activity of the morning and provided a pleasant hour of ecumenical Christian fellowship. The Metropolitan offered grace in the Syriac dialect of Aramaic, which he proudly announced as the language of Jesus.[3]

Our guests from the Monastery ate with obvious relish. Helen had prepared macaroni, great mounds of which they readily consumed. The tall pile of coarse brown bread on a plate in the center of the table disappeared with amazing rapidity. Omar brought another; it too was soon gone. Tea was served with the meal, but immediately afterward Sowmy reminded me that "His Grace" was accustomed to coffee after lunch. I persuaded them to wait until we had repaired the Isaiah Scroll, for this task was one I did not want to delay a moment longer.

First three columns of Isaiah "A" Scroll, after repairing

While Brownlee worked on the floor with the smaller scroll, I stretched the beginning columns of the Isaiah Scroll on a long table. Scotch tape was all we had to use, but I carefully applied it to the back of the breaks to avoid any possible damage to the script. Setting the various pieces in their proper places was like working a huge jigsaw puzzle. The Syrians stood close by, keenly watching every move. The Metropolitan leaned so close to my shoulder as I bent over the scroll that his beard tickled my neck. I dared not complain! With each successful placement, he uttered an ejaculation of delight.

Finally, every available inscribed piece, except one very small piece containing only five letters (see p. 127), was in its proper place. Much to my disappointment there were still six breaks for which no pieces could be found. The edges of two or three showed evidence of recent tears. I queried the Syrians about the possibility of their having them somewhere else, but they assured me that all the pieces must be with the scroll or in the satchel.

Several small fragments of leather from the outer margins of the Isaiah Scroll, bits of ancient repair material and linen thread, remained in the satchel, and a few had fallen to the table during the repair work. There were a few which the Metropolitan claimed belonged to a "cover" which had been attached to the scroll when he first saw it. These I gathered onto sheets of paper, and the Metropolitan suggested that I keep them as souvenirs.[4]

A taxi was to come for the Syrians at four fifteen; it was after three o'clock before the repairing was finished. Hastily we returned the scroll to the copy-board to continue the photographing. Helen, meanwhile, served the Syrians the promised coffee.

When finished, the Isaiah Scroll took twenty-nine sheets of film; that left only seven for the smaller scroll. The shape of its columns made it quite unsatisfactory to include two columns on each film. With eleven and a half columns to go, however, there was no other choice. The final six exposures were soon completed.

With half an hour to spare, I was determined to take a few color shots. The special camera and plates had been carefully prepared for the purpose that morning, so the shift could be made quickly. Then it was that I made two exposures of Columns 32 and 33, with the rest of the scroll rolled on either side—a picture which has been published probably more often than any other one related to the scrolls. A similar picture of the first four columns was also made in color, the red corduroy background providing an ideal setting.

Finally, there was one more picture I insisted on getting—a record shot of the occasion. Quickly loading my best camera with a roll of color film and attaching the flash gun, I lined up Sowmy and the Metropolitan against the basement wall; focusing and adjusting the camera, I handed it to Brownlee to snap the picture after I ran to join them. Sowmy and I each held a scroll, but the Metropolitan insisted on holding only his staff.

The taxi had arrived. Two scrolls and a small fragment of another had not been touched. I urged the Metropolitan to let us keep them long enough to repair and photograph. They would be kept in the School safe and returned promptly at two thirty Tuesday afternoon, I promised, remembering my Monday appointment at Khirbet Mafjir. Apparently their confidence in us had been won, for they agreed to leave the documents.

As the taxi pulled away from the gate, I slowly returned to the laboratory to put things back in order. I was exhausted. Every move seemed to require more effort than I could muster. It was more than an hour later when I wearily climbed the stairs to my second-floor room and slumped into the chair by my desk. My mind wanted to examine the other scrolls, but my body rebelled. Finally, placing the scrolls in the safe in the School office, as promised, I went to the dining room for a leisurely dinner.

Brownlee, too, was feeling the strain of the day's activities, so after dinner we cleared the dining room table and played ping-pong. We had found this a pleasant diversion so many times during those months when we could not leave the School after dark. About eight thirty, having been rejuvenated by the relaxation, I felt the call of those undeveloped films in the darkroom, and I could not resist.

Father Sowmi, Metropolitan Samuel, and author, holding Isaiah Scroll, February 21, 1948

The room in the basement which was used as a photographic laboratory was really a large closet with a bench around three of its walls, some shelves, and a light-sealed door. Most of its equipment I had brought from home. There was no running water, nor any drain; the nearest source for water was a tap in the courtyard about a hundred yards away. Large metal water jugs were used to haul the water to the room, and five-gallon kerosene cans held the waste. Despite the heavy rains which had broken the long drought of the year before, we were careful to conserve all the water we could. Thus we emptied the tanks of waste water in various places on Mahmoud's lovely garden.

The special fine-grain developer had to be mixed before processing could begin. Only twelve films could be developed in my tank at one time, and it was almost midnight before the first dozen films were hanging up to dry. All were perfect and assured success for the rest. A sense of elation swept through me as I viewed the sparkling-clear negatives, copies of what I firmly believed was the oldest Biblical manuscript yet known to man.

Once again I wearily trudged the three flights of stairs to bed. It had indeed been a never-to-be-forgotten day.

5

Progress Under Pressure

S UNDAY morning I awakened at four o'clock. My mind was racing with thoughts
about the scrolls. *I must have more rest,* I argued with myself, and I tried to relax
both mind and body. By then I could appreciate fully the ecstasy of Tischendorf, who
in 1859, after fifteen years and two additional trips to St. Catherine's Monastery at
Mount Sinai, finally discovered the huge Greek Codex Sinaiticus in a steward's room.
He was allowed to have the bulky manuscript in his own room that night, and avidly he
poured over the vellum folios. Later he wrote, ". . . that night it seemed sacrilege to
sleep."

In Jerusalem during 1948, however, we could not enjoy the silence and peace of
an isolated monastery like St. Catherine's. At exactly 6:24 that Sunday morning a
terrific explosion shattered the brief stillness of the Holy City. Our building trembled. I
bounced out of bed and with one step reached the west window, where I flung open
the shutters. Over the roof tops, like a huge mushroom, rose an ugly black cloud of
smoke. Again the sirens began to wail. Pandemonium broke loose. *The Central Prison
has been bombed,* I thought, remembering that once before it had been attacked unsuc-
cessfully. We learned later, however, that two trucks loaded with explosives had been
parked in front of a hotel on Ben Yehudi Street; they had exploded with frightful

destruction and loss of life (forty-nine people were reported killed). The Christian Lord's day seemed especially chosen for such atrocities by both Jews and Arabs.

There was still an hour after breakfast until guests were to arrive to accompany us to church. Retrieving the negatives from the darkroom, I began to sort and examine them. The single columns were two-fifths as large as the originals, and under my magnifying glass the script became almost natural size. With the actual forms of the script now available for several columns, I was eager to check again my impressions about their relation to the Nash Papyrus. The identification still seemed so incredible.

The previous Thursday when I was examining the scrolls for the first time, Brownlee went to the American Colony to invite Mr. and Mrs. John Whiting to accompany us to the Scotch Presbyterian Church on Sunday and then join us for lunch. These good folks had been so kind to us that we wanted to reciprocate in some way, and we knew it was their custom to attend services in the somber, stone St. Andrew's Church which commands a dominating position overlooking the Valley of Hinnom on Jerusalem's southwest boundary. The Reverend Clark Kerr, then pastor of the church, referred to it as "the church on the brink of hell."[1]

Mrs. Whiting arrived at nine thirty without her husband, who had been detained as a result of the bombing that morning. As I descended the steps from the School courtyard to the driveway by the garage to get the car, suddenly—zing!—a bullet whined overhead, just missing the tile roof of the School. Others followed in quick succession. Puffs of smoke appeared simultaneously near the foot of Mount Scopus to the northeast. Shielded by the garage, I dashed to get the School station wagon.

We drove to the church by way of military zone "B," taking the road past the American Consulate and King George Avenue. We had been accustomed to taking the Jaffa Road past the Jaffa Gate and across the bridge at the Birket es-Sultan; that route, however, led through the now treacherous Montefiore District.

Although we had special zone passes to admit us, we had to register with the guards at each zone. One hundred yards from the church we registered for zone "A" and were given slips which permitted us to enter the zone "for prayers."

Though the day was gloriously bright, the unheated stone church was uncomfortably cold. During the singing of the hymns, I was amused to note puffs of frosty breath emitted from the singers' mouths! With a sermon most helpfully suited to the troublesome times, the silent meditation of the communion service, and the warmth of fellowship in the lounge afterwards, our jangled nerves were quieted. We returned to the School, refreshed and thankful.

Mr. Whiting joined us for the lovely lunch prepared by Omar. We had not known, however, that the Whitings could not eat oranges, which had become our almost-daily dessert. I inquired of Mahmud whether anything else might be available, and he said there was nothing. My look of disappointment was more than the faithful gardener could bear, and a few minutes later he brought a Jericho banana for each guest (he had gone to a nearby store to buy them in the interim!). This was the kind of service of which the American School could boast from its loyal Arab servants. Even the Ameri-

Zion's Hill from tower of Church of the Redeemer

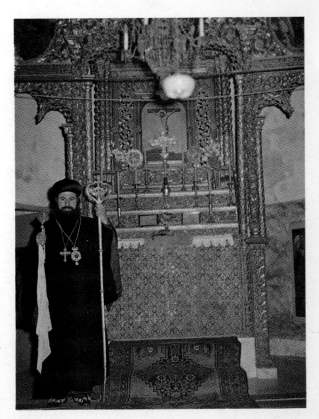

Metropolitan Samuel beside altar of St. Mark's Chapel

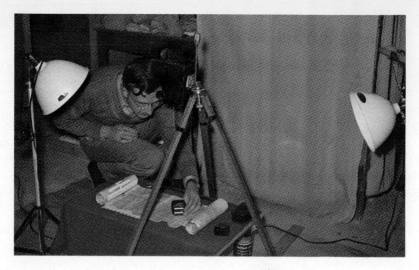

Author photographing Manual of Discipline in A.S.O.R.

Isaiah "A" Scroll opened to columns 32-33

can consul general, whom I visited the previous Wednesday, had expressed envy over our good fortune with such enterprising servants.

The youthful exuberance of both Brownlee and myself, of course, bubbled over with excitement concerning the scrolls during the dinner-table conversation. After lunch I took one of them from the safe to show our guests, gently pulling back only a few inches of the larger one to reveal a little of the writing. It had already been apparent that great care would have to be exercised to avoid further damage to the brittle leather.

Within a few minutes of our guests' departure, I hastened to the task of examining and repairing the two scrolls. Looking like altar candles, and not much larger, the cream-colored rolls immediately impressed me with their similarity of color and texture. Carefully I began to open the smaller one, only to find that severe cracks and complete breaks were frequent. It was obvious from the newness of the breaks that the scroll had not been very carefully handled. The unusually high humidity of the winter months, however, apparently had softened the leather sufficiently to allow careful opening.

All the Scotch tape in the School had been used to repair the first two scrolls. Adhesive tape was the only other possibility. It would strengthen the cracks greatly, I reasoned, and if applied to the back it could in no way harm the text, despite the unorthodox procedure. I systematically raided all available first-aid kits. A strip of tape was placed on the back of each major crack, most of which covered the entire 9½-inch width of the scroll.

The first scroll contained only four columns of text on two sheets of leather sewn together with what looked like the same kind of thread as found on the Isaiah Scroll. One sheet had three columns, and the other a partially filled single column. The first column was badly broken and demanded much repair. Its beginning edge was torn and quite irregular, though none of the text was missing. The upper right corner showed some stitching, which indicated that previous columns had been attached. A strange angular symbol appeared in the margin to the left of the first column. Along the left edge of the last column, obviously the end of the manuscript, were stitching holes, which indicated that some more leather had once been attached.[2] With the entire scroll unrolled, its cracks and breaks strengthened with tape, I left it opened on the table while I turned to the other one.

The second scroll was obviously longer, for there were more turns of leather to be seen at the ends. Its first column, though broken across the middle, was much easier to open. Stitching holes along the right edge implied the possibility of previous columns, or perhaps a cover.[3] The wide outer margin of the first column seemed to argue that this might be the beginning of a scroll. The first line of the text was unreadable, for scallops cut deeply into the text at the top as well as the bottom. They were not as severe, however, as those on the lower margin of the smaller scroll.

After the cracks in the first two columns were repaired, the rest of this scroll began to unroll more easily. Only small cracks needed reinforcement. While repairing the first two columns, I noticed that the script of the scroll appeared identical to that on the

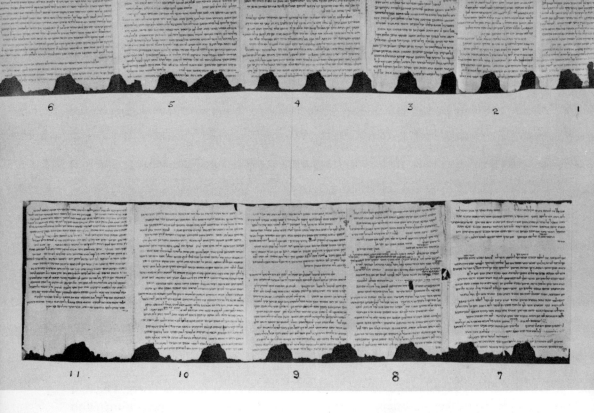

Complete text of "Manual of.Discipline" (1QS), after completion of repairing

other one. The same scribe must have copied this manuscript! Perhaps the two scrolls were related.

Three columns of text appeared on the first sheet of leather; and the next two sheets, which were opened before me within a matter of minutes, had two columns each—a total of seven columns on three sheets.

Suddenly, at the very end, the final evidence for the relationship of the two scrolls appeared. All along the upper half of the left edge the stitching thread was still in place where another sheet of leather had broken away; a fragment from the adjacent sheet, about an inch long and a quarter of an inch wide, was still in place. Along the whole lower half of the same edge a half-inch strip of leather, also from the other sheet, remained stitched in position. Traces of two letters were on the very edge. Here were the missing pieces from the beginning of the other scroll!

Quickly I placed the end of the second scroll against the broken beginning of the first one. Every piece fitted perfectly! Besides, the fragments of two letters completed the letters at the beginning of two lines of text. A marginal mark at the beginning of a paragraph also was completed by the join. There was now no doubt about it—this was all one scroll with eleven columns of beautifully preserved text.

Carefully I pressed the broken beginning edge of the first scroll down onto the left half of the adhesive side of a strip of tape. Then, to match the end of the other scroll accurately, I started at the bottom with the two broken letters. Pressing the broken end gently against the adhesive, gradually I worked up the column to be certain that every point was joined correctly. The two scrolls were now one! The five Syrian scrolls turned out to be four![4] Since we then had no idea concerning its contents, we simply called it "Jerusalem Scroll #1" (today it is called the "Manual of Discipline," or 1QS).

There was no time to attempt an identification of the manuscript, for I was determined to photograph it first. Supper would be called within a short while, so I hurried to the basement to prepare copy equipment and films for that important step. But then I remembered—there was only one more sheet of the proper kind of film left!

Exactly where I found some more film, my memory and my records fail to indicate. That the entire eleven columns of the scroll were photographed after supper that evening is clearly stated in my records. From somewhere eleven sheets of "Kodak Super-XX Panchromatic" film appeared.[5] By midnight all the negatives for this scroll were drying in the darkroom. Though made on film which I would normally reject for manuscript copying, this set of negatives, ironically, proved to be the best of all.

The Museum station wagon was to stop for me at eight thirty Monday morning for Mr. Iliffe's project at Khirbet Mafjir. Somewhat reluctantly I prepared to fulfill this commitment. With gadget bag filled with camera and supplies, I sat on the front steps of the School at the appointed time—no station wagon appeared! As the precious minutes away from the manuscripts ticked away, my impatience mounted.

Fortunately, a pleasant diversion appeared across the street: a large flock of fat-tailed sheep and black goats, shepherded by two Bedouins, was approaching. With movie camera in hand, I dashed across to the field to record this pastoral scene in the heart of Jerusalem. The flock came directly toward me, providing an unusual opportunity for close-ups. With gesticulations, a few words of Arabic (including the all-important word *bachshish*), and expressions of friendship, I persuaded the shepherds to pose with their flocks. With a dozen feet of film recorded, suddenly a shout from behind prompted me to turn about. Some hundred yards away, his arms waving wildly, an Arab raced toward me, his white *keffiyeh* flapping behind his head. Other than the *keffiyeh*, he was dressed in Western business clothes, and it was English I heard spoken when he came closer. He was very agitated and was scolding me for taking pictures of the shepherds, who continued to stand quietly with their animals gathered around them.

The gist of the tongue-lashing he gave me was that American tourists liked to take pictures of Arab Bedouins and then belittled the Arabs when they returned to America. Restraining my own rising anger at the rude intrusion and misrepresentation of my intentions, I stopped his flow of invectives. As reassuringly as possible, I emphasized to him my love for the Arabs and my genuine concern for their welfare. I surprised myself with the eloquence of my little pro-Arab speech. His anger seemed to abate, and he turned to the shepherds as I proffered them a few piasters. What he said in Arabic to them, as he motioned them away, I will never know; but to me he said, "Please don't be mad at me." I assured him all was forgiven.

It was 9:45 when the Museum car finally arrived, the driver quite apologetic over the delay. Besides the driver, only the Museum photographer and a visitor from England were in the car; Mr. Iliffe had been detained. I was disappointed, for I had hoped to discuss the manuscripts with him. We had not been long on the way, however, before I bubbled forth with statements concerning my work on the scrolls.[6]

The respite from my long confinement in Jerusalem added to the pleasure of the trip to Jericho. It was my first opportunity to see the spring flowers in their native habitat, a sight for which I had longed. Splashes of green speckled with red anemones and yellow daisies bedecked some of the Judean hills. Soon, however, as we sped down the tortuous Jericho Road, the grass and wild flowers were confined to a narrow strip along each side of the road. The wilderness we were entering was perpetual. This was the rugged terrain made famous by the Galilean Carpenter who began a parable, "A man was going down from Jerusalem to Jericho . . . ." Deep gorges, rocky crags, barren slopes, and desert sand greeted the eye in every direction. The black ribbon of road twisted like a snake down toward the Dead Sea, with numerous blind corners which might harbor waiting bandits. The speed with which the driver maneuvered the sharp, plunging turns made me wonder if he expected the parable to be repeated. Recent ambushes along that road gave him good reason to be fearful.

Once in the great plain of the Jordan, we continued through Jericho without stopping. The sight of huge bougainvillea vines, etched against the distant barren cliffs of the Judean plateau and surmounted by a brilliant sky, whetted my photographic appetite. On we sped past 'Ain es-Sultan (Elisha's Fountain), which supplied ancient Jericho with water, and Tell es-Sultan, the great deserted mound of Canaanite Jericho. A mile to the north, we left the main road and soon found spread before us the fascinating ruins of Khirbet Mafjir, the eighth-century A.D. Umayyad winter palace of Caliph Hisham.

The archeologists and their assistants welcomed us and escorted us to the great mosaic-floored bath, some ninety feet square, which had just been cleared. It was the smaller mosaic, discovered the year before and a few paces to the west, however, that was my photographic assignment. A temporary gabled metal roof had been erected over the reconstructed walls to protect the beautiful mosaics laid out to simulate Persian carpets, even with corner tassels, on the desert sand. My problem was how to get up near the top of the roof in order to get the photographs. We decided to stretch two large beams between the two main rafter trusses and place a large drawing-board on them to form a platform on which to work. The draftsman had to stop his drawing while I borrowed his board.

With camera and flash gun dangling from my neck, I scrambled up the roof supports onto the beams we had placed there. Inching my way along, I pushed the drawing-board ahead until the right position for the first of the mosaics had been reached. Later I commented in a letter, "I may have looked like a monkey, but I would have been grateful for the dexterity of that animal under the circumstances!" What I did not know at the time was that the beams and rafters were covered with dust-filled creosote, and I had worn some of my better clothes for the occasion!

By the time I was certain that the best possible pictures had been obtained, considering the circumstances, it was twelve thirty; the station wagon was to leave for Jerusalem at twelve forty-five. Hastily I took a few general scenes of the large, newly-discovered mosaic, promising to return at a later time to do that mosaic more carefully for the Department of Antiquities (that promise could never be fulfilled). Needless to say, under those circumstances there was no time to talk with the archeologists about manuscripts.

As the Museum car emerged from the palm-lined streets of Jericho onto the straight open road to the south, I noticed in the distance a long line of armored Jewish potash trucks ascending the road from the Dead Sea on the way up to Jerusalem. I pointed out the line to the driver and he too sensed the problem that lay ahead. On that circuitous road through the Judean hills we would be slowed to a snail's pace by those trucks and in danger of snipers who often ambushed the convoys. The driver's foot pressed the accelerator to the floor as he attempted to get to the junction of the two roads before the convoys. Three trucks had already started up the mountain road before we darted in ahead of the fourth one. It was some comfort to see armed British Tommies sprawled over the bags of potash, keeping watchful eyes on the dangerous road. With skillful maneuvering by our driver, the station wagon finally careened past the leading truck. Soon we could relax, to enjoy once again the variegated terrain of the wilderness of Judea.

We arrived in Jerusalem in time for a late lunch. A brief nap after lunch helped me recover from the strenuous morning, and soon I was back in the darkroom to develop the rest of the negatives of the Isaiah Scroll. By dinnertime all the films had been processed and readied for final washing. There had not been a single mishap!

Washing and hanging large numbers of sheet film is a tedious process, and hazardous without special frames; it is easy to chip and scratch the delicate emulsion. Thus after dinner it was late before all the negatives were safely hung to dry. There was still one project that had to be done before morning, when I planned to make color photographs of the repaired scroll which had to be returned to the Monastery that day. But the color films taken of the Isaiah Scroll, I felt, had to be developed first, so that I could be certain the factors being used were accurate.

Experience had shown that to obtain accurate color pictures, one must develop the latent images as soon as possible after taking the pictures. To process color films, however, an exacting series of fourteen steps must be followed. It had never been done in Jerusalem before; therefore, I had assembled the necessary equipment in the American School basement that previous September. A trunkful of supplies and equipment had been brought to process the 150 rolls of Ansco Color Film and twelve dozen sheet films I planned to use.[7] Since all the required solutions must be held to an exact 68° temperature, the fall months had posed a major problem of chilling the water which came from the tap and was far above the required temperature. During the winter, on the other hand, the water was too cold. By February, processing of color films had become a routine, so that I could count on completing each batch—either four rolls or twenty-five sheet films—in a little over two hours.

It was already after ten o'clock when I started the process on twelve sheet films, including the ones used for the Isaiah Scroll the previous Saturday afternoon. Brownlee meanwhile was in his room trying to decipher the difficult script on the small fragment of leather which the Syrians had left with the two scrolls. Periodically he came to the basement to report on his progress and interpretations. By midnight I was so weary that I appealed to him to help with the final steps on the color films, particularly to bring water from the courtyard tap and to haul the heavy cans of waste water to the garden.

As one by one I pulled the transparencies out of the final fixing bath, my weariness was overcome by elation. Every one was perfect! There was the Isaiah Scroll in full natural color!

6

More Problems

MY last day before leaving Des Moines, Iowa, the previous July had involved the usual frenzied scramble any family with small children experiences before a major move. Helpful friends graciously invited us into their home the night before, since we had to move all our furniture to storage. To complicate matters, an important discussion about a new position had to be scheduled for that last morning. The officers of the International Council of Religious Education,[1] who were in Des Moines for their annual meeting, wanted to discuss with me an opening which had developed on their staff. In anticipation of the appearance of the *Revised Standard Version of the Bible* about 1950 (it actually appeared September 30, 1952), they were seeking the services of an "educational representative" to the Protestant churches. They wondered whether I would consider such a position.

With my mind focused on getting my family to California and myself to Palestine, I found it difficult to evaluate the sudden proposition. To give up my trip to the Holy Land to begin the job at once was unthinkable, I emphasized. The position could wait, they said. It meant leaving teaching; I had been engaged in it for three years, and I loved it. At the time, therefore, I could only assure the officers that the proposition was interesting and that I would give it careful thought while in Jerusalem. On August 9, while on the way to New York, I stopped in Chicago for another brief discussion with them.

During the subsequent months I had weighed the idea carefully and decided it was the kind of service I would like to render. In the meantime, some doubts had arisen about my being invited to the position after all; others were also being considered. Perhaps an awareness of the competition served to sharpen my enthusiasm, for I began to feel some apprehension over the long delay in the matter. By February no decision had been reached in the Council headquarters in Chicago.

All thoughts concerning such matters had now been erased from my mind by the appearance of the manuscripts. It was while I was hard at work Monday afternoon (February 23, 1948), developing the negatives of the Isaiah Scroll, that a cablegram was brought to the darkroom door. It had been sent from the States on February 18, five days earlier, the very day my adventure began.[2] In it were the words which a week before I was anxiously awaiting —an invitation to join the Council staff. Now, however, the message came as another interruption in the midst of an exciting discovery.

After a rapid reading I set the cablegram aside to continue the all-important developing. My decision would be seriously complicated by the manuscripts, I realized. Such a position with the Council would demand much travel, frequent lecturing, but little time for research. The manuscripts would demand much time for research and quiet study. But the idea of being related to the Standard Bible Committee and sharing with the members the oldest known Old Testament manuscript seemed to lend an element of providence to the proposition. I decided to "sleep on it."

By six thirty Tuesday morning I was in the darkroom gathering up the finished negatives of the Isaiah Scroll and the color transparencies. Each negative had to be identified, labeled, and filed in its proper order, a task more complicated than I had anticipated. Without the original scroll before me to determine the proper order, it became necessary to match overlapping sections of columns near the edges of the negatives. Repeated examinations of the negatives led to a growing conviction that they would not produce adequate prints for a quality publication. *Would it be possible,* I pondered, *to get some 13 × 18 centimeter sheet film to rephotograph each column on a sheet? Even if the film could be secured, could I persuade the Syrians to let me have the Isaiah Scroll long enough to do the job properly?* Such a request would take diplomacy, and time was running out! These thoughts gave birth to a determination to begin the diplomacy that afternoon, when we had promised to return the other scrolls.

The Isaiah Scroll color transparencies developed the night before had proved that my data for color-copying was accurate. It was a routine matter, therefore, to make a full-color record of each column of Jerusalem Scroll #I.[3] The small leather fragment with disintegrated script was also reproduced in color at the same time.

There was even time before the promised return of the manuscripts to the Syrian Monastery at two thirty to make color transparencies of the famed "Gezer Ostracon,"[4] which was kept in the safe at the School. Found at the ancient site of Gezer, west of Jerusalem, the small piece of pottery is incised with three of the earliest known alphabetic letters, probably written about 1,600 B.C.[5]

To be doubly certain of a safe return of the precious manuscripts to the Syrian Monastery, I had arranged for the Syrian *kawas* (footman) to meet Brownlee and me at the New Gate to the Old City, which entered off Suleiman Road just north of Allenby Square. By using that entrance we could avoid the hazardous Jaffa Gate so near the embattled Yemen Moshe Quarter. Immediately before leaving for the appointment, we paused at the entrance to the School long enough to complete our records with some movies of the scroll. Wrapping it carefully, we started for the Monastery. Brownlee carried a large, thin volume of the published Chester Beatty Papyri,[6] with which I hoped to impress the Syrians concerning the need for quality publication.

By-passing the perilous Damascus Gate, we cut across the open field opposite the School, crossed the Nablus Road, and continued through another vacant field to the Arab Musrara Quarter along Godfrey de Bouillon Street. We usually called it "Gazelle Street," since we had seen a baby gazelle there several months ago. Lined with modern Arab homes and shops,[7] this street joined Suleiman Road about a hundred yards north of the New Gate and almost adjacent to the property of the huge Convent of Notre Dame. At this point the Old City wall reaches its most westerly extension and surrounds an area dominated by Christian monasteries and churches, as well as the Latin, Greek, and Armenian patriarchates.

The New Gate was a huge, steel, double door which could be opened to allow large vehicles to enter the market place just inside. Now, however, the Gate was barricaded with masses of coiled barbed wire; only a small door, a section of the large one, was used for admittance. As we emerged onto the stone-paved market place, two men dressed in khaki stepped forward to greet us and motioned to us to follow. The rough, narrow corridors between towering stone walls provided a feeling of security. Our guides seemed to know almost everyone we met. No one questioned us. The guides knew no English, and our few words of Arabic were soon exhausted, so we walked in silence. Aware of the diplomatic move I was planning and the need for restraint, I sought guidance in prayer.

At St. Mark's Monastery we were greeted with extremely cordial expressions by Metropolitan Samuel and Father Sowmy. With the usual formalities (including demitasse coffee) ended, I launched into the discussion of the scrolls and the next steps to be taken. Unrolling before them the repaired scroll, I explained how the two scrolls had fitted together. They seemed delighted with the news.

One thing they most wanted to hear, of course — what we really thought about the antiquity of the scrolls — was the thing I most cautiously refrained from revealing. I reiterated a promise, made earlier, that I would provide them with a written progress report as soon as possible.

With appropriate introductory remarks, I showed them the Chester Beatty volume. This is the kind of publication that should be undertaken with their scrolls, I emphasized. But such work demands patience and considerable investment, I continued. To avoid revealing my firm convictions, I punctuated every sentence with *in sha' Allah* (a common Arabic expression meaning "If God wills") and such expressions as "providing your manuscripts prove to be what I hope they will." Brownlee sat discreetly silent, or occasionally added a word of endorsement to my remarks.

Another prime concern about the scrolls was their safety in wartorn Jerusalem. It seemed strategic to discuss this matter, too. They argued that their Monastery was as safe as any place. I was not at all convinced. The library in which they kept the scrolls was separated by a wall only three feet thick from the Jewish Quarter of the Old City, one of the worst trouble spots in Jerusalem. They assured me that there were rooms down beneath ground level in the Monastery where the documents could be secreted without possible danger, but I thought of the dampness of such places and what it would mean to ancient leather. Further discussion of this problem seemed fruitless.

Turning the conversation to the tightly rolled scroll from which it was believed the small fragment had come, I urged upon them the importance of having it opened by experts in America. Its advanced state of disintegration would demand the most careful treatment, I emphasized. Asking to see that scroll again, I mentioned that a hunch had come to me as I was developing the color films the night before. When they laid it before me, I turned the small fragment of leather which we were returning with the scroll upside down and checked the edges of a large broken place on the scroll with those on the fragment. The fragment's edges revealed fresh breaks. The Syrians bent close with intense interest. Suddenly the very place from which the fragment came was apparent! The fit seemed perfect. This fragment did indeed belong to that scroll, and thus provided evidence for the nature of its script. Something about the script—more likely it was the state of disintegration—led me to think then that this scroll might be older than the others. Although later I became less confident of the place of matching and abandoned any ideas of its being older, this bit of added drama during our interview appeared to strengthen the Syrians' confidence in us.

With the main items of discussion completed and the scrolls returned to their satchel once again, the Syrians invited us to examine their library of rare books. It was indeed an impressive collection, though most of the volumes were late medieval Biblical and religious treatises in Syriac, the sacred language of their church. A Syriac copy of the Gospels, with eight colorful miniatures, dated 1222, whetted my photographic appetite. Its illustrations of medieval art, I urged, should be photographed in color. A similar request had been denied a staff member of the Palestine Archaeological Museum, Sowmy said, and then added, "But we may give Dr. John the privilege." This testimony of their confidence made me rejoice.

Of passing interest at the time was a large dark leather scroll, the only other manuscript in scroll form that we saw in their collection. About twice the size of the Isaiah Scroll, it was quite similar to several Torah[8] scrolls I had previously seen. As a student at the University of Southern California many years before, my first contact with a Hebrew scroll had been one which Professor John G. Hill had secured for the collection in the Doheny Memorial Library. It was a small dark scroll of Esther which Professor Hill had claimed dated from the eighth century A.D. I later learned that no Hebrew manuscript with such features had been known to date from before the thirteenth century. Noting some of these same features on the large scroll in the Syrian library, I immediately concluded that it must be relatively modern.[9] It was clearly not related to the ones on which we were working. Sowmy commented that this scroll had not been found with the others.[10]

Bidding farewell to the Monastery *kawas* at the New Gate, Brownlee and I returned by the route we had come. There was much to discuss. We were certain that the events of the afternoon had been providential. The warmth of feeling expressed by the Metropolitan's handshake as we parted convinced me that his confidence had been completely won. My prayers had been answered! An overwhelming sense of responsibility gripped me, and two days later I wrote in a letter:

The degree with which they were convinced amazed me, and I think i have them in the right frame of mind to do most anything. It will be terribly important, however, to maintain strict confidence and absolute integrity.

Another diversion kept me from the manuscripts that evening, for the films taken at Jericho had been promised to the Museum as soon as possible. The results of the color-developing that evening, however, were so amazing that I did not begrudge the time loss. About ten thirty Brownlee came to the darkroom to talk—just in time to help carry out the wash water. He followed me to my room and sat down on the bed to explain his understanding about the telephone call the previous Wednesday. The unanswered cablegram lay on my desk; letters had to be written, and I was impatient to get to work on them. Brownlee's attempt to clarify what had actually happened, therefore, failed to register.[11]

Borrowing his typewriter, I set to work on the letters, a chore that always took twice as long as it should. I tended to write too much, anyway, and now there was much more to relate. As I began, a terrific battle raged in the Old City, adding to the confusion of my mind. I was still typing feverishly well past midnight, when the mounting number of errors finally prompted me to stop.

On Wednesday morning an invitation to visit the Haram esh-Sharif (literally it means "Sanctuary of the Noble One"), the sacred area which surrounds the great Dome of the Rock where Solomon's Temple once stood, again tore me away from work on the scrolls. Through the gracious intercession of Anwar Khatib Tamimi, then Secretary of the Muslim Supreme Council, the Director of the Haram, Ismail el Ansan, had granted me permission to take whatever photographs I wished. Such an opportunity was too good to miss. The elegant Dome, with its glazed blue exterior tiles emblazoned with quotations from the Quran in white stylized Arabic script, and its richly decorated interior, was a photographer's paradise.

With the darkroom work pressing for completion and detailed letters to write, there was no opportunity for leisurely study of the manuscripts that afternoon. More color films had to be developed. That evening the tedious task of printing three copies of each of the manuscript negatives was begun. Brownlee developed the prints while I manned the printing-box. By eleven o'clock, when I sensed that my uncomplaining assistant was catching cold from the chill of the basement room, we stopped. Dozens of prints were ready for washing. Those from the test negatives were washed and put on plates to dry, to be ready to send to the United States the next day.

A dental appointment near the post office the next morning at ten thirty prompted me to eat an early breakfast and finish the letters that must accompany the cables carrying my decision regarding the new position. I had hoped to write a letter to Dr. W. F. Albright, also, but the hour of the appointment drew near. Taking stationery, pen, and envelopes with me, I set out for the dentist's office near Allenby Square.

Chaplain Klein was on his way to town at the same time, so we strolled along together discussing the scrolls and the Syrians, whom he also knew very well. At Allenby Square we parted. The dental work did not take long, but I was there long enough to share a little of my experiences with the scrolls. Apparently I radiated my feelings more than I realized, for while the dentist was working he said, "You are the first happy man who has been inside my office since November!" As I left he added, "I think you must be the only man in all of Palestine with a real joy in living!" As a Palestinian Arab he had good reason to be pessimistic, and I hoped that my own joy provided a tiny ray of light in the midst of his gloom.

At the post office I sent a cable of acceptance to the Executive Director of the International Council of Religious Education and one to my wife informing her of my decision. Having posted the letters, I sought a quiet corner of the building to write the good news about the manuscripts to Dr. Albright. In a scrawling hand and with cautious reserve, I wrote to the world-renowned scholar:

Enclosed are some sample prints from a manuscript which I have discovered here in Jerusalem in Dr. Burrows' absence. . . . If you are right about your dating of the Nash Papyrus, then I believe that this is the oldest Bible document yet discovered! . . .

My first thought when seeing these scrolls was to get them photographed and a copy to you for study. I firmly believe the script cannot be later than the 2nd Cent. A.D. (Dura Fragment), and it has some indications to show it may be earlier than the Nash Papyrus. I am so busy with the photographing of them that I can't take time now to make the careful study that they demand for more accurate dating. I am personally convinced that their age is great. . . .

. . . I know you will understand my concern about the safety of the MSS, so will keep this absolutely confidential. Should there be an announcement now, there is great danger that they might be destroyed.

With less reserve I also wrote the same day to my good friend in California, Dr. Edgar J. Goodspeed:

The most exciting thing, however, is my chance discovery of what I am convinced are the oldest Bible documents yet found. The most important one is a complete scroll of the Book of Isaiah with very few lacunae! If Dr. Albright is correct in dating the Nash Papyrus in the 2nd century B.C., then this is as old or older!! . . . Unless I am entirely no good as a paleographer this discovery should create a sensation in the

United States. It is for one thing the first ancient Bible MS. found *in Palestine*. Its provenance is claimed to be from the Dead Sea area. I am tracing the story as best as possible. . . .[12]

The first news of the discovery was now on its way to the United States, but not for publication.

7

A Frantic Search
for Film

APPEARING much like the bar of a British pub, or an American tavern, the darkroom shelves at our School were stocked with all the liter-sized wine bottles I could beg or borrow for my chemical solutions. Some of the corks still wafted an odor of the contents they once sealed; many of the labels still proclaimed this or that brand of fine vintage. Penciled notations, however, now indicated the contents as "First Developer," "Color Developer," or "Bleach."

For the sake of economy in time as well as space in my luggage, I had purchased gallon-sized containers of the three key chemical formulae required for color developing. Once the dry powders were put into solution, the two developers and bleach had to be used within two weeks to assure quality results. Even then, they had to be sealed in tightly stoppered bottles to prevent oxidation. Wine bottles proved to be the only proper-sized ones available for the purpose in Jerusalem. The rest of the chemicals needed for the process could be easily weighed out as needed from bulk supplies.

The time limit on the last batch of chemicals had almost expired. To utilize the remainder of these chemicals, therefore, it was necessary on Thursday and Friday (February 26-27, 1948) to concentrate on color developing.

Some studying could be done during the processing, I had found, as long as one hand could be free to agitate the films in the tanks. A timing clock prevented me from getting too engrossed in study. It was hardly a scholarly procedure, but a new theory was growing in my thinking about the date of the Isaiah Scroll, and I sought every possible moment to consider it.

During Thursday afternoon, while developing some more of the sheet films, I began another review of Dr. Albright's article about the Nash Papyrus. The peculiar "looped *alephs* and *taws*"[1] of Nash were puzzling. They did not appear on the Isaiah Scroll, so far as I could tell. Was this a scribal idiosyncrasy, or a later development, or possibly an earlier?

When developing sheet films, I seldom knew which pictures were involved until the first development had been completed. Turning on the lights for the second exposure, I discovered among the films some columns of Jerusalem Scroll #I and those of the small dark fragment. On the latter I noticed evidence that the disintegrated script seemed to show more clearly than on the original fragment. Since the script was reversed on the transparency and still opaque, however, such an impression had to await completion of the process. During the final fixing bath, when I eagerly drew one of the transparencies out of the tank and held it to the light, my impression was confirmed. The script was clearer than on the original fragment![2] Perhaps now we could make out the contents. The words *'nsh' l'r'* clearly marked the beginning of a sentence, but what did they mean? These forms were not familiar from Hebrew. Could they be Aramaic? There was no time to check. The processing had to be finished.

That evening, while processing two rolls of the Haram pictures, I returned to the further study of Dr. Albright's article. His "Class IV" discussion included some fourth-third-century B.C. Hebrew papyri from Edfu in Upper Egypt.[3] Some of the letter forms from these papyri, included on Albright's chart, impressed me as being closer to the Isaiah Scroll than to the Nash Papyrus. The *aleph* (A), *kaph* (K), perhaps *mem* (M), *nun* (N), and especially *taw* (T) seemed to suggest that our scroll might be somewhat older than Nash. This might put it as early as 200 B.C., I reasoned.

What was going on in Palestine about 200 B.C. that might account for manuscripts being hidden in a cave by the Dead Sea? The name Antiochus Epiphanes presently came to mind. A Seleucid ruler of Syria in the early second century B.C., he hated the Jews and persecuted them. I seemed to recall that he particularly sought to destroy Hebrew manuscripts. It was he against whom the Judean Maccabees arose in revolt. Could these manuscripts have been secreted in the cave by some Jews who feared the destruction of their sacred scrolls at that time? It seemed like a perfect historic situation to account for the early script. This would really make the discovery fabulous, I suddenly realized.[4]

The bell on the time clock suddenly jerked me out of the age of Antiochus. Color processing had to be exact! A few minutes later the two rolls were finished. On them were the pictures from inside the Dome of the Rock; their beauty was startling. With the films still dripping wash water, I dashed up the stairs to show them to the Secretary of the Muslim Supreme Council, Anwar Tamimi, who was a temporary resident at our

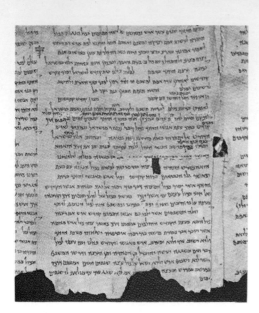

"Manual of Discipline," column 8

"Habakkuk Commentary," column 7

"Genesis Apocryphon" with fragments

Large fragment of "Genesis Apocryphon

Dr. Burrows and his students at the A.S.O.R. library in Jerusalem

A.S.O.R. visit to Haram esh-Sharif, October 1947

School. His delight was exuberant. Perhaps he could contact the *Life* magazine correspondent (whom we had met at the Haram the day before) and suggest he do a story with these pictures. Intrigued by the idea, Anwar promised to pursue it in the morning.[5]

It was late, but I had just remembered the negatives of Jerusalem Scroll #I. Nothing further had been done to identify it. Tired as I was, I set to work with magnifying glass held against the back-lighted negative of Column #I to try a translation. The first two lines were so broken, I started in the middle of the second, where the text became continuous. "To do the good and upright before him, according as he [the subject was obviously God] commanded by the hand of Moses and by the hand of all his servants the prophets . . . ," I laboriously deciphered, checking and double-checking the form of each letter in each word. With only consonants and no vowels to be sure of the pronunciation of the words, the first reading of an ancient Hebrew manuscript is often tedious.

As more words became clear—"evil," "doers of good," "to do truth and righteousness and justice"—sayings in the Wisdom literature seemed to be suggested. I thought of Proverbs and Ecclesiasticus in the Old Testament and the Apocrypha. The documents sounded like Scripture; but after repeated checks, I could find nothing in the Bible that followed the exact words. It was well past midnight when my eyes would focus no longer on the fine script, and I dropped into a heavy sleep.

A more practical problem continued to plague my mind. The Isaiah Scroll must be rephotographed. Where could the proper film be found? Suddenly that night I remembered a scene in the Palestine Archaeological Museum the week before. While photographing the Jerash objects in one of the offices there,[6] I had noticed in the nearby shipping room a long wooden box being unpacked. Dozens of packages of fresh 13 × 18 centimeter film had just arrived from England! It was a British film ideally suited for copying manuscripts. I had been told that it was ordered for the detailed copying of the huge mosaic floor uncovered at Khirbet Mafjir. Could I persuade the Museum authorities to let me buy some of that new film to rephotograph the Isaiah Scroll?

I decided to approach Mr. Iliffe the next morning. Having done him a favor by taking the Khirbet Mafjir mosaics in color, I reasoned, perhaps he would return the favor now. Taking the beautiful mosaic transparencies, a half dozen or more prints of the Isaiah Scroll, and some of the small scroll, I set out for the Museum shortly after breakfast the next morning.

The Palestine Archaeological Museum commands a dominating position on a high prominence overlooking the northeast corner of the Old City of Jerusalem. Its white sandstone hexagonal tower and broad exhibit-gallery wings are glaring to the eyes in the intense Palestinian sunlight. It is an impressive sight from near or far. A gift of John D. Rockefeller, Jr., to British Mandate Palestine during the early nineteen thirties and built at a cost of one million dollars, it is one of the finest museums in the world. With utmost patience and amazing ingenuity Mr. Harry Iliffe, the curator, aided by a few others, skillfully planned each exhibit. The two naturally lighted exhibit-galleries, radiating from the large entrance rotunda, spread before the visitor with artistic décor the archeological remains from a vast history of the Holy Land—from most ancient paleolithic to medieval Arabic times, about 75,000 years of human habitation in that area.

We at the American School were privileged with passes, which we seldom had to show, to use the Museum galleries and library for study at almost any time without the usual entrance fee. Our travel opportunities having been so greatly restricted, we found the galleries a constant source of challenge and stimulus to our archeological interests. Brownlee and I had examined intently every item in the exhibit cases. We studied carefully the elaborate descriptions and historical information in guide books provided in Hebrew, Arabic, and English.[7] Already I had been allowed to make color photos of almost a hundred objects, a priceless collection of lecture illustrations. The Museum was a part of us, and we almost a part of it.

Although my conversations with the Syrians had revealed a reticence on their part toward the government Department of Antiquities (whose offices were in the Museum), I saw no reason to refrain from discussing the manuscripts there. The logical question—why the documents had not been known to the Department of Antiquities before—failed to enter my mind. I was not a detective.

When I inquired for Mr. Iliffe at the outer office that Friday morning, I was informed that he had left suddenly for Baghdad. R. W. Hamilton, Director of Antiquities, was in, and I asked whether he could see me. In a short time one of the guards ushered me through a small door marked "Private" and down a long corridor to Mr. Hamilton's office. The guard politely announced my arrival as we entered a large paneled office made cozy from the chill of winter by a briskly-burning fire on an open grate. A chocolate-colored dachshund, curled on a rug before the fire, stirred as we entered.

Mr. Hamilton, whom I had met casually on several previous occasions, arose from behind a heavy walnut desk well stocked with books and papers which bespoke a scholar at work. A somewhat slight, wiry, sandy-haired Britisher, he had impressed me as a dedicated scholar without the usual distant austerity. His cordial, personable greeting made me feel at ease. As he offered me a chair beside his desk, he beckoned to the guard to bring coffee.

We wasted little time with formalities. Handing him the color transparencies from Khirbet Mafjir, I asked if he would see that they were delivered to Mr. Iliffe. He expressed much delight over the results and thanked me profusely, all of which encouraged me to launch into the manuscript story.

Placing several of the prints of the two scrolls on his desk, I began to unfold with unrestrained, youthful exuberance all I knew about them. The fact that it was my understanding that the scrolls had been in the Syrian Monastery for many years, of course, was included. I emphasized my conviction that, on the basis of paleography, the scrolls must date from at least as early as New Testament times, and even mentioned my new theory about Antiochus. He examined the photographs closely and seemed to be pleased with what he saw and heard.

Pointing to some of the prints containing more than one column, I explained the problem of enlarging them to their natural size for adequate publication. Then, with some hesitation, I mentioned having noticed the large shipment of fresh film received by the Museum a week earlier. Would there be a possibility, I inquired, of my buying about seventy sheets of this film to redo these two scrolls? Hopefully I awaited his reply as he examined the prints further. He took a few sips of coffee, then began to explain the importance of that shipment of film to the Museum. It was probably the last they could obtain from England, with the circumstances in Palestine so rapidly disintegrating. There was barely enough, furthermore, to complete the Khirbet Mafjir mosaics. My heart sank.

As I shared more of the story, and he examined print after print, I continued to hope that he might, after all, change his mind about the Museum film. He suggested several places in Jerusalem where he felt certain I could obtain the necessary film. Finally, after almost an hour, I was convinced that there was no more hope. Thanking him for his suggestions and refreshments, I started back to the School.[8]

It was not quite eleven o'clock when I arrived back at the School that morning. There was just time to finish the rest of the Jerusalem Scroll #I color films, if I hurried. Enough developers remained for one more batch. Hastening to the kitchen, I asked Helen to delay lunch a few minutes so I could do these films. The results were perfect; that scroll was now thoroughly recorded. Always my concern for the safety of the scrolls lent an urgency to the photographic process. Perhaps the original scrolls, lying so close to the disputed Jewish Quarter, would be victims of the repeated bombings any day, I reasoned.

Except for some further translation of Scroll #I late that evening—now with the aid of the color transparencies—the rest of that day had to be devoted to letters, following up the cables sent the day before. Many personal problems, greatly complicated by the manuscript discovery and the acceptance of the new position, had to be discussed with my wife, who was eight thousand miles away. To record all that was happening in Jerusalem as well demanded many hours of writing.

Washing and drying the great mass of prints we had made Wednesday evening continued into that same day. The primitive method we were forced to follow for washing prints made it a laborious chore. Many changes of water on the prints required frequent interruptions of whatever I was doing. Among the last prints put out to dry that afternoon were the rest of those from the smaller scroll (then called Jerusalem Scroll #II).

That evening I gave a set of Scroll #II prints to Brownlee. He immediately went to work on a translation.[9] It was then he discovered the key to the scroll which linked it with the Book of Habakkuk. The second line on the first full column (Column 3) begins, "For this is what it says . . . ," and follows with the last phrase of Habakkuk 1:6

and all of verse 7: ". . . to seize habitations not their own. Dread and terrible are they; their justice and dignity proceed from themselves." Then comes the phrase, "Its meaning [or interpretation] concerns the Kittim . . . ," and continues with an application apparently to contemporary history. At intervals Brownlee came to my room to report his discoveries of quotations from the Book of Habakkuk scattered through the columns. Each quotation was followed by an interpretation. The scroll was apparently some type of commentary on Habakkuk! During the next weeks Brownlee spent many hours of work on the translation of the entire document.

By nine o'clock the next morning I was on my way to the Old City to begin the search for film. Proceeding to Allenby Square, I turned down Jaffa Road. Midway from Allenby Square to the Jaffa Gate was a small photo shop owned by the personable C. Raad. He was the logical first contact, Mr. Hamilton and I had agreed; his skillful photographic work was much appreciated by scholars and laymen alike. Having been a photographer for Allenby's army in 1917, he knew Jerusalem like a book. He could converse with almost anyone who entered his shop, for he knew the basics of about fifteen languages. Already I had come to appreciate him as a trustworthy and warm friend, as well as a helpful businessman.

As I entered his shop (one of the few still doing business along Jaffa Road), the short, stocky, gray-haired Mr. Raad was bustling about, waiting on a number of customers. While waiting my turn, I studied the display of pictures mounted on the walls and under the glass counter-tops. Many of them were scenes taken during the British conquest of Palestine in the First World War. After the last customer left, I related to Mr. Raad the important project for which I needed his help. He had some 9 $\times$ 12 centimeter film, he assured me—enough to do all the Habakkuk Commentary properly—but he had no 13 $\times$ 18 centimeter film. He very much doubted that any could be found in all Jerusalem. He suggested, however, that I visit a certain shop in the market place inside the Jaffa Gate. They ought to have some, if anyone did, he said.

I asked him to hold the 9 $\times$ 12 centimeter film for me and continued on down Jaffa Road to the Gate. My pass was all that was necessary this time to gain a quick entrance. Being Saturday, there was little activity in the market square. At the shop no encouragement for my quest could be given. Another shop was suggested, down King David Street and among the suqs (covered streets in the bazaars, a characteristic feature of many oriental cities). There I was told the same story, but this shopkeeper said he thought he could get some film for me if I would come back in a few days.

It was already past noon when I started through the Old City toward Herod's Gate. At each photo shop among the suqs I stopped with the same request. Several dealers assured me they would get some film if I would come back in a few days. Footsore and discouraged, I finally made my way back to the School.[10]

That afternoon I persuaded Brownlee to abandon his study of the Habukkuk manuscript photographs and assist me with the rest of the prints of the Isaiah Scroll and Scroll #I—the "Sectarian Document," as I began to call it, since it was religious but obviously not Biblical. We chatted and theorized about the scrolls as we worked, following the same system we had used the previous Wednesday evening. Each print was numbered on the back to facilitate assembling later. Prints began to pile up; every tray was put to use. By four o'clock many more prints had been exposed than were developed. Brownlee was then handling six prints at a time in the developer. Suddenly we heard the crunch of tires on the gravel driveway—it must be the Director returning from Baghdad, we agreed.

Leaving Brownlee with his hands deeply immersed in developer, I dashed out through the garden to find Dr. and Mrs. Millar Burrows emerging from Mr. Abudi-yeh's green Studebaker. Without consideration of their feelings after the long, wearisome trip, I urged Dr. Burrows to come to my room at once. It was very important, I insisted. Dr. Burrows seemed a bit bewildered by my sudden outburst. He complained of being tired and pleaded for a chance to get a cup of tea.

Stopping by the darkroom, I announced their arrival to Brownlee and told him that I was going to my room to prepare for Dr. Burrows' visit. Brownlee agreed to continue developing the exposed paper. Bounding up the stairs three at a time, I hastily laid my plans. Already I had begun to assemble a set of Isaiah Scroll prints into a small scroll by trimming a group of the prints to match, attaching them with Scotch tape. About a third of a scroll was in one continuous strip. This I laid out on my desk. Then a set of Habakkuk Commentary prints were laid side by side in proper order. Only a few prints of the "Sectarian Document" were available, but they were laid out with a miscellany of others, including some color transparencies. With lamp adjusted for best light and a magnifying glass ready, I impatiently awaited the sound of steps along the corridor.

Remembering the efforts Dr. Burrows had put forth on my behalf in connection with the new position so recently accepted, I located the cablegram. Just then I heard the sound of steps outside my door. Offering Dr. Burrows the easy chair placed beside the desk, I handed him the cablegram.

Hardly had he finished the sixty-six words of the message when I launched forth with the manuscript story, much of which I am sure was lost from my torrent of words. When I paused momentarily, Dr. Burrows inquired, in a fatherly tone of voice (perhaps trying to calm my flow of words), "What have you done about this?" and pointed to the cablegram. The decision to accept, I began, was complicated by these manuscripts, but I had finally sent it. "Remember, John," he cautioned, "you cannot eat these documents." At the moment his words seemed almost facetious, but the passing years have proved their wisdom.

He began to examine some of the prints with my magnifying glass, as I returned to their story and my reasons for believing that they represented the most ancient manuscripts of their kind known. Finally I paused to give him a chance to respond.

Continuing to examine them, slowly and quietly, and with characteristic scholarly caution, he queried some points concerning the paleographic basis of my enthusiastic claims. Pondering some of the prints further as I pressed the paleographic arguments, he finally terminated the discussion by pointing out that certainly the manuscripts were important and should be published as soon as possible. He assured me that the A.S.O.R. would back such a publication. Agreeing to go with me to see the manuscripts at the Monastery the next Monday, he turned the conversation to other matters relating to our two weeks alone at the School.

As Dr. Burrows left, I suddenly remembered Brownlee still at work in the basement and returned to the darkroom to relieve him of the monotony of developing prints. We finished the printing after dinner that evening. A total of almost 250 prints from seventy-eight columns on the three manuscripts and one fragment had been completed. We now had three complete copies of each of the scrolls, even though for two of them I was still not satisfied with the quality. The search for more film had to continue.

8

The Truth is Revealed

EVEN Jerusalem's weather seemed to be trying to hold back the mounting fury of strife, as winter continued to delay the approach of spring. Another blanket of cold settled over Jerusalem on Sunday, the last day of February. At St. George's Cathedral I huddled close to a small stove beside a great pillar in the bone-chilling stone structure. Despite the din of gunfire just north of the church, I found the solemn prayers and intoned chants of the formal service were quieting to my overcrowded mind.

After the service Mrs. Bertha Vester of the American Colony invited me to lunch. Brownlee joined us for a pleasant afternoon with the members of the Colony.[1] It was a day of much-needed rest. Not until that evening did I turn again to the matter of the scrolls.

To satisfy Metropolitan Samuel's impatience for the results of our study, I had promised him a written preliminary report as soon as possible. It now seemed important to prepare it. That evening I started to draft a statement which would give some of the information he sought, but emphasized mainly our continuing interest and assurance of full cooperation. Brownlee's and my convictions concerning the antiquity of the scrolls, however, I deliberately omitted. Since it appeared that Dr. Burrows was unconvinced, my earlier concerns about persuading scholars had already been confirmed. It would not be dishonest, I reasoned, to refrain from revealing my own convictions to the Syrians.[2] The document was completed early the next morning (March 1).

Before leaving for the Monastery to show Dr. Burrows the scrolls, I finished splicing together the prints of the Isaiah Scroll. This miniature scroll, I was certain, would impress and delight the Metropolitan. In the meantime Dr. Burrows went to get a pass from the Arab Higher Committee to gain admittance to the Old City.

At the Monastery we were most cordially received, as usual. Presenting my statement, I explained that it was merely a "preliminary report" to keep them informed of our progress. The Metropolitan's enthusiastic reaction to the miniature scroll made from the photographs justified my efforts to construct it. Though less than a third the size of the original, it made an impressive scroll which could actually be read if one's eyes could stand the strain. A set of prints of each of the other scrolls was also presented to him.

The Syrians readily offered to show Dr. Burrows the scrolls. He examined each one intently but with very little comment. When he came to the small fragment belonging to the fourth scroll, he noted the letters *l'r'* and exclaimed, "This is Aramaic!" What I had thought might be true while examining the color photograph the previous Thursday, and had failed to follow up, now was confirmed. The large, tightly rolled scroll, to which I was still confident this fragment belonged, must therefore be Aramaic. The full import of that little discovery was to be long in coming to light, unfortunately (see p. 131).

Having been assured by a photo dealer in the Old City the previous Saturday that a supply of large film could be obtained, my next move was to convince the Metropolitan that a second set of negatives for the Isaiah and Habakkuk scrolls was necessary. Opening the small scroll of photographs to illustrate the great magnification that would be necessary, I urged him to allow us to redo the two scrolls with large film. Dr. Burrows agreed that we should strive for a high-quality publication and lent support to my urging. He assured the Syrians that the A.S.O.R. would provide the necessary funds to carry out the project properly. The Metropolitan maintained some hesitancy, but we left feeling that the point had been won.[3]

With the manuscripts now available to us in photographic form, we agreed that the courses begun the previous October should be dropped, except for Dr. Burrows' lectures on the topography of the Bible. On alternate days, therefore, we concentrated all our academic efforts toward translating the scrolls. Dr. Brownlee worked on the "Habakkuk Commentary," and I on the "Sectarian Document." Since October, Brownlee and I had studied Hebrew epigraphy under Dr. Burrows' guidance. We had worked through the Mesha, Siloam, and the other earliest-known Hebrew inscriptions. The Christmas holidays intervened just as we had begun to translate the Ugaritic Keret Legend[4] from photostats made for us at the Museum. All these sessions had been a valuable prelude to these new studies. Now we met every other afternoon for almost two hours to discuss the scrolls. Seldom has a graduate seminar had the exciting privilege of analyzing ancient Biblical manuscripts never before translated. Ours was unique.

Sometime early that week an incident occurred in the School library which assured me that Dr. Burrows was rapidly becoming convinced about the antiquity of the scrolls. While seeking some published Hebrew paleographic evidences, Dr. Burrows and I were checking the shelves when he found a reproduction of the Dura Fragment.[5] Pointing to some of the letters, he remarked, "Your scrolls are certainly older than this." His cautious approach to the matter was a testimony to his pre-eminent scholarship.[6]

Between classes that week I spent most of my time in the Old City making the rounds of the photo shops to see if any 13 × 18 centimeter film had been found. It soon became apparent that every photo dealer was scouring every other photo shop to get the coveted film. The question was, who would discover some first? Monday afternoon and Tuesday morning (March 1 and 2, 1948) I heard the same story—"We will have some by tomorrow." When I went to Raad's shop Monday afternoon to get some trial enlargements he had made of sample negatives from the three scrolls, the urgency of my quest for film was punctuated: the enlargements were disappointingly poor.[7]

Discouraged by the constant unfulfilled promises, on Tuesday I went back to Raad's to get the 9 × 12 centimeter film he was holding for me. He was delayed in his darkroom when I arrived, so I went to see a banker friend about getting some Palestinian money to pay for all the photo supplies. Having lost my Crusader cross, which a shopkeeper had given me months before as an expression of his concern for my safety, I went to Kort's Curio Shop and bought another. (Even the most militant Muslims and Jews would not stoop to wearing a cross.)

Early Wednesday morning I was again in the Old City. One shop had been particularly certain that the film I wanted would be available. As I entered the shop, the proprietors were beaming with cordiality. Their smiles soon gave way to apologies; the film was not there yet. They pleaded with me to wait a little while; a boy had just gone to get it. They served me coffee and tried to make conversation, but I paced the shop impatiently. Presently the boy burst into the shop, gleefully waving two boxes of film.

I examined the gray unfamiliar boxes. "Gevaert, Studio-film, Ultra Panchro Normal, made in Belgium," the labels read. "This is portrait film," I exclaimed, as once again my heart sank. Furthermore, I needed six dozen, not two. This was the only kind of film available in all Jerusalem, they claimed. They had scoured the city thoroughly. Four more boxes would be there the next day, they assured me. But then my eye caught a stamped date on one of the boxes—"1 Sep 1947." My disappointment exploded. This film was long outdated, besides being good only for portraiture! Whoever heard of photographing ancient manuscripts on outdated portrait film?

Trying to conceal my disappointment, I groped for a decision. *Should I give up, or try using such impossible film?* I had worked with films unsuited to specific jobs before. Perhaps this film could be adapted to the situation, I reasoned; and six months was not too long after the expiration date, if the film had been in a cool, dry place. I decided to take the chance.

How much did they want for it, I inquired? One Palestinian pound[8] per package was the immediate reply. I was dumbfounded. Normally, outdated film could be purchased for half-price in the States, and film as far outdated as this would be thrown away by any respectable dealer. But here they were asking twice the normal price! I wondered if they stated this price to begin the usual Oriental bargaining.

Offering them half a pound per package, I emphasized the worthlessness of the film, but they were adamant. They did not want to bargain, I could quickly see. Realizing that business was at a standstill without tourists in troubled Jerusalem, I did not have the heart to press the matter. They were as desperate as I was. I paid the £P2 and promised to return for the other four packages the next day.

Shaken with discouragement, I made my way to St. Mark's Monastery to deliver a special cardboard box I had made the night before to protect the "Fourth Scroll," as we called it. The Metropolitan was alone in his office when I arrived, Sowmy having left for a few days of vacation. This was the first time he was absent from our interviews, and I missed his help as interpreter.

We inserted the delicate Fourth Scroll in the cotton-padded box, only to find that it was a trifle too snug; the end of the box bulged. I had miscalculated the length of the scroll, one end of which was quite irregular. The small fragment had been mounted between pieces of glass. The Metropolitan expressed gratitude for my efforts.

With the scroll and fragment lying before us, I cautiously approached the problem of opening the poorly preserved document. Dr. Burrows and I had agreed that in view of the rapidly disintegrating circumstances all around us, we should make the attempt to photograph whatever could be preserved from the scroll. Who could tell what might happen to it any day? The reasons I advanced seemed to impress the Metropolitan, and we concluded that I should proceed with the work as soon as possible.

First, however, the Isaiah and Habakkuk scrolls must be rephotographed. Would he bring the scrolls to our School on Friday, I inquired, assuring him that at last the film was available. Carefully concealing my trepidation concerning the nature of the film, I showed him the two boxes purchased earlier that day. He agreed to bring the scrolls to the School on Friday. Gleeful over both the promise to let me work on the Fourth Scroll and the assurance that I could soon rephotograph the others, I hastened back to the School to begin the arduous preparations that would be necessary.

Early on Thursday I was again in the Old City to retrieve the rest of the film. To my utter amazement the drama of the previous day was repeated: again the film was not there; again there was a long delay as the shopkeeper tried to smooth my ruffled feelings with the usual lame excuses; finally the boy arrived with the four packages of film. Hastily I examined each one. Two were of similar make to the ones purchased the day before, but the date was "Jul 1946," almost two years outdated![9] Two others were a Kodak portrait film of about the same vintage. Again I remonstrated over the price, for I was sure that only a portion of such old film would be usable. Again they were adamant, and reluctantly I gave them the £P4. As much disgusted with my own inability to cope with Arab business methods as with being robbed in such a way, I stomped angrily out of the shop. I strode rapidly toward Raad's shop on Jaffa Road, wondering if I were destined for failure in this most important task.

Having found a photo tank of sufficient capacity to develop these large films at our School, I sought Raad's help for an adequate quantity of developer in which to immerse the films. Furthermore, I must have a high-contrast, yet fine-grain developer to overcome the low contrast of portrait film. Raad did not have the formula for "D-11"[10] developer which I suggested, but he assured me he could mix up a good fine-grain developer of adequate contrast for my purpose. He would have a gallon ready Friday morning, he promised.

A cold, steady rain was falling Friday morning (March 5), but I determined to go to St. Mark's Monastery anyway. Folding some newspapers to make a semblance of an umbrella (an item not to be found at the School), I started toward the door. Dr. Burrows followed me, trying to dissuade me from going; he was concerned for my safety as well as for my health. I argued with him. I had to get the scrolls and the developer to proceed with the rephotographing. Then he told me that the American consul general had advised us all to leave, in view of the mounting hostilities. Our safety was in jeopardy, and the consul could not help us.

I was still determined. As I opened the door, Dr. Burrows said, "Remember the word *Mesichi*, John." As I dashed away in the rain, I wondered why he told me that Arabic word. Suddenly it dawned on me—that is the same as *Mashiach* in Hebrew, the word for "Messiah"; it is the equivalent of "Christian," a Greek word. I found myself saying on numerous occasions thereafter, *Ana Americani Mesichi* ("I am an American Christian"). It always bothered me, however, for I seemed to be saying, "I am an American Messiah."

That day I did not need to use the word. It was not even necessary to show my passes, for the barriers were mostly deserted. The officials must have reasoned that no one would start trouble on such a nasty day. By the time I reached the Monastery, I was dripping wet. The Syrians lighted a kerosene stove in the Metropolitan's office and brought me hot coffee.

My discomforts were soon forgotten, for early in the conversation I mentioned what Dr. Burrows had told me—that all Americans were being asked to leave Palestine. Their response jolted me. They began to plead with me not to leave; for, they said, they were counting on me for further help. I was amazed, for I had assumed my work would be finished as soon as the scrolls were rephotographed. Some moments passed as the Metropolitan and Father Sowmy, who had returned the day before, conversed in Arabic. I waited with bated breath.

Slowly and deliberately Father Sowmy began: "We have been keeping something from you, Doctor John, until we were certain we could trust you. The scrolls have not been in our Monastery for forty years, as I told you. They were purchased last August from some Bedouins who live near Bethlehem."[11] He went on to say that Father Yusif, a priest of the Monastery, had gone with the Bedouins to visit the cave from which the scrolls had come. Its location he designated only as "near 'Ain Feshkha by the Dead Sea." There he had seen one of the jars in which the scrolls had been found, and many fragments of broken ones. Also, there was a pile of small fragments and cloth wrappings which the Bedouins had tossed aside as worthless.

Two of the jars had been taken to Bethlehem by the Bedouins and were being used as water jars, he continued. Ever since I had mentioned the value of the jars for dating the manuscripts that first day when I visited the Monastery, they had been trying to obtain the jars, he said. They had contacted the Bedouins, he added, but had failed to get the jars.[12] It was their plan, the Metropolitan interjected, as soon as things quieted down in the country, to go to the cave again, and they were anxious to have me go with them! The cave, which had previously appeared so remotely significant, suddenly rocketed into prominent focus.

All the more like a tale out of *Arabian Nights*, their story threw me into a state of confusion. Questions flooded my mind, but until I had time for reflection, little could be gained from raising them. Thus I turned the conversation to the major purpose of my visit that morning—to take the Isaiah and Habakkuk scrolls to our School for rephotographing.

Sowmy decided to accompany me, for which I was most thankful. I had not relished the thought of carrying such valuable documents alone through the Old City of Jerusalem so fraught with dangers. Departing through the Jaffa Gate, we went to Raad's shop for the gallon of developer. It was ready, as promised, so within minutes we hailed a taxi and were on our way to the School. With the scrolls safely secluded in the office of the School, Sowmy bade me farewell, promising to return for them on Monday.

Dashing across the courtyard, I burst into the Director's apartment to unfold the latest news to Dr. Burrows. He, too, seemed dazed by the revelation. If the cave had been so recently discovered by Bedouins, it was a matter of archeological urgency to get there to prevent further damage. Excavation would require the permission of the Department of Antiquities. What should be our next steps?

9

Planning an Expedition

BEING very much occupied with the affairs of the School on his return from Baghdad, Dr. Burrows left the negotiations concerning the scrolls in my hands. I kept him well informed of my discussions with the Syrians, but there were many details which did not seem important enough at the time to communicate. The new revelation about the scrolls received on March 5, however, prompted much discussion in the Director's apartment the next morning.

Excavation of the cave was now imperative, but excavations take time to prepare. Much careful planning is necessary; yet we were already being asked by our American consul to leave. This was no time to plan an expedition. Time was running out.

Even if there had been no dangers, our position, we realized, was difficult. The scrolls were the possession of the Syrians. Our privileges with the documents depended on their good will, which we had carefully cultivated. They alone knew the location of the cave; that it was somewhere in the vicinity of 'Ain Feshkha was all we knew. As an archeological institution the American School could not conduct an excavation without the permission of the government Department of Antiquities. The Syrians, however, were clearly opposed to working in cooperation with that Department.[1]

To publish the manuscripts, we needed to preserve the friendship of the Syrians.

The country was reaching a state of anarchy as the Mandate Government was withdrawing. Many functions of the government had been turned over to Arabs, as I had discovered when I went to get a bread ration renewed more than two weeks before. Were the antiquities laws really in force? Saving the scrolls and their place of origin for scholarship seemed of primary importance. One conclusion was clear. We must try to get the Syrians to take us to the cave. It was agreed, therefore, that I should discuss the procedure privately with Mr. Hamilton, Director of Antiquities.[2]

Further discussion regarding an expedition to the cave had to wait. We could have the scrolls at the School for only three days. Every effort must be bent toward getting the kind of negatives that high-quality publication demanded — with outdated portrait film! The rest of Friday and all day Saturday (March 5-6) were devoted completely to that task.

The School was equipped with a fine Zeiss 13 × 18 centimeter view camera for archeological purposes. With its excellent Zeiss lens, I was confident that high-quality copies could be made, given the proper film. Everything was now in readiness for the first tests, and tests there must be with such poor film. A sheet of film from the oldest box was loaded in a holder. With one exposure made, I immediately developed it in total darkness, using the tray method.

With the film in the hypo, I switched on the lights. It was black all over — not even the unexposed edges showed the usual creamy-white color. The film was fogged by age; it was useless! I waited until the hypo had completely cleared the undeveloped silver haloid from the film, then held it to the light. Black fog penetrated some two inches into the film, leaving only the center of the negative usable, and even there the contrast was very poor. Was the whole box like this?

Removing a sheet of film from the very center of the same package, I ran a second test. When that negative was developed, only a very narrow strip of fog appeared around the outer edges. This was usable, though still lacking contrast. A third test with a sheet nearer the top of the package again proved usable. My hopes began to rise. About half the films in that box could be used. There would be barely enough film, I calculated after the third test, assuming that the two more recently dated boxes would be entirely good. Hopefully I figured on eight usable sheets from each of the other boxes.

Starting with the center sheet of each box of film, I loaded holders in the order of what I figured would be the better film down to what was probably poorer. After twenty exposures I was ready to use the large developing tank. Each film had to be loaded into a special metal frame to hold the film upright in the open tank, the entire process being done in total darkness. I had performed much more difficult photographic tasks before; but now even my hands trembled a little, and beads of perspiration gathered on my brow despite the chill of the room. My mind vacillated between concern for what failure would mean, and confidence based on the three tests. With no more film available in all Jerusalem, I dared not fail! I prayed for guidance, though I expected no miracles. The film was either usable or not; though a man of faith, I could not expect God to change the facts.

With the films safely in the hypo bath, I mustered courage to turn on the lights. One by one I lifted the films. Some were distinctly usable, several were too fogged with age; as expected, it was mostly the last films that proved worthless. This was a little comforting, for it meant less effort to retake them. On closer examination it was obvious that even the usable ones were very much lacking in contrast. Some compensation for contrast is possible in the printing process, I knew, but I feared these films might be beyond the range for adequate correction. Perhaps it was Raad's developer, I reasoned. Another test must be run.

With the holders reloaded, I returned to the copy-board and made another test exposure. This was developed for the required fifteen minutes in a tray of D-76 developer (a fine-grain film developer, but one used primarily where high contrast in negatives is not required), the only other film developer available. To my amazement and joy, it showed a marked improvement in contrast. Unfortunately, I had only two quarts of D-76 left, only half enough to fill the large tank. There was only one way to proceed—develop six films at a time in a tray, despite the hazards involved with such large films. A slight increase in developing time would further improve the contrast, I realized; about eighteen minutes for each batch should be just right. The process would be tedious, but it promised results.

Except for carrying water and a few other minor jobs, there was little anyone else could do to help me in the exacting task. Therefore, I worked mostly alone. There were fewer distractions that way. By ten thirty that night I could go on no longer. All the next day the same arduous procedure continued. It was a relief, on Saturday afternoon, to turn to the smaller film and camera for the Habakkuk Commentary copies. With each column of that manuscript on a sheet of film, beautiful negatives resulted. Besides, Mr. Raad's film was not outdated. By late Saturday night only twelve of the large films needed development to finish the two scrolls.

With only one more day to keep the scrolls, there was yet another project I was determined to complete—a full-color reproduction of the Isaiah and Habakkuk scrolls. The color transparencies of the "Sectarian Document" had convinced me that similar transparencies of the other scrolls were imperative. For detailed study they would be priceless, perhaps as valuable as having the scrolls themselves. Sunday, therefore, was not a day of rest. It rained all day, anyway.

Of the color sheet-films which the Ansco Company had given me, fifty-four sheets remained, exactly enough to do the Isaiah Scroll. With no chemicals mixed, not even a test exposure could be developed, for that would take four hours. There was hardly time to do that and make all the exposures before the manuscripts had to be returned. All fifty-four sheets would have to be exposed without developing even one.

With only six plate-holders for my color camera, trips to the darkroom were frequent. Guests came for lunch, and a tea had been planned for late afternoon. Only the Isaiah Scroll was finished that day.

For the Habakkuk Commentary it was necessary to start using a supply of Ektachrome film, an Eastman color film which had been on the market for only a few months at that time. Several packages had been ordered the previous summer but

End view of "Genesis Apocryphon" before unrolling

failed to arrive by the time I left New York. Interminable difficulties arose over getting the film to Palestine and through customs at the Lydda Airport, where it finally arrived via air parcel post. Now, perhaps, it would prove worthy of the efforts we had expended to get it. Sunday evening I studied the instructions which accompanied each box, realizing that there would be no chance for test-developing or retakes. By the time the Syrians came for the scrolls Monday afternoon, therefore, the Habakkuk Scroll had also been recorded in color, but without certainty of the results.[3] In addition, the remainder of the large black-and-white negatives were developed.

When the Syrians arrived to pick up the two scrolls on March 8, they brought the "Sectarian Document" and the "Fourth Scroll," as we had requested. We wanted to check some points on the former, since our class discussions of our attempted translations required it. Furthermore, our plan was to begin to work then on unrolling the "Fourth Scroll." In the meantime, however, Father Sowmy had urged the Metropolitan to withdraw his permission to unroll that scroll. We were disappointed when they announced their decision, but agreed with their claim that we had plenty to keep us busy. They did consent to leave the scroll with us until the end of the week. Then Dr. Burrows drove the Syrians back to the Jaffa Gate in the School station wagon, despite the fact that recently several station wagons had been stolen at gunpoint in broad daylight.

That evening I examined the "Fourth Scroll" in minute detail, attempting by measurements to calculate the extent of its contents. There might be as many as 400 lines of text, I estimated, if the scroll could be opened without too much damage.[4] Though a delicate task, I felt confident that it could be opened without too much loss.[5] A peculiar kind of disintegration along the inscribed lines was particularly puzzling, for none of the other documents exhibited a similar phenomenon. To what extent the interior had been affected by it, we could only speculate. At many points deep cracks penetrated several layers of the thin leather.

For the next two days I remained at the School, unable to do more than attend classes and study, with intermittent periods of rest. Having broken out with boils, which called to mind a serious abcess I had suffered the previous October, I felt weak and enervated.

Since we could not open the "Fourth Scroll," I spent much of Wednesday studying it as I rested. I wondered if there might be a place on the tightly rolled scroll where some of the script could be clearly seen. While gently probing the softer side near the center, I discovered a jagged vertical crack two inches long which formed a line of demarcation between the brittle, disintegrated part and the softer part. It joined an irregular horizontal crack which ran, except at the beginning, through the center of a line of what was obviously script, and almost across the width of the scroll to another irregular vertical crack. At the other end of the first vertical crack, hardly a half inch of soft leather separated it from another horizontal crack, which again passed through a line of script completely across the scroll. Gently lifting the thin brown leather at the point where the two cracks met, I could see the margin of a column and beginnings of some lines of script on the underside. The first vertical crack was along the left edge of another column. As I lifted the piece a little higher, suddenly the leather at the other end of the vertical crack gave way, and a fragment 2 inches wide by 3½ inches long broke loose from across the entire width of the softer part of the scroll.

Five lines of text plus fragments of two other lines from the right half of a column, including the right margin, were now exposed. The script, written on the hair side of the skin, was clearer than on the small fragment we had puzzled over and failed to decipher. It was obviously the same script. The expression *wl' mn kwl* ("and not from any") appeared three times on the fourth line and seemed obviously Hebrew, but there were other clearly Aramaic words on the fragment. Several words defied decipherment. The script ran together at crucial points, where the leather appeared to have taken the ink like a blotter. All the script was quite different in this regard from the other scrolls, for its lines were heavier, as though the scribe had used a dull-pointed reed pen. Perhaps, however, he used a thinner ink which tended to penetrate the leather deeper and may have been responsible for the peculiar disintegration along the inscribed lines.[6] The usual lines of ruling, probably made with a bone instrument, both for the margins and to guide the script, showed prominently.

My earlier hasty conclusion that this manuscript might be older (see p. 58) than the Isaiah Scroll I could now clearly see was wrong. The script was paleographically more developed. It represented a later period, more like the late corrector's hand on the Isaiah manuscript. Closer scrutiny left the impression that it belonged chronologically with the Habakkuk Scroll. Nothing on this fragment, unfortunately, provided any clues for identification. That it was not Biblical became clear as soon as I tried to trace some of its phrases through a concordance. Here was apparently another sectarian document.

By Thursday morning (March 11) I felt strong enough to photograph the "Fourth Scroll" and the newly removed fragment. Using both color and black-and-white-films, I recorded end views as well as back and front views of the scroll with both fragments.

Meanwhile the formidable task of making four sets of prints from the new Isaiah Scroll negatives prompted me to appeal to Dr. Burrows for help. He agreed to provide funds to have the prints made, if Mr. Raad could undertake the task. There was no question about the reliability of Mr. Raad, but the location of his shop on Jaffa Road gave me some concern for the safety of the negatives. The great respect which Mr. Raad commanded among both Arabs and Jews, however, was in itself a protection. With a boxful of the Isaiah Scroll negatives in hand, I walked to Mr. Raad's shop that same morning to discuss the project with him. He was, of course, most happy for the business and assured me that he could handle the large number of prints safely and quickly. It was agreed that the negatives should be delivered to him in groups, as he was able to work on them.

Although I had hoped to visit the Museum for a discussion with Mr. Hamilton that afternoon, the efforts of the morning were all my strength could endure. Thus the rest of that day and evening were spent working on the translation of the Jerusalem Scroll #1 (1QS). Gradually the nature of this scroll was becoming clear. In our class discussions we struggled particularly with the meaning of the word *yahad,* which occurred repeatedly as a noun. No meaning found in Biblical usage seemed to fit. Dr. Brownlee suggested the translation "community," and Dr. Burrows "communion." Dr. Burrows had suggested that the document read considerably like the Book of Deuteronomy, but now we concluded it was a sort of code-book of some esoteric community or Jewish sect, perhaps the Essenes. Later, Dr. Burrows likened the document to a Methodist "Discipline," and that name seemed to fit best. Thus we called it "The Manual of Discipline."

During our class discussions the problem of the paleography of the scrolls arose repeatedly. Dr. Brownlee had examined some ossuary[7] inscriptions at the Museum that week and claimed that they convinced him that the scrolls could not be later than the first century A.D. This, too, made me eager to visit the Museum again.

Friday morning was my first opportunity to get there. While waiting for an appointment with Mr. Hamilton, I examined the ossuaries in the Roman section of the North Gallery and found two with names incised in Hebrew. One of them had been inscribed by a semi-skilled hand, the other with a crude cursive. A similarity to the script on our scrolls was immediately apparent, especially the final *M* and *T*. Later that morning I examined many other ossuaries stored in another part of the Museum. The great irregularity of the script, the obviously unskilled hands that produced most of them, and the medium in which they were incised made comparison difficult and conclusions from them hazardous. There was no doubt, however, that here was important additional evidence to add to that which we already had.[8]

When I saw Mr. Hamilton, unfortunately I failed to tell him about the newly revealed date of the discovery.[9] Our discussion centered around the problem of excavating the cave, not its discovery. Referring to the apparent reluctance of the Syrians to cooperate with the Department of Antiquities, I emphasized the dilemma created by our working with the Syrians in this project without permission from his Department. We considered it very important, I continued, to maintain the friendship of the Syrians; and thus my visit with him was without their knowledge. My main question was, how could we proceed without violating the law? Though many other details of that discussion are lost to my memory, I vividly recall these points and his suggestions: he said that I should go with the Syrians to the cave and "photograph everything *in situ*," i.e., without disturbing anything. Then, if there were any potsherds or other objects on the surface, we should gather them together carefully and take them to the American School. Finally, we were to report back to him so that he could go to the School to see what had been found.[10]

With the way cleared for us to visit the cave legally, I hastened to St. Mark's Monastery to discuss the matter with the Syrians. At the same time I returned the "Manual of Discipline" to them, as promised. Cautiously I approached the subject of going to the cave as soon as possible. Soon we would have to leave Palestine, I emphasized, and we were anxious to see the project through to completion, if possible. Putting it on a personal basis seemed at the time the better approach. Their response was one of concern for our safety; they did not think it possible at that time to get to the cave without serious danger. We would have to go through Jewish-controlled Kallia near the potash factory by the Dead Sea. I recognized, of course, that they knew more about the circumstances surrounding the cave than I; therefore, I decided not to continue the discussion that day.

Interruptions in the pursuit of matters relating to the scrolls and their study were now frequent as the urgency to leave the country became pressing. Our efforts to arrange for transportation were almost frenzied. No word had reached me since October about my reservation from England. Most of my letters to home were devoted to those problems and reflect the situation. Our state of confusion increased with all the confusion around us. We jumped from one thing to another, trying to take advantage of what opportunities were open to us. Research was decidedly intermittent.

During that week, as a result of some further study on paleography, I had abandoned my theory about the scrolls being deposited in the cave during the persecutions of Antiochus between 175 and 168 B.C. That would have meant that the latest of the scrolls, such as the Habakkuk Commentary, the "Fourth Scroll," and the corrector's hand on the Isaiah Scroll, must also date from before 175 B.C. These latter certainly were not that close to the Edfu Papyri, or even the Nash. From a paleographic standpoint the period of about 100 B.C. to A.D. 50 seemed much more feasible. Also I began to feel that the Isaiah Scroll was not as old as the Nash Papyrus, contrary to what I had suggested in my letter to Dr. Albright. Association of the deposit, therefore, with the revolt of the Jews in A.D. 66-70, as suggested by Ibrahim Sowmy, now seemed much more likely.

Eager as I was to see the results of the color work on the Isaiah Scroll, early Saturday morning (March 13) I mixed the necessary chemicals and prepared the darkroom for that purpose. Loading a specially arranged tank with twenty-four sheet films, I was ready to start the processing immediately after lunch.

At noon, as had been agreed the previous day, I met the Syrian guard at the New Gate. I was carrying the "Fourth Scroll" snugly in its box under my arm. When I handed the scroll to the Metropolitan, he informed me that plans were already being made for him to visit the Syrian communities in the United States. At that time, he assured me, we could arrange for proper treatment of the scroll. It was then agreed that I should retain the two fragments, which I had mounted between pieces of glass, for further study and preparation in the United States.[11]

Again I had hoped to bring up the matter of visiting the cave, but on arrival I had been introduced to a British officer who was making a routine visit to the Monastery. He was in charge of the Mandate forces at Jaffa Gate, I learned. A lively conversation ensued, quite unrelated to the scrolls. By the time the officer was ready to leave, it was so near lunchtime at our School that I left with him. As we sauntered up King David Street toward the Jaffa Gate, he continued to relate stories about the interminable problems involved in his administration of that troublesome sector of the Old City. His incredible experiences punctuated the frightful dilemma which the British were facing as they prepared to relinquish the Mandate. I felt a new admiration for them in the face of such a thankless, heartrending task.

Further insights into the local problems came from a discussion that evening with Anwar Tamimi. Strange sounds from underground were being heard each night near the Haram. The Muslim Supreme Council officers were worried about the possibility of Jews tunneling under the Haram from the Jewish Quarter. Together, in the School library, we examined detailed archeological maps of the Old City, and the many underground channels which we discovered on the maps appeared to justify their concerns.

As a result of the preparations in the morning, it was possible to put two sets of twenty-four films through the color process that afternoon and evening. It proved an exciting task, for the results were again perfect. To see forty-eight sparkling-clear columns of the Isaiah Scroll in full color momentarily erased the tragedies of Jerusalem from my mind.

A bitter cold rain again descended upon Jerusalem during the night, and I remained at the School for the next two days, devoting my time to study, completing the color-developing, and writing letters. In the midst of writing to my wife on Monday morning (March 15), the mail arrived with the long-awaited reply from Dr. Albright (my letter to him had not arrived in Baltimore until March 8). Starting on the wrong side of an air-letter, he wrote:

Dear Trever,

Your air-letter of Feb. 25th, with its enclosures, arrived this morning and I immediately got out my magnifying glass and started in. I am now having the prints enlarged so I can study the script to better advantage. My heartiest congratulations on the greatest MS discovery of modern times! There is no doubt whatever in my mind that the script is more archaic than that of the Nash Papyrus, standing very close to that of the third-century Egyptian papyri and ostraca in Aramaic. Of course, in the present state of our definite knowledge about Hebrew paleography it would be safe only to date it in the Maccabaean period, *i.e.*, not later than the accession of Herod the Great. I should prefer a date around 100 B.C. The script is in every respect older than that of the Dura parchment fragment.

In my excitement I began writing on the wrong side of the sheet! I repeat that in my opinion you have made the greatest MS discovery of modern times — certainly the greatest biblical MS find. The spelling is most interesting, resembling that of the Nash Papyrus very closely. The tendency to hyper-correction in writing כי as כיא is most extraordinary. Burrows will now have a chance to forget the events in Palestine for a while. Let us hope that nothing happens to your precious finds!

I don't anticipate any very significant textual corrections of the text of Isaiah, but the new material will revolutionize our conception of the development of Hebrew orthography. And who knows what treasures may be concealed in the remaining rolls!

....

It is a very fine thing that you have been able to get such an important result as this discovery from your difficult year in Jerusalem. You can imagine how my eyes bulged when I saw the script through my magnifying glass! What an absolutely incredible find! And there can happily not be the slightest doubt in the world about the genuineness of the MS.

....

Cordially,

W. F. Albright

His exuberance amazed and delighted me. Holding the letter and racing down the stairs, I burst into the Director's apartment. Breathlessly I read it to Dr. Burrows. His response, as usual, was reserved but obviously enthusiastic.[12] When I read the words about forgetting the events in Palestine, however, his comment was, "Little does Albright know." That very day it was rumored that our water supply had been poisoned! Bombings and battles by then were nightly affairs, as anarchy seemed to be closing in upon us. Every day we were forcefully reminded of the troubled present as we ventured into the exciting ancient past.

That evening as I examined a map of the area around 'Ain Feshkha by the Dead Sea, a sudden inspiration struck me. We could avoid the danger zone south of Jericho which worried the Syrians. Nebi Musa, an isolated Muslim sacred shrine in the desert northwest of 'Ain Feshkha, was within walking distance of the cliffs among which the cave was located. If we could make our headquarters at Nebi Musa, we could approach the cave from the plateau above. Hastening to Anwar's room, I broke in on his study to share the idea. He looked at the small map I carried and agreed that such an approach was possible. He said he knew the man in charge at the Nebi Musa shrine and was certain he could arrange for us to stay there.

In the School library were large survey maps showing clearly every feature of the country in detail. Examining the area on these, I found a trail leading from Nebi Musa directly to the point above where I thought the cave must be. There were some steep parts, but with donkeys we could maneuver the terrain. With this plan, perhaps, the Syrians might be persuaded to take us there.

Again I sought Dr. Burrows. He looked at the detailed maps and exclaimed, "There must be a hitch in this whole thing somewhere." How right he was!

10

First News Released to the World

ASNOWSTORM in Jerusalem is a rarity, but the cold drizzle that had persisted all day (March 15) turned to snow during the night. Jerusalem and the Mount of Olives, blanketed with snow the next morning, were sights of amazing beauty. Our cameras were swiftly put into action.

Arab children, on their way to school, exhibited an ecstasy of delight. Mahmud, frustrated with concern over the School garden, went about with a broom, knocking the fluffy white from bushes and hedges. Some of it he gathered into a small snowman, complete with simulated corncob pipe, for another servant's children,[1] who danced around it with ecstatic glee. As the sun broke through the clouds about mid-morning, the fairyland all about us soon evaporated. It was winter's last thrust, for by the end of the week we were favored with the full bloom of spring.

With letters to mail at the post office, more Isaiah Scroll negatives to deliver to Mr. Raad, prints to pick up, and another visit to St. Mark's Monastery on my schedule, I set out for town. At the Monastery I was deterred from plunging immediately into discussing our plans for visiting the cave. The Metropolitan had just purchased a camera from Mr. Raad and wanted me to show him how to use it. Eager to be cooperative, I proceeded with a lesson in the fundamentals of candid photography. To shorten the process I invited him to our School, where better instruction could be given, using some new color film that the Ansco Company had graciously sent.

Confident that our new plan for getting to the cave would elicit the full cooperation of the Metropolitan, I outlined it in detail, tracing on a small map the proposed route of approach from Nebi Musa. My enthusiastic presentation met with a cool reception. The Metropolitan, it seemed, wanted to accompany the expedition to the cave; for the spiritual leader of the Syrians, such a route would be too arduous and hazardous, Father Sowmy explained. Furthermore, he reiterated, if we waited until the troubles were over, we could approach the cave quite easily from the Jordan Valley. Discouraged, yet puzzled by their reluctance, I returned to our School.

Immediately I discussed the situation with Dr. Burrows, and we decided that probably the time had come to reveal to the Syrians the importance of their manuscripts. We decided, therefore, to work out a typed statement about the scrolls in the form of a news release. Dr. Burrows then invited the Metropolitan to the Director's apartment Thursday morning.

Wednesday evening (March 17) I prepared a suggested draft of the statement, in which our convictions regarding the great age of the Syrians' scrolls were emphasized. Dr. Burrows revised it and typed several copies for the meeting the next morning. As we worked, another battle, following several thunderous explosions, raged north of our School, reminding us that time was running out.

Metropolitan Samuel arrived promptly at ten thirty the next morning and was ushered into the Director's sitting room, where Dr. Burrows and I awaited him. After the formalities, which Dr. Burrows conducted with consummate skill as a host, and when the Metropolitan was comfortably seated beside a crackling fire, Dr. Burrows handed him a copy of the news release to read. He explained that we would like his permission to release the statement to the press in America. Silence ensued as the Metropolitan looked over the words for more than a minute. Returning the paper to Dr. Burrows, he asked him to read it aloud; he could understand it better that way, he said. As Dr. Burrows read, the Metropolitan's eyes began to sparkle with obvious delight. Slowly he lifted himself to an erect position on the edge of the overstuffed chair; when Dr. Burrows had barely finished, he exclaimed proudly, "I want you to know that these are *my* scrolls!"

Recovering from our amazement at the nature of his response, we indicated some of our reasons for believing that the Isaiah Scroll was the oldest known existing copy of a book of the Bible. Again we raised the matter of the safety of the scrolls, which once before had failed to make an impression on the Syrians. Such valuable scrolls were not safe in their Monastery, we emphasized. Remembering their monastery near the Jordan River at the traditional site of the baptism of Jesus, I suggested that perhaps there was some safe place there to secrete the scrolls from wartorn Jerusalem.[2] With our joint emphases and his sudden awareness of the great value of the scrolls, our concerns obviously registered more deeply. He assured us that the scrolls would be removed to a place of safety.

Dr. Burrows then pursued the matter of publishing the scrolls and invited the

Metropolitan to the School library to see some of the publications of the A.S.O.R. The library, which during previous weeks had been thoroughly cleaned and neatly arranged by Mrs. Burrows, deeply impressed the Metropolitan. Dr. Burrows drew several of the many A.S.O.R. volumes from the shelves to show him. Then, opening the huge volume of government survey maps lying on a large table, I traced the route from Nebi Musa to 'Ain Feshkha and again urged the importance of visiting the cave as soon as possible. Dr. Burrows stressed the urgency of gathering materials which might strengthen our dating of the scrolls before the scholarly world. Since the weather seemed to be breaking, we said we would like to make arrangements to go the following week. Again the Metropolitan seemed hesitant.

Inserting a roll of color film in his camera, I spent the next hour explaining the step-by-step process of taking pictures with it. We took several in the sun-flooded courtyard garden. I promised to develop and check his results if he would finish the twenty-exposure roll soon.

During our interview Cook's Travel Agency had called to report their receipt at last of a reservation for me on the *Queen Elizabeth*. Rejoicing over this news and absorbed by the events of the morning, I completely forgot to return a call from Anwar Tamimi. (The man in charge of the Nebi Musa shrine had been in Anwar's office at the Haram.) Shortly after five o'clock Anwar came to my room to scold me for my failure to return his call. With abject apologies, I urged him to make an appointment with the man for Saturday.

Dr. Burrows meanwhile dispatched the news release with a letter of instructions to the A.S.O.R. office in New Haven, Connecticut. The first public announcement about the great discovery was on its way to the United States. (It was not released, however, until April 11.)

Again that night a severe battle raged close to our School, following a violent explosion. Amid the din I pondered my return schedule, and the next morning tried to arrange for transportation to England. Complications proved interminable; communications with the outside world were poor, and demands for transportation out of the country were many. Visas were required by every country, and took time to procure. Any schedule was at best only tentative.

Arriving in the office of the Metropolitan Friday afternoon (March 19), I found him very agitated. He was worried about the safety of Father Sowmy, who had failed to return from Jericho as promised. Furthermore, a Syrian layman had come from the Y.M.C.A. that very morning with a request which greatly disturbed him; he seemed reluctant to talk about it, but made some vague allusions to Jews trying to get the manuscripts. Finally he divulged that Dr. Judah Magnes, President of the Hebrew University in Jerusalem, was urgently requesting the Metropolitan to take the scrolls to the Y.M.C.A. for him to see.[3] The Metropolitan seemed to fear that it was some kind of a trick to get the scrolls. Once before an allusion to some Jews' knowing about the scrolls had led me erroneously to think that Dr. E. L. Sukenik, Professor of Archaeology at the Hebrew University, was perhaps involved.[4] Wondering if the Syrians were secretly negotiating a sale of the scrolls to the Hebrew University, I asked the Metropolitan directly if Dr. Sukenik knew about the scrolls. With some hesitation he revealed that Dr. Sukenik had not only seen the scrolls, but also was trying to buy them.[5] The matter had been dropped for some time, he continued, but now Dr. Magnes was making new overtures. What should he do?

Knowing nothing of the complex background to the Metropolitan's statements (see pp. 112-113), I could not understand the reasons for his expressed concerns. For him, it seemed to me, the solution was relatively simple: he should report to Dr. Magnes that the scrolls were being handled by the A.S.O.R. and that Dr. Burrows was the one with whom to discuss the matter. Since both the A.S.O.R. and the Hebrew University, whose opening ceremonies we had attended the previous October, were academic institutions, such a method of handling the problem seemed most logical. Suddenly aware of what a sale of the scrolls then would mean to all our efforts toward publication, I emphasized to the Metropolitan that such a move would be a serious disservice to the A.S.O.R. Thus I laid additional stress on the importance of letting us handle the arrangements.

Seemingly relieved by my suggestion, the prelate voluntarily turned the discussion to visiting the cave. He had a theory, he said, which made him particularly anxious to visit the cave personally—he was confident that the original "Ark of the Covenant"[6] was in that cave! Utterly amazed, I groped for words. What could possibly have led him to such a conclusion? Father Yusif, he explained, when he visited the cave the past summer, had reported seeing in the cave a piece of wood under which was a stone. His theory had developed from this bit of evidence, and he wanted to investigate the matter personally.

This kind of conclusion is always somewhat irritating to one trained in making enthusiasm wait upon proof, and I emphatically warned the Metropolitan that such a procedure would be a violation of the law. We would have to withdraw all our cooperation if he persisted in such a scheme, I continued. It was then that I revealed to him the fact that I had already told the whole story to the Director of Antiquities and had received specific instructions about how to conduct the visit to the cave.[7] Furthermore, I emphasized, it was impractical to think that anything else as valuable as the scrolls might be found in the cave. Certainly the Bedouins had already removed the best materials, and the most we could hope to find would be only fragments and other insignificant items. The fact that the scrolls clearly showed the late sectarian nature of the deposit would preclude the discovery of anything belonging to Solomon's Temple, I added. My torrent of arguments obviously convinced him, for he agreed that the visit to the cave should be done with the cooperation of the Department of Antiquities.

Just then Father Sowmy arrived from Jericho with reports of fighting between Jews and Arabs in the region near the cave. In fact, he added, the Arab tribes in the region were feuding among themselves. The fears of the Metropolitan were renewed; my hopes for a visit to the cave began to dwindle. During the somewhat heated discussion that ensued, a battle broke out in the Old City, not far from St. Mark's Monastery, reminding me that I was supposed to be back at our School by four o'clock; it was then five. It was not safe to leave then, so I continued to try to allay their fears about going to the cave. The battle so near their Monastery, furthermore, provided another opportunity to emphasize the importance of getting the manuscripts to a place of safety.

As the din of battle subsided about five thirty, I insisted on leaving. Again they sent their *kawas* to usher me safely out of the Old City. We walked in silence along the deserted streets. The steel corrugated shutters of all the shops along Christian Street were drawn tight and locked. A deathly silence pervaded the entire city, broken only by the echoing clatter of our hard-soled shoes on the stone pavement. This time the *kawas* insisted on accompanying me outside the New Gate as far as the barbed-wire entrance to the Musrara Quarter midway along Godfrey de Bouillon Street. There the armed Arab guards checked my pass as we exchanged the usual friendly greetings, and I hastened alone toward our School.

Following my usual route between a row of apartment buildings at the north edge of the Musrara Quarter, I emerged onto the open field which separated the buildings from the Nablus Road. Hardly had I taken twenty long strides out into the rough, rocky field, when suddenly—zing!—a bullet whined a few feet above my head. Another zing!—and another!—followed closely. Puffs of smoke from the snipers' guns dotted some buildings directly ahead on the edge of the Mea Shearim Sector. Terrified, I dashed with all the speed I could muster toward Nablus Road and the shelter of the Palestine Pottery Works. My dash was spurred by the sudden fearful recollection that a British lady, on her way to worship at St. George's Cathedral the previous Sunday, had been killed by a sniper within a few feet of the very point where I heard the first bullet pass overhead. Several Arab boys returning from the Ibrahimiyeh College joined me behind the same wall, and we tried to comfort each other with senseless chatter as we crouched there, trembling in fear. The School was plainly visible across another open field. I watched to see if anyone appeared at the gate, so I could signal my dilemma to them. No one appeared.

Some minutes later the shooting subsided, and I made another dash to the gate of our School. Once in my room, I slumped into the chair by my desk, a cold sweat moistening my brow. Psychologically, we were living in Bible times!

With my equilibrium regained, I reported the discussion at the Monastery to Dr. Burrows. He suggested trying to contact Dr. Magnes immediately, but I urged him to let the Syrians follow my instructions and await a call from the Hebrew University. Dr. Magnes never called. Perhaps the Syrians did not follow my suggestions.[8]

All Jerusalem was buzzing with excitement early Saturday morning (March 20). During the night, word was broadcast that America had reversed her decision regarding Partition. Everyone I met was jubilant. Brownlee reported seeing some Arab boys waving American flags as they raced on scooters down the street near the Y.M.C.A. Besides, the warmth and beauty of spring was in the air.

When I called Anwar Tamimi at the Haram, he informed me that the Arab in charge of the Nebi Musa shrine was in his office. Dr. Burrows and I hastened to Herod's Gate, where we were met by a guard whom Anwar had sent. At the Haram we were ushered into the great Council Chamber; Dr. Burrows was offered the seat of honor. Presently Anwar ushered in several Arabs in long robes and *keffiyehs*—obviously men of the desert. Tea and coffee were served before a word was said concerning the purpose of the meeting.

With Anwar as interpreter, we outlined our plan for visiting the cliffs west of 'Ain Feshkha, via the shrine at Nebi Musa. We were deliberately vague about our exact purpose. The Arabs assured us it would not be difficult; the trip could be made in about an hour and a half by donkey, they said. The man in charge of the shrine offered to arrange for donkeys and other needs to be brought from Jericho. He would personally make the trip the next day, he said, since he wanted to investigate a shepherd's complaint in that region, anyway. Thus by Monday he could give us a firsthand report. In answer to my query about Sowmy's reference to Arab feuds, he assured me there were none. He claimed he knew every Bedouin throughout the area.

Encouraged by the assurances of the Arabs that our mission from Nebi Musa could be accomplished, Dr. Burrows and I returned to the School before noon. The beauty of the day and the news which brought a temporary respite from strife had prompted Dr. Burrows to arrange for a trip to Bethlehem. It proved a welcome interlude as well as a delightful excursion. That afternoon Brownlee and I visited the Garden of Gethsemane to take long-awaited spring pictures. That brief visit by taxi to the Mount of Olives had to substitute for the traditional Palm Sunday pilgrimage we longed to join from the site of ancient Bethany (modern el-'Azariyeh) to Jerusalem over the Mount of Olives. There was no pilgrimage the next day, for again sporadic shooting occurred during the night.

The rejoicing of the Arabs was short-lived, for Partition soon again appeared to be inevitable. The brief respite, however, enabled Brownlee and me to walk to St. Andrew's Church in Zone "A" for their service and for dinner with their pastor on Palm Sunday. The walk both ways was without incident, quite contrary to what we were destined to experience on Easter Sunday.

Impatiently I awaited the report from Nebi Musa on Monday (March 22). None came. Metropolitan Samuel arrived about noon with the Syriac New Testament to permit me to photograph its colorful miniatures. He was having trouble with his camera and left it for me to fix, a task that took the entire evening.

Tuesday morning the Syrians sent a taxi for me to return the New Testament. Having arranged to take a series of pictures in the Monastery, I also carried all my color equipment. On arrival I was surprised to find the man from Nebi Musa talking to the Metropolitan. He had not been able to make the trip, he explained, for it had rained. Discussing the situation with a number of Bedouins, however, he had learned that the Jewish Haganah army occupied all the region around 'Ain Feshkha right up to the base of the cliffs. We would be completely exposed on the cliff if we attempted to descend, he asserted. It was now clear that the expedition would have to be abandoned until peace was restored to the area. The Syrians assured me, however, that they would cooperate fully with the A.S.O.R. when the opportunity to visit the cave became possible.

Discouraged by the frustration of our hopes, I stopped at Raad's shop to find that he had completed all the prints of the new Isaiah and Habakkuk Scroll negatives. This was good news, at least; our photographs were now completed without mishap. Except for our class session, that entire afternoon was devoted to assembling the sets of prints, one for each of us—the Metropolitan, Dr. Burrows, Brownlee, and myself.

During the next two days efforts to obtain visas and other details related to our leaving consumed almost all of our time. Thursday (March 25), after a particularly

Complete text of "Habakkuk Commentary" (1QpHab)

frustrating morning when I tried to secure a visa for England, I returned to the School shortly after noon to learn that the Syrians had again sent their *kawas* with a taxi to conduct me to the Monastery. It was urgent that I go at once, the servants claimed, concerned more about my safety than the Syrians' request. Helen offered to fix lunch forty-five minutes early, so I could be safely back by three o'clock. (By then the almost-daily skirmishes began as early as three thirty or four o'clock.) Visions of some tragic accident to the precious scrolls occupied my mind as I hurried my lunch.

Arriving at the Monastery out of breath, hastily I glanced around, almost expecting to see evidence of bomb damage. Then I spotted the Metropolitan standing at the head of the stairway to the balcony; a broad smile lighted up his face. My fears melted into curiosity. As I followed him into his office, a portly stranger in Western clerical garb arose from the settee. He was introduced as the Rev. John S. Malak, formerly of Oregon, and a good friend of the Metropolitan. Little was said, however, for from his desk drawer the Metropolitan drew forth a folded sheet of paper and handed it to me. Opening the paper, I was startled and delighted to see a dark brown fragment of leather, its edges irregularly chewed and several gaping holes breaking its inscribed text.

Immediately its script reminded me of the Habakkuk Commentary. Parts of two columns were inscribed on either side of a margin. The left part, I was sure, would provide the right half of the broken column at the beginning of the scroll, which Brownlee had by then completely translated. Recalling how Brownlee had bewailed the absence of a portion of Habakkuk 1:6, about which a scholarly dispute had arisen, I wondered if this fragment would provide the missing words. The scroll had at least one more column, we now knew.

The Metropolitan said that he had opened a book to read that morning and had discovered the fragment, about which he had completely forgotten.[9] As I rejoiced over the new fragment, he went on to relate that Father Sowmy had left that morning for Beirut with the four precious scrolls. The safety of the manuscripts, he continued, was by then assured. It was a great relief to know that at last the scrolls were out of strife-ridden Jerusalem. By what route or means of transportation Sowmy had departed, I was not informed. That the manuscripts would be placed in a bank vault in Beirut was all the specific information revealed to me. The fact that removing antiquities from the country without an export license was technically illegal, was totally foreign to my thoughts. I rejoiced to know that the scrolls were safe.[10]

11

Jerusalem, Jerusalem!

EASTER Sunday (March 28) dawned clear and warm amid thunderous explosions and exchanges of gunfire not far from our School. Efforts to establish a truce for this holiest day of Jerusalem's Christian calendar had failed. Brownlee and I joined the handful of Christians at the Garden tomb for the traditional "sunrise" service. Normally, on that occasion, thousands of pilgrims crowded the lovely Garden, which formed a natural amphitheater around the sheer stone cliff with its rock-cut tomb. From here, many Christians sincerely believe, Jesus arose that first Easter.[1]

Plaintive music from a wheezy reed organ provided little support for the joyous Easter hymns, as halfhearted singers solemnly rendered the victorious notes. Myriad bells from the Old City pealed discordantly during much of the simple service. While a British Army chaplain intoned solemn words of prayer, distant dull thuds of bombs, mingled with the clatter of small arms and machine-gun fire, emphasized his pleas for divine assistance. A convoy, we learned later, was ambushed along the Hebron Road south of Bethlehem; four small airplanes circled the scene, and bombs were cast from their windows. The urgent words of the Rev. Edwin Moll's sermon were mostly lost amid the sickening jumble of sounds of battle and bells.

Hoping once again to attend the St. Andrew's Church service, Brownlee and I started at ten thirty to traverse the city by the route used successfully on Palm Sunday. Descending a broad stairway connecting Jaffa Road and the lower Mamillah Road, we were crossing the latter when suddenly a barrage of gunfire streaked across the Mamillah Cemetery a few hundred yards to our right. Bullets whined above our heads; Arabs, from the tops of the buildings opposite us, returned the barrage. Like dozens of others caught in the cross-fire, we darted into the nearest open doorway. Within a few minutes the firing ceased. Cautiously we emerged from our shelter, hoping to reach a stairway where we could descend into the bombed-out no man's land of the Jewish commercial center. From there we thought it would be safer to get around to Julian's Way and up to the Y.M.C.A. a half mile farther south. We hugged close to the buildings as we approached the Mamillah Cemetery.

We were barely ten paces from the stairway when once again the firing broke out above us. We could see the puffs of smoke near the housetops across the Muslim cemetery. Again we dashed to the nearest building entrance, joining a considerable crowd gathered for refuge. Presently, on a stairway directly ahead, who should appear but our good friend Anwar Tamimi! Amazed to see us in the crowd, he motioned us up the stairs. He led us into an office where armed Arab soldiers, whose checkered red *keffiyehs* revealed their Trans-Jordanian origin, were seated along three walls.

Anwar queried us about our purpose in somewhat scolding tones. A little sheepishly we explained our hopes to attend the Easter service at St. Andrew's Church. Promising to help if he could, Anwar chatted in Arabic with the soldiers nearest his desk; a good deal of head-shaking by the soldiers indicated their opposition to his proposal. Being in an office of the Muslim Supreme Council, surrounded by armed Muslim soldiers on Easter Sunday at churchtime, suddenly struck me as ironical. I might have laughed except for the tension of our plight.

In dashed another armed Arab, who spoke excitedly with Anwar. Turning to us, he explained that the battle had now spread to the Montefiore District, making it impossible for us to get to the church. Declining his offer to send a guard with us to the School, we retraced our steps. As we started to cross the Nablus Road by the Palestine Pottery Works, where I had sought refuge from snipers ten days before, Brownlee left me to return to the School. I continued to St. George's Cathedral.

The service was well under way as I found a seat near the rear of the great nave, whose heavy stone wall seemed particularly welcome. Presently, to my delight, Bishop Stewart rose to preach. It was a brief but pointed sermon, based on the Johannine phrase, "They have taken away my Lord . . ." (John 20:13). Stressing the uniqueness of our experiences, which enabled us to share intensely the frustrations which the disciples must have felt that first Holy Week, the Bishop's consoling words touched each worshiper deeply. After the turmoil of the morning, I felt a strange peace within as I walked slowly back to our School. Still another battle broke out later that day, ending one of the most tragic holy days I have ever known.

Meanwhile our intermittent studies of the scrolls had progressed slowly. Dr. Brownlee rejoiced over the additional Habakkuk Scroll fragment, which supplied certain words he had hoped to find. Some scholars many years before had proposed that the Book of Habakkuk was written in the late fourth century B.C., and referred in 1:6 to the "Kittim," meaning the Greeks under Alexander the Great; the present reference to the seventh-century B.C. "Chaldeans" (*Kasdim*), they claimed, was a later emendation of the original text. The new leather fragment now provided a first-century B.C.—A.D. testimony to the accuracy of the text as it has been preserved—*Kasdim* was clearly in the text used then by the copyist. The next line, however, begins, "Its interpretation concerns the Kittim . . . ." The modern theory had already been propounded by interpretation by the ancient community two thousand years earlier!

Saturday, March 27, we held our last class session, during which we discussed the final two columns of the Habakkuk Commentary. Dr. Brownlee had, in the meantime, prepared typed copies of a transliterated Hebrew text and his provisional translation for each of us. I regretted my inability to do likewise for the Manual of Discipline, only a few columns of which we had been able by then to translate. Other responsibilities relating to the scrolls had cut too deeply into my study time.

With our plans for an expedition to the cave abandoned, I sought all possible information from the Syrians concerning the cave. One day I queried Father Yusif at length regarding his visit to the cave with George Isha'ya during August 1947. He described the small entrance to the cave, which he interpreted as resulting from the collapse of the front of the cave during an earthquake.[2] Consequently, he claimed, the scrolls, wrapped in many layers of cloth, were originally found protruding from the debris. He saw the piles of cloth, one complete jar amid much broken pottery, and some fragments of leather scattered on the floor of the cave.

He and Isha'ya spent the night just outside the entrance to the cave. The next day they tried to take the one complete jar but found it too much to carry in the August heat.[3] It was then that the Syrians expressed the opinion that the Bedouins may have happened upon the cave during one of their periodic trips from Amman to Bethlehem (they had found a ready market for American goods available in Amman but restricted by high import duties from Palestine).[4]

After repeated interviews with the Syrians, I still found many gaps in the story about the early history of the scrolls. It was to be many months before sufficient evidence could be gleaned to piece together what probably had happened (see next chapter).

As part of my continuing efforts to weld an enduring friendship with the Monastery people, I probed them concerning their plans and hopes for the future of their Monastery. Of primary urgency, they emphasized, was the establishment of a school adjacent to the Monastery. It was readily apparent that their educational outreach needed extending. My suggestion that the scrolls could be a means for bringing additional income to their Monastery met with an enthusiastic response.

Together we worked out a plan whereby a small museum would be developed within, or immediately adjacent to their Monastery property to house the valuable scrolls. Interest in the scrolls, I assured them, would be so great that thousands of tourists would flock to their Monastery to view the amazing documents. By charging a small entrance fee, they would be assured of a steady and sizable income to devote to educating their young people and clergy. To assist in this project, I promised to contribute most of whatever profits I might make in the United States from the sale of pictures of the scrolls and the Syriac New Testament miniatures.[5]

Our activities during those last few days reached a frenzied crescendo. There were still many pictures I wanted to take at the Museum, in our School, and in some of the local shops. Tuesday, March 30, the Metropolitan promised to take me to Bethlehem to arrange for a series of color pictures in the Church of the Nativity. Torrential rains that day and skirmishes along the Bethlehem Road frustrated those plans. Mr. Whiting of the American Colony wanted guidance in taking color pictures of his rare irises and some instruction in color-processing. The Museum photographer also wanted to be instructed in color-processing. The more pictures I took, the more processing was necessary. The demonstrations, therefore, actually made the task easier.

P. L. O. Guy offered, on April 3, to open some of the cases in the Museum so that I might get some special pictures without the glass reflections. A whole morning was gladly devoted to this welcome opportunity. Four more rolls of color film had to be developed, but the results were well worth the pressure the project created.

Last-minute preparations to leave sent us all scurrying in various directions. Dr. Brownlee left from Lydda by plane during a downpour on Tuesday, March 30; Dr. and Mrs. Burrows left in a convoy for Haifa early Friday morning to await a small Norwegian freighter, which failed to dock for two weeks; scheduled to leave by plane on April 8, I continued to work alone at the School. The Museum had promised me a collection of duplicate pottery in return for some films and supplies for color-processing I offered them. Packing the pottery for shipment in my trunk took the better part of another morning. The Metropolitan's camera again needed repair—an evening was devoted to that. Anwar had purchased Brownlee's camera and wanted instructions in using it. So the days sped by.

On Saturday afternoon Mr. Whiting came for further instruction on the use of a color camera and had been gone but a few minutes when the Metropolitan, Father Sowmy, and their friend, the Rev. John S. Malak, arrived for a final conference. They had come to work out the contract with the A.S.O.R. for the publication of the scrolls, they announced. Having been left with no authority, I could do no more than write down items which we agreed should go into the document, with a promise to communicate them to the A.S.O.R. officers in America.

With great solemnity they outlined the various points which they expected to be included in the contract: "1) The owner of the manuscripts is His Grace, Mar Athanasius Yeshue Samuel, Metropolitan of the Jerusalem Syrian Orthodox Church; 2) publisher, the A.S.O.R.; 3) period of agreement, at least three years; 4) the total number of copies printed must be indicated in the volume, and each one must be numbered; 5) several copies should be supplied to the Syrians to use as gifts; 6) if there is a profit from the sale of the volumes, what percentage would revert to the owner?; 7) before publication a copy of the prepared materials is to be sent to the owner for approval."

For the sake of the A.S.O.R. I suggested we add two more points: "8) During the period of the agreement, the rights for publication shall not be transferred to another institution without the consent of the owner, and likewise the owner will not grant any publication rights to any other party or parties during the period of the contract; and 9) if any or all of the manuscripts are sold during the period of the agreement, the purchaser will be bound to allow the same publication rights to continue."

Considerable discussion developed around the sixth point, for the Syrians wanted the matter made specific. It was hard to communicate to them the fact that the kind of publication that would be prepared could not be expected to produce profits. No large volume of sales of such technical books is common; seldom are more than a few hundred copies sold, and those have to be mostly subsidized. The possibility of any profits, I emphasized, was very remote.

Before they left, I urged again the importance of full cooperation with the School on any future visit to the cave. Failure to have an official of the School accompany them, I warned, would be a violation of the agreement worked out with the Department of Antiquities. They assured me that they would cooperate fully. Thus I felt confident that the best possible arrangements had been worked out for the publication of the scrolls and that the cave would suffer no further damage. With many warm and friendly farewells and fond hopes that the strife would soon pass, we parted.

Hardly had the Syrians left the School when Mr. Whiting returned for another demonstration of color-developing, including an experimental roll of iris pictures he had just exposed. Processing the four rolls taken at the Museum that morning occupied the evening. To complicate matters, the airline office called that day, asking me to be ready to leave early Monday morning. If my luggage were reduced to 100 kilograms (about 220 pounds), they said, they would carry it on the same plane. This meant giving Sunday over to repacking. Most of the books I had bought thus had to be sent by mail, despite the uncertainty of postal service, which by then had almost completely collapsed.

At the airline depot near the Y.M.C.A. early Monday, everything had to be weighed. First my two trunks were put on a large scale and, fortunately, totaled exactly 100 kilograms. Then, to my surprise, the man in charge asked me to get on the scales with my small bulging satchel and tightly packed camera gadget-bag. He put down my weight as 90 kilograms—198 pounds! Having lost over 20 pounds during the months of intense strain and activity, I weighed barely 130 pounds at the time. Subtracting the 20-kilogram allowance for free baggage, he charged me only 80 percent of an extra fare. For the first time in the Near East I had been charged less than I expected to pay!

With the transaction completed, the agent asked if I would do him a favor: Would I mail a bundle of his wedding announcements in Beirut? After the favor he had rendered to me, his request was indeed insignificant and easily accomplished.

Cautiously the driver of the airline station wagon drove through the almost-deserted streets of Jerusalem as I craned my neck to gain last fleeting glimpses of the Holy City. The evidences of the many battles were everywhere. Once-beautiful buildings, some barely completed, were now reduced to rubble or filled with round, jagged holes where trim rectangular windows had once been. Maneuvering the station wagon skillfully through the cement cones that marked the entrance to the Sheikh Jarrah Quarter, the driver nervously hastened through that hotly disputed zone and up the switchback on the south slope of Mount Scopus. At the top, well out of range of Jerusalem's danger zones, he stopped and allowed us to get out for a few minutes. Perhaps he felt the need of a respite after traversing the treacherous route.

As I stood scanning the scene in which I had been engulfed for almost eight months, I was sickened by the sight. There before me lay the results of those incessant conflicts near our school. The new part of Jerusalem was reduced to a ghostly shambles: not a building was unmarred; most were roofless, gutted frames of what once had been homes and shops. I could have taken a picture, but I did not have the heart to record the tragedy of this city which had become such an integral part of my life. Once again, as on a previous occasion when I stood on the Mount of Olives, the words of Jesus, weeping over Jerusalem, seemed to come forth: "Would that even today you knew the things that make for peace! But now they are hid from your eyes" (Luke 19:42, RSV).

Were it not for the grass and wildflowers which grew in rich variety along the side of the road, it would have been hard to believe that this was the height of spring in the Holy Land. Many fields, normally lush with growing grain by this time, were still barren or unkempt. Perhaps their owners had been too busy laying plans to defend their lands from the specter of war. Down the steep road that follows the rocky, terraced Valley of Aijalon, where once Joshua chased the five kings of the Amorites (Joshua 10:6-14), we plunged toward Lydda on the open plain.

Inside the heavily guarded barrier at the Lydda Airport, the usual complications of travel quickly dispelled my reflections on the tragedy of Palestine. At the customs post my carefully prepared list of contents did not dissuade the official from a thorough search of my luggage. Handing him the papers given to me by Mr. Iliffe at the Museum, I explained about the large sealed box of antiquities in my trunk. Looking over the papers, he inquired where my export license was. These were all the papers given me at the Museum, I countered; surely they must include an export license. For a while the situation seemed hopeless, but then he noticed that the Museum had placed a value of less than five dollars on all the items, so he decided to pass the matter by.[6] Later, on boarding the plane, I found my roped trunks securely strapped directly behind my seat.

With its supercharged motors roaring, the small DC-3 Middle East Airlines plane slowly rose from the runway. Almost immediately the pilot banked toward the west as though impatient to reach the safety of the open Mediterranean Sea, out of range of snipers' bullets. As the ribbon of sandy beach by Tel Aviv swept past below, a wave of relief engulfed me. Suddenly, for the first time since January, I felt safe!

Months of silence now descended upon the story of the scrolls.

12

What Had Happened Before

THROUGH many retellings, the fragmentary early published accounts concerning what transpired in the scroll story prior to February, 1948, have become legend-[1] To gather the evidence and sift the often-contradictory information about those obscure events has required many years, but what were probably the essential facts can now be related with a fair degree of certainty. Many details, therefore, are published here for the first time, others are corrected, and still others can now be further clarified. Still other details may never be recovered from their obscurity.

Late in 1945 or early 1946, according to the evidence,[2] a controversy arose among the Syrian Orthodox Christians of Palestine over the handling of a piece of Monastery property located between the Street of the Prophets and the Russian Compound in the western sector of Jerusalem. A small school had been operated there by the Syrian community, but certain business interests wanted to develop the area into commercial buildings. The priests at St. Mark's favored the latter as a source of income for their Monastery; most of the laity, however, wanted the school improved. The priests were planning instead to develop a new school beside the Monastery in the Old City. Considerable heat was generated over the matter, and as a result many lay members of the church became alienated from their religious leaders at the Monastery.

In order to keep harmony in their church, a layman by the name of Anton D. Kiraz attempted to mitigate the tension. A dealer in secondhand cars and an operator of a fleet of taxis under the title "Imperial Taxi Service," he had developed a prosperous business and owned one of the finer homes along the old Bethlehem Road just south of the Talpioth Sector of Jerusalem. Considerable publicity centered around his property in 1945 when Professor E. L. Sukenik excavated a first-century tomb there and found what he then believed to be Christian remains.[3]

When Mar Athanasius Y. Samuel—who had been associated with St. Mark's for many years—was consecrated Metropolitan of Jerusalem by the Patriarch in Homs, Syria, on December 22, 1946, Mr. Kiraz was the only member of the Syrian Orthodox community of Jerusalem who attended the service. To honor the newly consecrated Metropolitan, he gave a dinner party at the Villa Rose Marie in the German Colony of Jerusalem on January 22, 1947. Some forty members of the community, including the monks and priests of St. Mark's Monastery, were invited to the gala occasion.[4] Thus Mr. Kiraz endeared himself to the Metropolitan, who sought his counsel repeatedly on business and other matters. They were frequently together during 1947 and early 1948, and Mr. Kiraz often provided his taxis to assist the Monastery people.

At the extreme northwest shore of the Dead Sea, which lies 1,285 feet below sea level, a modern hotel had recently opened at the popular resort of Kallia, about six miles southeast of Jericho. Many tourists frequented the resort to enjoy the amazing properties of the highly saline Dead Sea water. On October 25, 1947, some members of the American School (including the writer) formed one such group of curious tourists.

From Kallia a broad, barren plain stretches for two and a half miles westward to sheer cliffs which mark the eastern edge of the rugged Judean wilderness. Six miles to the south the rapidly-narrowing plain is brought to a sharp point where the cliffs plunge to the Dead Sea at Ras Feshkha. Less than a mile north of Ras Feshkha warm brackish water emerges from a copious, bubbling spring at 'Ain Feshkha, around which reeds, marsh grasses, and other flora grow abundantly. A well-worn path follows the shore of the Dead Sea south from Kallia, past 'Ain Feshkha, and climbs the steep slope of Ras Feshkha onto the broad Buqei'a plateau of the eastern Judean wilderness (believed to be the Valley of Achor of Joshua 7:24-26). From there the path continues to rise as it winds westward through dry wadis, finally crossing the traditional Shepherds' Fields to Bethlehem. It was this very route which Ruth and Naomi, in the familiar Biblical story, would doubtless have taken between Moab and Bethlehem. David too, no doubt, explored the same route in his youth and probably sent his parents to Moab that way (I Samuel 22:3-4). Amos, who lived nearby in Tekoa, must have known the region intimately.

For almost three centuries the Bedouins of the tribe called Ta'amireh have roamed this wilderness east of Bethlehem.[5] By 1947 it was also true that the three Bedouin tribes of the area had found that the high duties imposed by the Mandate Government of Palestine on American goods—which were plentiful in independent Trans-Jordan's capital, Amman—offered a tempting opportunity for profit in their Bethlehem market place. Under cover of darkness they could ford the lower Jordan River, well out of range of the customs post at Allenby Bridge (where Father Sowmy's brother was a customs official), and following this shore path soon be lost in the desert fastness.[6]

It was during the early fall of 1946 that three Ta'amireh Bedouins descended with their flocks of sheep and goats to 'Ain Feshkha in search of water, forage, and warmth, as they normally do at that time of the year.[7] The two older herdsmen were Khalil Musa and his younger cousin, Jum'a Muhammed Khalil.[8] The youngest of the trio was their teen-age cousin, Muhammed Ahmed el-Hamed, whose nickname is "Edh-Dhib," because, they said, his father was "fierce like a wolf."[9]

Jum'a, according to his older cousin Khalil, had a penchant for exploring caves, for he felt confident that someday he would locate one in which a cache of gold had been stored in ancient times. Often, while tending the flocks, he would explore the rocky crags nearby to satisfy his curiosity.

Sometime during the winter of 1946-1947 (the Bedouins think it was November or December 1946), Jum'a, it was, who happened upon two holes in the side of a rock projection above the plateau where their flocks were grazing. The lower of the two holes was barely large enough "for a cat to enter," as Jum'a described it in several interviews; the one which was somewhat above eye level was large enough for a slender man to enter. Jum'a threw a rock through the smaller opening and was startled by the strange sound he heard; apparently the rock shattered an earthenware jar within. Thinking there might be a cache of gold within, he summoned the two other herdsmen to show them the curious holes.[10] In the gathering darkness of evening it was too late to

Plateau and cliffs where Caves I and II were discovered

Two Ta'amireh Bedouins with interviewers in 1962

attempt an entrance; the next day had to be devoted to watering their flocks at 'Ain Feshkha, so they agreed to explore the cave two days later.

Shortly after sunup on the third day,[11] while his two older cousins still slept near the flocks, Muhammed edh-Dhib quietly slipped away and climbed the 100 meters from their camp up to the intriguing holes. Placing some large rocks beneath the larger opening, Muhammed was able to reach up and grasp the rock overhang above the opening and hoist himself up sufficiently to permit his legs to enter the hole. Thus he eased himself down feet first into the cave and slid to the floor on his back.[12]

As his eyes became accustomed to the dim light, he saw about ten tall jars lining the walls of the cave, according to his own description. Several of them had covers. Some of the jars had small handles which apparently were used in tying down the covers to seal the contents.[13] In addition, the Bedouins claim that there was a pile of rocks which had fallen from the ceiling, and much broken pottery on the floor of the cave. All but two of the jars proved to be empty. One was filled with reddish earth; from the other one, a jar with a cover, Muhammed pulled two bundles wrapped in cloth which he described as "greenish" in appearance.[14] A third, the largest, was a roll of leather without any wrapping. From his description and hand motions during our interview, as well as from other evidence, it seems quite probable that the larger scroll was the now-famed Isaiah Scroll (1QIs^a) and the two smaller ones, the Habakkuk Commentary (1QpHab) and the Manual of Discipline (1QS).[15] Only these three manuscripts were taken by edh-Dhib from the cave that morning.[16]

When edh-Dhib returned to his older companions and showed them the three bundles, they were angered by the fact that he had gone alone and accused him of hiding some gold from them. This betrayal of his older cousins' confidence may account for edh-Dhib's absence from the subsequent events. Although edh-Dhib did go back to the cave with Jum'a and Khalil and help them remove two large jars, he seems to have had nothing further to do with the story, as he and his cousins testify.

When one of Jum'a's five sons arrived some days later, Jum'a carried the three scrolls to the Ta'amireh center southeast of Bethlehem. The jars meanwhile were left standing outside the entrance to the cave.[17] For several weeks the manuscripts were left in a bag hanging on a tent pole.[18] It was during this period, while the manuscripts were being shown to other members of the tribe, that the uninscribed cover on the Isaiah Scroll was apparently broken off and destroyed.[19] Also it was possible that the Manual of Discipline was broken into two parts at this time, though this matter still remains a mystery.[20]

During March, 1947,[21] Jum'a and Khalil Musa took the three manuscripts and the

Ibrahim 'Ijha, Bethlehem merchant

two jars (they had in the meantime secured them from the cave) to Bethlehem where they showed them to a carpenter and antiquities dealer by the name of Ibrahim 'Ijha, who promised to see if they could be sold. 'Ijha, when interviewed in the same shop (see Appendix I), where he continues to make ax and hoe handles from walnut branches and to deal in a few antiquities, says that he kept the scrolls for several weeks. During that time he showed them to another antiquities dealer, Faidi Salahi. The latter suspected that the documents had been stolen from a Jewish synagogue and thus warned 'Ijha against dealing with the Bedouins.[22] When, therefore, Jum'a inquired again about the manuscripts (apparently it was on Saturday, April 5, 1947),[23] 'Ijha returned them to him, explaining that they had no archeological value and that no one would buy them. The jars, however, were left in 'Ijha's shop.

Jum'a then carried the three scrolls to the market place of Bethlehem, where he chanced to meet George Isha'ya Shamoun (usually called Isha'ya, or just Sha'ya), a Syrian Orthodox Christian who frequented Bethlehem to sell *abayahs* (cloaklike outer garments) to the Bedouins. On being shown the scrolls Isha'ya offered to arrange for their sale, but Jum'a was suspicious of him. While they discussed the scrolls, Sheikh 'Ali Subh,[24] also a Ta'amireh and a friend of Jum'a, appeared; he suggested that they all go to Khalil Eskander Shahin (locally called Kando), a cobbler near Manger Square. They agreed to ask him "to guarantee George Isha'ya for £P5 to keep the scrolls." In Kando's shop, where Khalil Musa presently joined them,[25] an agreement was reached that the Bedouins should receive two-thirds of any price Kando and Isha'ya were able to get for the scrolls. Thus the Bedouins were persuaded to leave the scrolls in Kando's care.

During Holy Week (April 7-13, 1947) Isha'ya contacted St. Mark's Syrian Orthodox Monastery in Jerusalem and was invited to bring one of the scrolls there for the Metropolitan to examine. Sometime after Holy Week Isha'ya and Kando appeared at the Monastery with a piece of what is now commonly called the Manual of Discipline.[26] When they described the scrolls as having been "wrapped like mummies" and found in a cave by the Dead Sea, the Metropolitan decided that they might be from early Christian times and offered to buy them. Apparently Isha'ya and Kando were in no hurry, for the sale was not completed until July 19, 1947 (see below).

In the meantime, having been urged by Metropolitan Samuel and Kando, Isha'ya persuaded the Bedouins, Jum'a and Khalil Musa, to take him to the cave. According to Jum'a (see Appendix I), the three of them went together in a taxi from Jerusalem to the point where the Dead Sea road branches from the Jericho road. From there they hiked for an hour to reach the cave. Nothing seems to have been taken from the cave on that visit, but Jum'a said that before they left Isha'ya made a cairn of rocks to mark the site. Some weeks later, Jum'a met Isha'ya and Khalil Musa in the Bethlehem market place, and they were carrying two more scrolls from the same cave. Khalil Musa, when interviewed independently,[27] agreed that he went a second time to the cave with Isha'ya but asserted that they secured *four* scrolls from under the debris on the floor of the cave at that time.[28]

These four scrolls were taken to Kando, who has confirmed the fact that *four* scrolls were brought to him by Isha'ya and Khalil before any scrolls had been sold to St. Mark's.[29] Kando kept only one of this group, however, as payment for the advance he had made to Isha'ya on expenses for the two trips to the cave.[30] Khalil Musa and Jum'a wanted to keep the other scrolls since, as Kando put it, "they were partners" in the deal. It seems quite likely that the scroll which Kando secured at that time (probably in May or June 1947) was the Syrians' "Fourth Scroll," now called the "Genesis Apocryphon" (1QApoc).[31]

According to Jum'a's statements, the three manuscripts which Jum'a and Khalil kept were then taken to a friend of Khalil's by the name of Da'ud Musallam (see Appendix I), the cousin of the present mayor of Bethlehem, 'Ayub Musallam. Da'ud had a dealer friend in Jaffa by the name of Mahmud Avghani to whom he planned to show the scrolls; but when Avghani failed to appear after several days, Da'ud returned these scrolls to the Bedouins.[32] It was then, probably in June, 1947, that Jum'a and Khalil decided to take these three documents to Faidi Salahi, who purchased them for £P7 ($28.35). At the same time, Salahi secured the two jars for twenty piasters each (about 80 cents). It was this group of manuscripts and the two jars which Dr. E. L.

Sukenik purchased from Salahi for the Hebrew University on November 29, 1947, about five months later.[33]

It was probably Saturday, July 5, 1947,[34] when Kando finally arranged for Isha'ya to take Jum'a and Khalil [35] with the first group of four scrolls to Jerusalem to St. Mark's Monastery. Metropolitan Samuel, having been apprised of their coming, waited impatiently for their arrival. Isha'ya took the two Bedouins first to his home in the Katamon Quarter, where he gave them lunch, and then they went together to St. Mark's.[36] When they arrived, a priest by the name of Bulos Gilf, knowing nothing of the negotiations, met them at the gate and was repulsed by the appearance of the ragged Bedouins and their dirty bag with foul-smelling scrolls inside. Despite the appeals of Isha'ya that the Metropolitan was expecting them, Father Bulos was adamant and refused them admittance.[37]

Later, Father Bulos mentioned casually, and with disdain, the appearance of the Bedouins with Isha'ya at their gate. Metropolitan Samuel hastened to the telephone to call Kando in Bethlehem. Kando confirmed the story and added that while Isha'ya and the Bedouins were leaving the Old City, they met a Jewish antiquities dealer to whom the scrolls were shown. He offered to buy them and sought directions to the cave. When he asked the Bedouins to accompany him to his shop to get the money, Isha'ya warned them that it was a trick to turn them over to the government authorities, who would put them in jail.[38] Thus they all fled back to Bethlehem, and the four scrolls were again left in Kando's shop.[39]

Metropolitan Samuel meanwhile told Kando to "pay the Bedouins a good price" for the scrolls whenever he could again contact them. It was two weeks later (July 19, 1947) when Kando saw the Bedouins again.[40] He told them of the prelate's offer and paid them £P16 ($64.80). When Kando delivered the four scrolls to St. Mark's Monastery, he received £P24 ($97.20), according to his agreement with the Bedouins.[41]

Eager to learn more about the place of origin of the scrolls, Metropolitan Samuel persuaded Isha'ya to take someone from the Monastery to the cave. About the middle of August, Isha'ya took a priest of St. Mark's (Father Yusif) to the cave, traveling by way of Kallia in a car. Father Yusif reported back with the same information which Isha'ya had provided, as already related in the previous chapter. The location of the scrolls in a jar in a cave by the Dead Sea, and their fragile state of preservation, strengthened the prelate's belief that the scrolls might date from early Christian times.

Meanwhile the Metropolitan had contacted a member of his community who was an assistant librarian at the Palestine Archaeological Museum, Stephan Hanna Stephan. Being an Arabist only, he had little basis for a judgment about Hebrew scrolls; but he did claim that they were worthless—certainly not as old as the Metropolitan alleged. He is reported to have said that they were "not worth a shilling."

Metropolitan Samuel then called Father S. Marmardji, a friend and teacher of Arabic at the Dominican École Biblique in Jerusalem. He examined the scrolls but seriously doubted the prelate's claim for their antiquity. A few days later—it must have been before the end of July[42]—the Metropolitan invited Marmardji to bring Father J. van der Ploeg, an Old Testament scholar who was staying at the École Biblique, to St. Mark's Monastery to examine the scrolls. Because of his interest in Syrian Orthodox history,[43] van der Ploeg had already visited St. Mark's Monastery twice several months before.

Seated in the Monastery lounge, the Dominicans were brought four scrolls on a large platter.[44] Van der Ploeg examined the largest one, which was apparently rolled with the central part exposed, and found the script difficult to read at first. Having prepared a doctoral dissertation thirteen years before on some texts of Isaiah, his eye happened upon one of them on the scroll before him. Soon he detected others. It was he, therefore, who first identified the scroll and informed the Syrians that their scroll contained the Book of Isaiah.

When told that the scrolls had been found in a jar and were two thousand years old, van der Ploeg was incredulous and asked the Metropolitan to produce the jar as proof. At the Dominican School that afternoon, van der Ploeg discussed the prelate's claim for his scrolls' great antiquity with the eminent archeologist and retired professor of the École Biblique, Father L. H. Vincent.[45] The elderly Dominican scholar so impressed van der Ploeg with the possibility of forgery, through several notable examples, that he determined to await the Metropolitan's proof from the pottery. Since the latter was never produced, he left Palestine on December 11, 1947, believing that the manuscripts were probably medieval and of relatively little importance.[46]

Among the buildings owned by the Syrian Monastery near the Street of the Prophets was a clinic rented to a Jewish doctor. During the summer of 1947 the doctor died. Dr. Maurice Brown, another Jewish doctor, learned of the vacant clinic and sought to rent the property; thus he visited St. Mark's Monastery sometime that August.[47] With the rental arrangements completed, Metropolitan Samuel produced the scrolls and asked Dr. Brown's advice about their value. Having no opinion to offer, the doctor assured him that expert advice could be obtained and that he would arrange for it immediately.

Dr. Brown called the president of the Hebrew University, Dr. Judah L. Magnes, and advised him to send a Hebrew specialist to examine the scrolls. Dr. Magnes in turn communicated the request in a note to the head librarian. Two librarians arrived at St. Mark's in a few days, and the Metropolitan showed them the scrolls, explaining this time that they had been kept for many years in a library of their monastery near the Dead Sea. He asked their advice about the age of the documents, their contents, and whether the University library might consider their purchase. The librarians considered the documents to be of Samaritan origin and decided that an expert in that field should be consulted.[48]

Since the librarians spoke Hebrew to each other, their comments were not understood by the Metropolitan. To him they said only that they must consult an expert before offering any suggestions. It was at least two weeks before they called the Syrian

Monastery again. Then they learned that the Metropolitan was to be away for some time.

Apparently Dr. Brown also called a Jewish antiquities dealer by the name of Sassun; for that same day, after the librarians had left, Sassun appeared at the Monastery, asking to see the documents. His suggestion was that the Metropolitan should send pieces of the scrolls to antiquities dealers in Europe and America to have them evaluated, but the Metropolitan was opposed to such an idea. Sometime before the first of October Sassun offered £P100 ($405) for the five scrolls.[49]

Late in August the Metropolitan sought counsel from his close friend and confidant, Anton Kiraz, concerning some complications in the prelate's personal affairs. (Kiraz had learned about the scrolls only a few weeks before.) When Kiraz revealed that he was planning to leave shortly for a vacation trip to Lebanon and Syria, Metropolitan Samuel urged him to delay until after the Feast of St. Mary on August 28 in order that he might accompany Kiraz. On September 5 they left Jerusalem, the Metropolitan carrying the scrolls in a small leather satchel. They entered Lebanon via the coast road at Ras en Naqura and soon were in Beirut.

Leisurely they traveled in the area for several days, visiting the Cedars of Lebanon, Tripoli, and other places. At Homs, in Syria, the Metropolitan remained with the scrolls at the Syrian Patriarchate, while Kiraz continued his vacation trip to Aleppo to visit a friend. On his return Kiraz again stopped at Homs to visit the Patriarchate; there he learned that the Metropolitan had decided to remain a few more days. Kiraz continued on to Jerusalem without him and arrived there on September 19.

His Holiness, Mar Ignatius Aphram I, Patriarch of Antioch,[50] was highly respected in the Syrian community for his learning; the Metropolitan therefore sought his advice. With deep interest the Patriarch examined the scrolls but could not share the Metropolitan's belief in their great antiquity. He suggested they might be as much as three hundred years old but doubted any greater antiquity. He counseled the prelate, however, to seek advice from the professor of Hebrew at the American University of Beirut. The idea appealed to the Metropolitan, who proceeded to visit the University in Beirut on September 22. The professor of Hebrew, unfortunately, was on vacation. Thus the Metropolitan returned to Jerusalem on September 26[51] without obtaining any further light on the scrolls.

About the first of October, Metropolitan Samuel called Kiraz to inform him of his return and urge him to come to the Monastery at once. On arrival Kiraz found the prelate much agitated over his worsening personal affairs. Without revealing the specific cause for his dilemma, he told Kiraz about Mr. Sassun's offer of £P100 for the scrolls. Since the Metropolitan was in urgent need of funds, he asked Mr. Kiraz how much he would give for the documents. According to Kiraz, he gave the prelate £P25 and said, "Let's be partners in whatever the scrolls may bring."

The following day Kiraz relates that again he was called to the Monastery at the behest of the troubled Metropolitan. This time he unburdened to Kiraz a story of duplicity at the hands of a friend whom he had trusted. The prelate seemed desperate. Kiraz, on hearing the tragic story, assured Metropolitan Samuel that he would solve the problem, even if he had to mortgage his home to do so. Leaving another £P50, therefore, Kiraz urged that the prelate be patient; it would take time to work out a solution to the dilemma, he counseled. Kiraz was true to his word, though it took him almost nine months to solve the problem. Thus arose Kiraz's claim to partnership with the Metropolitan in the further explorations regarding the scrolls.[52]

More eager now to learn the value of the scrolls, Metropolitan Samuel again called Mr. Stephan[53] at the Museum. He requested that Stephan bring some Hebrew grammars to St. Mark's to enable the Metropolitan to study the scrolls himself. The books taught the prelate very little, but he continued confident of the antiquity of the manuscripts.

In a few days Stephan called to say he was bringing an expert in Jewish antiquities to the Monastery. Shortly thereafter Mr. Stephan arrived with Mr. Tovia Wechsler, who was shown the scrolls and recognized the Book of Isaiah among them. He also saw what he thought was a scroll of *Haftarot*.[54] Blank spaces in the text, which he seems to have interpreted as the spaces between the selected readings, influenced his decision. Apparently he was influenced also by the numerous marginal markings. The *Haftarot* scroll, he told the Metropolitan, had indications of recent usage—the blackness of ink corrections on it led primarily to this conclusion.[55] When the Metropolitan claimed great antiquity for the scrolls, therefore, he said Wechsler's reply was, "If that table [a small table in the Monastery office which I later used when examining the same scrolls —see p. 34] were a box and you filled it full of pound notes, you couldn't even then measure the value of these scrolls if they are two thousand years old, as you say." Though intended to discourage the Metropolitan, Wechsler's remark provided the prelate with some hope for the scrolls' value.

Probably the best known of all the stories relating to the Dead Sea Scrolls is that which involved the late Dr. E. L. Sukenik, Professor of Archeology at Jerusalem's Hebrew University, when he returned from a prolonged leave of absence in the United States during 1947. Since his story has been dramatized on television and related in numerous popular books, only a sketch is necessary here.[56]

An Armenian antiquities dealer, whose shop was near the Y.M.C.A. in Jerusalem's "B" Zone, left an urgent telephoned message at the Hebrew University on Sunday, November 23, 1947, to have Dr. Sukenik call him immediately about an antiquity. That afternoon when he called the dealer, Sukenik was unable to learn the nature of the discovery; but he agreed to meet the dealer the next morning at the gate to Zone "B." There, through the barbed-wire barricade, the eminent archeologist saw a ragged fragment of leather inscribed in strange Hebrew characters. The dealer told him of its discovery by Bedouins who were seeking to sell many such pieces to their mutual friend, Faidi Salahi, an antiquities dealer in Bethlehem. When Sukenik noted a resemblance between the script on the fragment and that which he had often seen scratched on first-century ossuaries, his initial skepticism soon gave way to excited curiosity. He therefore offered to buy the fragments for the Hebrew University and urged the Armenian dealer to get more samples of them from the Bethlehem dealer.

Thursday, when at Lake Success the United Nations were approaching a final vote on the Partition of Palestine, the Jerusalem dealer again called, suggesting that Dr. Sukenik come to his shop. There he saw more leather fragments with the same kind of script. Now convinced that the fragments must be genuine and ancient, he arranged to go to Bethlehem, at great personal risk, to meet Faidi Salahi. Had it not been for the decision at Lake Success the next day to delay the final vote on Partition until Saturday, the twenty-ninth, Sukenik probably would not have been able to go. That day of respite gave Sukenik courage to believe that there would be no violence for at least another day.

To clarify this situation, it should be pointed out that, as a member of the Palestine Archaeological Advisory Board, Dr. Sukenik had a means readily available for securing the materials without risk.[57] A call to the Director of Antiquities, R. W. Hamilton, would at that time have assured a safe procedure for bringing the manuscripts and the cave under scholarly control.[58] Faidi Salahi, furthermore, as a licensed antiquities dealer, was technically required to consult the Department of Antiquities prior to any attempt to sell such materials elsewhere.[59]

Together, the Armenian dealer and Dr. Sukenik made the trip to Bethlehem by bus that Saturday. In an upstairs apartment not far from the market place they met Salahi and were shown the two jars as well as the bundles of leather scrolls and fragments which Salahi had purchased from the Ta'amireh Bedouins the previous summer. Sukenik persuaded the dealer to let him take the scrolls to Jerusalem, promising that he would give his decision about purchasing them within two days through the Armenian dealer.

That evening he found that two different documents were contained in the bundles. One seemed similar to the Book of Psalms but was obviously not Biblical (it is now called *Hodayoth* or "Songs of Thanksgiving," 1QH). The other was a description of a battle "between the Sons of Light and the Sons of Darkness" (now commonly called the "War Scroll," 1QM). As he studied the ancient script, the news of the affirmative vote for Partition was announced over the radio. Sukenik joined the Jews of Jerusalem in their paroxysms of joy, his own excitement generated as much by the manuscripts as by the United Nations news.

Despite the increasing tensions and disturbances which followed the decision to partition Palestine, Dr. Sukenik succeeded in obtaining the two jars from Bethelem and in purchasing another scroll on December 22. The latter was apparently the poorly preserved and fragmentary copy of Isaiah (1QIs^b), the nature and contents of which were not revealed until it was opened during the summer of 1949.

Quite by accident one day in early December, Dr. Sukenik mentioned the scrolls to one of the librarians who had been sent to St. Mark's Monastery the preceding August. Immediately the librarian remembered his experience there. He left Dr. Sukenik puzzled, however, by his reference to the Syrian scrolls' having been in a monastery library near the Dead Sea for many years. Sukenik sought Dr. Magnes' permission to handle future negotiations with the Syrians and forthwith set about to make the contact, but to no avail. Jerusalem was by then too sharply divided.

During December and the early part of January, 1948, Metropolitan Samuel was again in Syria. On his return he consulted Mr. Kiraz about the next steps with the manuscripts. It was then that Kiraz remembered the excavation of the tombs on his property by Dr. Sukenik of the Hebrew University; surely Dr. Sukenik could evaluate the scrolls, he suggested. It was agreed that Kiraz should pursue this approach. Wrapping the scrolls in Arabic newspapers, Kiraz took them to his home, where he wrote a somewhat vaguely worded letter to Sukenik. It took three days to arrive at a point barely a mile to the northwest!

Immediately on reading the letter, Dr. Sukenik thought of the scrolls mentioned by the University librarian and contacted Kiraz to arrange a meeting place. Kiraz suggested that they meet on February 4 in Zone "B" in the office of the Y.M.C.A. librarian, Mr. Malak Tannourji, who was also a member of the Syrian Orthodox Church. Knowing that during those days seldom was a Jew at the Y.M.C.A., Dr. Sukenik carried a few books on pretense of returning them. As he entered the building, he was relieved to notice Kiraz sitting on the terrace among a group of Arabs.

Soon Kiraz sauntered into the librarian's office, having allowed time for Sukenik to meet Tannourji. When the Syrians drew forth three of the scrolls from a desk drawer,[60] the appearance of their script immediately reminded Dr. Sukenik of the scrolls which he had already purchased.

Gradually the story of the origin of the Syrian scrolls emerged from the conversation, and Sukenik realized that it tallied with what he had already heard from Salahi. Assuring Kiraz that he would buy the scrolls for the Hebrew University, Sukenik requested the privilege of taking them to show President Magnes and some of his colleagues. According to Kiraz, he was offered £P100 for the documents;[61] but he replied that he would have to discuss the offer "with his partner," the Metropolitan. The three men agreed to meet again in the same place Friday morning, February 6. During the interim Dr. Sukenik copied several chapters from the Isaiah Scroll. The two other Syrian scrolls (one portion of the Manual of Discipline and the "Genesis Apocryphon") remained in Mr. Tannourji's desk drawer.

Dr. Sukenik later reported that when the men again met in the same office Friday morning, the first words of Kiraz were, "What will you offer?" According to both Kiraz and Tannourji, Dr. Sukenik offered £P500 ($2,025)—£P250 for each of the partners to the scrolls. Again Mr. Kiraz demurred on the grounds that he must consult his partner. Dr. Sukenik then promised to give Mr. Kiraz an extra £P500 if he would persuade the Metropolitan to conclude the deal.[62] Another meeting was planned for the Yugoslav Consulate, according to both Kiraz and Sukenik, when Kiraz was to bring the Metropolitan, and Dr. Sukenik the president of the Hebrew University.[63]

Kiraz and the Metropolitan now realized that the scrolls must be worth a great deal; but the problem was, how much to ask? Meanwhile Mr. Tannourji counseled Kiraz to get another appraisal, reminding him of the story of the Codex Sinaiticus. He

Bethlehem from the tower over the Grotto of the Nativity

Cliffs among which Caves I and II were discovered

Entrance to Cave I

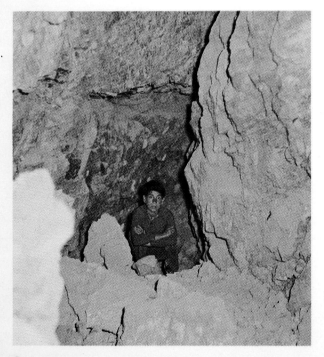

Interior of Cave I

suggested that the A.S.O.R. would probably be a good place to get an opinion. Days went by while Sukenik waited impatiently for a call about the meeting at the Yugoslav Consulate. It never came.

For more than a week the Syrian scrolls remained in a paper bag at the home of Mr. Kiraz. Father Sowmy meanwhile had been in Lebanon for almost a month; the Metropolitan awaited his return, for apparently he valued the monk's opinion highly. On his arrival in Jerusalem about February 17, Father Sowmy expressed strong opposition toward the negotiations with Dr. Sukenik.[64] The suggestion that the A.S.O.R. be consulted, however, he supported. He recalled, in fact, some pleasant associations with the American School some ten years before. The Metropolitan therefore requested Kiraz to return the scrolls to the Monastery, which he did that same day. To find out who could be reached at the A.S.O.R., Father Sowmy called Bishop Stewart at St. George's Cathedral and was given the names of Drs. Millar Burrows and William Brownlee. He then called the A.S.O.R., and asked for Dr. Brownlee, who was away at the time (see Chapter I and pp. 175-176).

When later the Syrians decided to accept my suggestions about the best procedure for handling the scrolls, apparently they said very little to Mr. Kiraz. Toward the end of February, however, Kiraz wrote to Dr. Sukenik, saying that they had decided to wait until after the troubles were over before selling. During March and April Dr. Sukenik continued to try to contact Kiraz, calling Mr. Tannourji several times in an effort to reach him. After the episode in late March, when Kiraz offered the photographs to Sukenik (see pp. 89-90, 91), however, there were no further communications between them.

13

The Scrolls Arrive
in America

OFF the runway at Haifa, where on April 5, 1948, we stopped for half an hour, the small plane darted out over the Bay of Acre and headed north. The pilot kept a safe distance from the coast, thus providing a breathtaking panorama of Galilee and the lofty Lebanon ranges. Sloping gently down to the narrow ribbon of cultivated coastlands with their deep undulations formed by many rivulets, the majestic peaks stretched away for endless miles. The sea below was spread like a carpet, its brilliant blue as deep as the lapis lazuli of King Tut-ankh-amen's jewels before which I had stood enthralled at the Cairo Museum.

Beyond the hills of Galilee, Mount Hermon poked its snow-capped peak above a bracelet of fluffy cumulus clouds surmounted by a deep azure sky. Streaks of snow penetrated like arrows into the lower slopes of the historic mountain. It was a photographer's paradise. Swiftly the ancient cities of Tyre and Sidon passed below, and in a matter of minutes we were swooping down over the red sand and Aleppo-pine watersheds that guide the planes into the busy Beirut airport. Mount Senin, still heavy with winter's snow, rose high above the red-tiled roofs of Beirut, which sits on the Lebanon slopes as though guarding the broad entrance to St. George's Bay.

The peace and beauty of Lebanon, the cordial hospitality of two gracious missionary families who entertained me, and the sights and scenes of more Biblical history soon soothed nerves that had been shattered by the strife I had now left behind. Nahr el-Kelb (Dog River) on the famed route of the conquerors; Jebeil, ancient Byblos of the Egyptian story of Wen-Amon, and the Gebal of the Old Testament; the ski slopes of the regal Cedars of Lebanon above Tripoli; exotic Baalbek in the lush Litani Valley between the Lebanons; the bazaars of Damascus; caves and streams behind Sidon—all these brought refreshing inspiration and memorable experiences. Study of the manuscript photographs, safely stored in their leather satchel, was therefore postponed.

Somewhere in Beirut the scrolls themselves were secreted. My closest link with them was a visit one day in the home of Karim Sowmy, a cousin of Father Butrus Sowmy. There I met again the latter's brother, Ibrahim, and was introduced to the Syrian Metropolitan of Beirut, who was to become the Patriarch of Antioch[1] nine years later.

For almost two weeks I waited for a boat that failed to arrive, and finally boarded another headed for Marseilles. As the outline of Beirut faded into the gathering twilight, a wave of nostalgia gripped my whole being and I lingered at the stern until the last twinkling light dropped below the horizon. During the four subsequent restful days on the gently rolling S.S. *Transylvania,* a Rumanian ship crowded with refugees fleeing the tentacles of communism, I spent many hours comparing the text of the Isaiah Scroll with that of the traditional Hebrew Masoretic text.[2]

It soon became apparent that the text of the ancient scroll was substantially the same as the traditional text, as Dr. Albright had presaged in his letter; but small variations were numerous. The differences tended to fall into a few broad categories, by far the largest of which constituted the liberal addition of certain consonants used as vowel letters to aid pronunciation. After the fifth century B.C., when Hebrew fell into disuse as a living tongue, being supplanted by the more common Aramaic, aids to pronunciation became imperative for new generations of readers. This feature on the Isaiah Scroll seemed to add another argument for its antiquity. Already the appearance of the outside of the scroll, darkened by many hands and repaired at many points, had indicated a much-read scroll. The text, too, now presented additional evidence for its use in public worship. Its many marginal marks argued further in this direction.

A second category included the many obvious errors of the scribe. Though his script was skillfully executed, he lacked that meticulous care which was the mark of the best scribes. Occasionally he corrected an error by inserting the proper letter above the line, or by an erasure. Other errors were left, as already noted, to be corrected by later hands.

Minor grammatical differences appeared fairly often; and variations in spelling, particularly of Biblical names, were also frequent. It was apparent that the discussion of these so-called morphological and orthographic features would occupy scholars for years to come.

Additions of *and, the,* and some prepositions, and occasionally an omission of one of these, were numerous. Important variations which would affect a translation or the meaning were few. None was startling or what might be considered a significant difference. It was obvious that some superior readings would emerge and ultimately be accepted by Biblical scholars, but certainly there would not be many.[3]

A tally of the first column, for instance, produced these results: of a total of 91 variations of all kinds from the Masoretic text, 51 are additions of vowel letters, 7 others are minor spelling variations, 13 are grammatical differences; 8 are probably errors (not including 5 corrected by the scribe); 11 are additions of articles, conjunctions, or prepositions (in addition, one *and* was omitted); and only 2 are significant word additions. Of all the 91 variations, only the 2 word additions and 2 variations in spelling would be worthy of much discussion. Thus, as has been repeatedly stated, the ancient Isaiah Scroll is a witness to the antiquity and faithful preservation of the traditional Masoretic text from at least as early as the first century B.C. The manuscript, on the other hand, clearly reveals that its scribe was no slavish literalist.

By no means, however, could this scroll be called a Masoretic text. It definitely represents another textual tradition, a factor which lends great significance to its discovery. On the problem of whether there was one or more authors for the original Book of Isaiah, the scroll makes no contribution. It was obviously copied at least a hundred years after the text of Isaiah had reached its present structure. A much older manuscript—one at least antedating the third century B.C.—would be necessary to shed significant light on that problem. An interesting marginal marking at the beginning of Chapter 40 on Column 32 is the only point worthy of comment in this regard. It very probably served as a guide to the reader to point out a major transition in the passage, as the same mark does elsewhere in the manuscript. The numerous marginal marks seem to divide the book into Scripture lessons.

During his much longer sea voyage on a freighter, Dr. Burrows was able to collate the entire manuscript, while I finished less than a dozen columns in the few days while crossing the Mediterranean and the Atlantic.

Arriving in London on April 25, I became aware for the first time of the fact that our news release about the scrolls had been flashed around the world. The next day's papers, furthermore, carried Dr. Sukenik's release about the scrolls which he had purchased for the Hebrew University. More scrolls had come from the same cave! My amazement at this announcement was as great as that of every other Bible student. When the A.S.O.R. release had appeared on April 11, I was high up in the Lebanons enjoying the fellowship of skiers and the enthralling beauty of the ancient cedars. No one in Lebanon mentioned seeing the release, but at the British Museum many scholars were buzzing about the discovery. I quickly discovered that my knowledge of the background of the story was an "open sesame" to scholarly circles. Normal scholarly reserve over the startling news was immediately apparent, but several scholars seemed to consider my statements more enthusiasm than wisdom.

In London I eagerly sought out the great manuscript expert, Sir Frederick Kenyon, whose profound writings had made a deep impression on me. When I unfolded some of the scroll story, the aged papyrologist seemed to thrill to my tale of adventure, which touched so intimately his long life of scholarly concentration. Not a Hebraist, however, he had no opinion to offer.[4] While touring Oxford and Cambridge

Universities, I visited Dr. G. R. Driver of Magdalen College, Oxford, and Dr. J. L. Teicher, who was cataloguing Hebrew manuscripts in the Cambridge University Library. They pumped me with questions; but, to judge by their later writings, they did not share my convictions concerning the antiquity of the scrolls. At the Cambridge Library Dr. Teicher brought forth the original Nash Papyrus, which I examined with avid interest.

Crossing the Atlantic on the H.M.S. *Queen Elizabeth*, after the fourteen-day voyage on the lowly S.S. *Marine Carp* the previous August, was like moving from the slums to a king's palace. Reveling in the wonders of that great ship, I found concentration on manuscript study most difficult. Even the swift pace of the "Queen," however, was not enough to satisfy my impatience to be reunited with my family, still far away in California.

Early on the morning of May 15, in Las Vegas, Nevada, that longing was fulfilled. Having promised my brother to address the Community Church of nearby Boulder City the following morning, it was there my journey ended. In my sermon the next morning I could not refrain from unburdening my heart of some of the tragic scenes I had left behind in the Holy Land.

Even as I spoke, eight thousand miles away Jerusalem was embroiled in one of its worst blood-baths, despite the U.N. intention that it be internationalized. As the British forces withdrew on the morning of May 14, all bedlam let loose. A voluntary truce committee had been set up on May 13, comprising the three consuls general of the United States, France, and Belgium. They strove desperately to achieve a cease-fire, which was agreed to for the morning of the sixteenth but failed to be observed. During the holocaust that followed, St. Mark's Monastery suffered severe damage, and fragments from a bursting bomb struck and killed Father Butrus Sowmy.

Two days before, Anton Kiraz had driven the Rev. John Malak and his two sisters to Beirut. Having lost his home and all but one of his cars, Kiraz was now one of the many thousands of refugees who fled with only the few possessions they could carry. Metropolitan Samuel meanwhile went to Madeba in Trans-Jordan.

The summer weeks sped by, as my attention was turned to the task of becoming oriented into a new position. The International Council of Religious Education had arranged a schedule of many speaking engagements related to my responsibilities as Representative of the Committee for the Revised Standard Version of the Bible. Lectures, addresses, special short courses, sermons, and a host of other tasks dominated my daily life. I even forgot to submit the proposed publication contract discussed with the Syrians in Jerusalem. A letter from Dr. Burrows in late May, inquiring about the arrangements I had finally been able to work out, jolted me to action. Quickly I dispatched the points agreed upon, but it was months before the A.S.O.R. could get their revised agreement through to the Metropolitan.

Unexpected complications arose, as Dr. Sukenik pressed for equal rights to publish the Syrian scrolls on the basis of an agreement he claimed to have with Mr. Kiraz. It was the first we had heard of such an agreement, though now the deeper meaning behind the Metropolitan's concerns expressed on March 19 seemed to be coming to light (see pp. 89-90). I prepared a summary of my understanding of the situation for Dr. Burrows, but it lacked the specific details needed.

In the meantime we began to prepare some preliminary articles that would give as complete as possible a picture of the discovery and what it entailed, as far as we then understood it. It was agreed that I should write an abbreviated account of the story for the *Biblical Archaeologist* (September, 1948), a publication by the A.S.O.R. for laymen; and that Dr. Burrows would follow it with a summary of the contents of the three scrolls thus far studied. For the more academic *Bulletin of the American Schools of Oriental Research*, I was asked to prepare a descriptive summary of the four scrolls in the possession of the Syrians and an analysis of the method of dating documents through paleography. For this same journal Dr. Burrows was to summarize the results of his collation of the Isaiah Scroll and Dr. Brownlee to present his tentative translation of the Habakkuk Commentary.[5] Meanwhile Dr. Sukenik published a more elaborate monograph in Hebrew as a preliminary report on two of the scrolls of the Hebrew University.[6] In it he included a transliteration of Isaiah 42 and 43, which he had copied out when the Syrians' scrolls were in his hands February 4-6, as recounted in the previous chapter.[7]

Each of the publications carried sample photographs of the texts, so that by the end of 1948 portions of each scroll, except the Hebrew University Isaiah Scroll (1QIs^b) which had not yet been opened or identified, had been made available to scholars. With these sample photographs before them, the scholars of the world trained their guns of expected criticism upon our conclusions, and the first "battle of the scrolls" began in earnest.[8] That December Dr. Burrows, Dr. Brownlee, and I presented papers before the annual joint meeting of the Society of Biblical Literature and Exegesis, The National Association of Biblical Instructors, and the American Schools of Oriental Research, when the largest gathering of scholars in the history of these meetings crowded into a huge lecture hall at Union Theological Seminary to hear our firsthand reports. The world of Biblical scholarship was thoroughly aroused.

All three of us were greatly handicapped by the various complications of our personal lives in trying to write our reports. Both Brownlee and I were particularly frustrated by the necessity of beginning new jobs. Brownlee not only faced his first year of college teaching at Duke University, but also was making plans to be married. My work with the I.C.R.E. kept me traveling so much that pullman cars, hotel rooms, and seemingly every place except the quiet of a private study were used for research and writing. Everywhere I went, a satchel well stocked with photographs of the various scrolls was my constant companion. The work on the paleography, at that time the only sound basis for dating the scrolls, demanded extensive library resources which could be found in only a few of the finest libraries in the country. Generally I was hundreds of miles from the nearest library resources when some strategic point demanded checking.

Every letter on the entire Habakkuk Commentary, on a dozen columns of the Isaiah Scroll, and on the columns of the Manual of Discipline was carefully examined to be certain of the standard forms used by each scribe. A chart of letter forms, which was crucial to illustrate my thesis and to establish it visually, was prepared mostly in hotel rooms and private homes where I was entertained during a series of addresses in various communities across the United States.

About the middle of August, 1948, a letter from Metropolitan Samuel at last arrived. He was replying to my note of sympathy which had been sent through a Beirut address as soon as I learned of the tragic death of Father Sowmy. The first truce which had been successfully negotiated by the newly appointed United Nations mediator, Count Folke Bernadotte, lasted only from June 11 to July 9. The resumption of hostilities on July 9 produced thousands of additional refugees who were flooding into Trans-Jordan and other Arab countries. The pitiful plight of the refugees touched the Palestinian religious leaders deeply, and superhuman efforts were put forth to cope with the heartrending situation. All thoughts about our neatly contrived plan to bring tourists to a museum featuring the scrolls at St. Mark's Monastery were now obsolete. The Monastery was badly damaged, and thousands of Syrian Orthodox Christians were suffering. The Metropolitan therefore was thinking of the scrolls in terms of ameliorating the situation to some degree. Already the Patriarch had suggested he visit their communicants in America, at which time he had planned to bring the Fourth Scroll for scientific treatment. Now it was imperative that he come to seek help in a larger way. In his second letter, which reached me late in September, he wrote:

As you know our Convent in Jerusalem is partly damaged and we lost all our income and my people were obliged to escape from the Calamity leaving everything, house, furniture and even their clothes and are dispersed in the surrounding countries and as the hard times of Winter are coming they need everything. Lately I visited them and I found that 3000 of them are in immediate need of help. To help them is practical and real Christianity.

Feeling the situation intimately, both Dr. Burrows and I saw the plans of the Metropolitan as a hopeful means of aiding many suffering refugees. Thus, we encouraged him to come to America with the scrolls. We offered to do what we could to expedite a sale. He sought my help to finance his trip, but I was in no position to offer such extensive assistance; my intermittent efforts to arouse interest in the plight of the Arabs had met with paltry success.

We began to consider how we might be able to assist toward a sale of the scrolls. In the light of Dr. Sukenik's claim to equal rights, a major obstacle stood in the way. Cautiously I raised the matter in a letter to Metropolitan Samuel, who was then in the Patriarchate in Homs. His handwritten reply, dated September 14, 1948, contained a firm denial of the claim.

Meanwhile Dr. Ovid Sellers, then Dean and Professor of Old Testament at McCormick Theological Seminary in Chicago, was able during the first truce to reach Jerusalem on July 7 to assume the duties of Director of the A.S.O.R. Together we had discussed the scroll story at length before his departure; but the chaotic situation which followed two days after his arrival in Jerusalem, with the end of the first truce, left no opportunity for him to pursue negotiations. Mere survival was the predominant concern. He gave yeoman service under most trying and dangerous conditions. Joining forces with other foreign religious leaders, he sought to elicit aid from America for the thousands of Arab refugees.

Early in September, Metropolitan Samuel visited Dr. Sellers and showed him some newly acquired scroll fragments which were carried in a flat tin box. Shortly thereafter Professor Sellers was seriously injured when the plane in which he was riding from Beirut to Jerusalem was shot down by a fighter plane over the Sea of Galilee. For weeks he was hospitalized.

Despite the war and such tragedies, curiosity about the scroll discovery was increasing throughout the Near East. Not until November was peace restored to Jerusalem. In January restrictions on travel were relaxed sufficiently to revive hopes for a visit to the cave. When Dr. Sellers was finally able to visit St. Mark's Monastery, he learned that the Metropolitan had already left[9] and that Father Bulos was in charge. He reminded them of their promise to cooperate with the A.S.O.R. in visiting the cave, and was introduced to George Isha'ya, who demanded an advance of £P75 ($303.75) and other exhorbitant requirements to take anyone to the cave. Negotiations with the Monastery therefore ceased; the cave had to be rediscovered.

Already, in December, 1948, Belgian Captain Philippe Lippens, an observer for the United Nations who was housed at the King David Hotel in Israeli Jerusalem, was thinking about how the manuscript cave might be reached. When transferred to the Arab side of Jerusalem, he visited the A.S.O.R., St. Mark's Monastery, and the École Biblique to gain what information he could. Father R. de Vaux, Director of the École Biblique, showed him a few published articles which had recently reached their library. A vague reference in one of the articles to the location of the cave and the story of our failure to reach it fired his enthusiasm. On January 24, 1949, he succeeded in obtaining an interview with Major General Lash, the British Commander of the 3rd Brigade of the Arab Legion at Ramallah. General Lash called Brigadier Ashton, his archeological advisor, who in turn contacted G. L. Harding, Chief Inspector of Antiquities, in Amman, Jordan. Harding confirmed the importance of the cave project. Thus, General Lash dispatched Brigadier Ashton with two Bedouins and Captain Akkash el-Zebn to search the area mentioned in my article.

On January 28 Captain Akkash el-Zebn spotted a strange-colored disturbance of the earth high up on the cliff; it looked a little like the results of an excavation. On closer examination it proved to be what they were seeking. A guard was posted, and Mr. Harding was called. Though dubious at first, Harding soon found evidence to associate the cave with the manuscript discovery. He began at once to arrange for the excavation.

A lengthy tour of addresses kept me in Southern California during January, 1949. Among other things forwarded from my office about the middle of the month was a note written in longhand on the back of one of Metropolitan Samuel's calling cards. Dated January 6, from Alexandria, Egypt, the brief note said that he would arrive in New York on January 28 aboard the S.S. *Excalibur* and asked that I meet him at the dock. My scheduled tour would not end until February 1 in St. Paul, Minnesota. Dr. Burrows therefore made plans to meet the boat, neither of us knowing that a reception committee of some twenty-five Syrian Orthodox communicants was being organized at the same time in West New York. I satisfied myself with an *ahlan wa-sahlan* (Arabic words of welcome) cablegram to the boat, a letter to be delivered at the dock, and a promise to visit the Metropolitan on February 4 in Jersey City.

On the twenty-eighth the S.S. *Excalibur* wallowed in heavy seas not far from New York (while in Jordan Captain Akkash el-Zebn was climbing up to rediscover the manuscript cave). Unable to remain to see the delayed boat dock on the afternoon of the twenty-ninth, Dr. Burrows too wrote his *ahlan wa-sahlan* in a letter to be delivered to the Metropolitan by the chairman of the reception committee. He then returned to New Haven.

On February 4 I found my way to the Hotel Plaza in Jersey City to greet the Metropolitan. It was a happy reunion in the midst of a host of Syrian Orthodox people who surrounded him. Not knowing how much his people knew about the scrolls, I waited for him to initiate the subject. Little was said until most of the friends had left; then, in the presence of only two Syrian laymen, opportunity was given for me to ask some of the myriad questions I had listed.

An engagement his friends had planned for the evening prevented any lengthy discussion. Having registered at the same hotel, I spent the evening in my room, recording the results of the interview. About ten thirty the telephone rang, and Metropolitan Samuel asked if I would come to his suite—at last he was alone. For over two hours we sat discussing the problem of how to raise funds to aid the refugees. We agreed to draft an appeal to be printed and sent to members of his church in this country. Then, for sentimental reasons, I asked if I might see the scrolls again. From a closet he drew forth a shining new leather satchel, from which I tenderly lifted out the Isaiah Scroll. Opening the precious document to Column 32, I read aloud the familiar words of Isaiah 40:1-8, which conclude, "The grass withers, the flower fades; but the word of our God shall stand for ever" (RSV).

14

The Mystery of the Daniel Fragments

DURING the long train trip from the Pacific Coast to New Jersey, intense expectancy had dominated my mind. Eagerly I sought to examine some new scrolls which, according to his letters, the Metropolitan had purchased during the previous summer.[1] Then there were the new fragments, carried by the prelate in a metal cigarette box, which had been shown to Dr. Ovid Sellers in Jerusalem the previous September. It was with difficulty, therefore, that I restrained my keen anticipation when, on arrival, I found Metropolitan Samuel surrounded by many Syrians in the hotel suite.

When only an attorney and a cousin of the late Father Sowmy remained, the Metropolitan did not seem hesitant about discussing the manuscripts; apparently these men knew about the documents. Presently from the closet he drew forth two sizable bundles and handed them to me. Hopefully I unwrapped the protective paper only to discover within two large rolls of shiny white parchment, as new as last June's college diploma. Though smaller than most similar scrolls I had seen, the first column of each revealed in an elegant script the familiar opening Hebrew words of the Book of Genesis. They were quite modern Torah scrolls, not even as early as the huge Torah scroll I had seen in the St. Mark's Monastery library (see pp. 58-59). Without hesitation

I asserted that these scrolls would not even deserve the designation of "antiquities."

Next he handed me a flat tin cigarette box which fitted Dr. Sellers' description. Gently lifting the cover, I found a layer of cotton under which lay fragments of familiar dark-brown, ragged-edged leather. Hardly a letter of script was immediately visible, but the appearance and faint odor emitted immediately associated the group with the cave scrolls. This matted mass of leather fragments, and under it a sizable piece of papyrus, recalled at once the description Dr. Sellers had given of the fragments he had seen (see p. 121). These must be the same ones, I concluded.

The largest of the group, measuring $3\frac{1}{2} \times 2\frac{3}{4}$ inches overall, was a folded mass of at least three different kinds of leather welded together at one corner by an area of disintegration which had reached the gelatinized stage. Separation of the fragments, it was apparent, would be difficult because of this gluey, fused section. On top was a loose piece which had become folded over the rest like a cover. Pulling it gently back, I discovered a somewhat flowing script which appeared to be semi-cursive. Letters were run together, but not intentionally connected by ligatures (1QDan*b*). There was some similarity to the Manual of Discipline, it seemed.

Adhering to the right side of the mass, and lying on top of each other, was a series of smaller fragments of a very thin, light-tan leather inscribed in an exquisitely fine hand. Though more perfectly executed, it reminded me of the insertion on Column 28 of the Isaiah Scroll. Several fragments from this same scroll could be clearly seen projecting in layers beneath the upper one, probably parts from other turns of the same scroll. Three other fragments with the same beautiful script were lying loose in the box (1Q34*bis*).

On the back of the mass was still another kind of leather, considerably lighter, though mottled, but folded so that nothing of its script could be seen. The whole mass gave the appearance of two scrolls which had been lying atop each other and deliberately squashed under someone's foot in ancient times.

Also in the box was a coarse piece of leather with very irregular edges, partly broken from disintegration and partly from having been eaten by insects. It measured about 2 by $2\frac{1}{2}$ inches overall. Only a few crude letters had been preserved on its surface (1Q19*bis*).

The most unique fragment, however, was a piece of papyrus about an inch wide and 2 inches long, a vertical piece broken from a column which had been inscribed in coarse Hebrew characters. Some of the letters had partially flaked away. Not a single word was complete (1Q70*bis*). Hebrew papyri have been rare among manuscript discoveries.

Several small fragments in the box seemed to belong with those in the matted mass, to judge by their texture, color, and script. Six uninscribed fragments, some with pieces of cloth attached, looked like what had been described in the early reports as "pitch," supposedly used to seal the jars in the cave. It was clear, however, that these were merely pieces of fused leather from the outer disintegrated crust of some of the scrolls. Through the many centuries of exposure in the cave, even in the extremely dry climate of that wilderness area, the outer turns of leather had become reduced to a gluey, amber-colored mass. When dry, this crust would crack easily and fall away unless handled with great care. Under humid conditions it would bend like plastic or hard rubber.

While I studied the fragments, the Metropolitan related the story of their origin. In view of the fact that we had been unable to get to the cave the previous spring, during the fall he had decided to send "one of his men"[2] to the cave to see whether it still remained in the same condition as when Father Yusif visited it in August, 1947. The Jews had left the region, having destroyed the Potash Works and the hotel at Kallia, thus allowing for easy access to the cave. He went on to say that these fragments were picked up along with a large piece of cloth at that time. Otherwise the cave was in the same condition as it had been the previous year. Even one complete jar was still there.[3] Why the jar was not removed, the Metropolitan was unable to explain. But see p. 197, n. 35.)

From my many questions about the early history of the scrolls, the idea of publishing the story arose. Assuring the Metropolitan that such an article would probably be appreciated by the *Biblical Archaeologist* editor, I set about to gather notes toward that end. He requested that I compose the article, then let him review and correct it until we were certain it represented the most accurate account possible. Urging him to think the whole story through carefully, I warned that such an article was bound to receive very critical scrutiny by scholars.

For over an hour later that night, when we were alone, I questioned him about various details of the story, jotting down copious notes in which I included every name he mentioned. When the name of Anton Kiraz arose, I asked casually how he came into the story. The prelate mentioned Dr. Sukenik's excavation on Mr. Kiraz's property in Talpioth and the fact that Dr. Sukenik, knowing that Kiraz was a Syrian, had written to him, requesting to see the Syrian scrolls. It was in January, while Father Sowmy was in Syria, that he had decided to let Kiraz show the scrolls to Dr. Sukenik for his evaluation, he continued. He did not give permission, he emphasized, for the scrolls to be left with Dr. Sukenik for several days.

Of primary concern to the prelate, however, was the drafting of a statement to be printed and circulated to his people as a means of raising funds for the many Syrian refugees. After discussing its proposed contents at great length, I agreed to draft a suitable statement the next morning.

A typewriter was delivered to my room in the hotel at eight thirty, but the Metropolitan insisted that I join him at breakfast before starting to work. Taking advantage of our privacy, again I pressed him with more questions. He seemed somewhat irritated by my incessant queries about dates and chronological relationships of events, but I insisted that these were essential to establish the record. After breakfast, I first typed all the notes about the scrolls. A rough draft of the fund-raising statement had been barely completed when the Metropolitan called to invite me to join some of his friends at lunch.

After lunch his people gave us another opportunity to be alone, but again most of the time had to be spent in further discussion of the statement. Occasionally it was possible to interject a question which had arisen that morning while I typed the notes about the scrolls. When I left that afternoon, therefore, it was with considerable confidence that the essential accuracy of the story about the discovery of the scrolls had been recorded.

Another series of speaking engagements took me to the Pacific Northwest during late February and early March. The following weeks were crowded as I attempted to prepare a first draft of the proposed article on the Metropolitan's story. In addition, the article on the paleography of the St. Mark's scrolls for the *BASOR* and an accompanying chart, were already overdue in Baltimore, Maryland. Taking advantage of the long train rides and the isolation and quiet of numerous hotel rooms between engagements, I gradually assembled the materials. The draft of the Metropolitan's article, containing many blank spaces for names and details to be filled in, was finally dispatched for his review prior to our next meeting.

In the meantime word reached me in Oregon that Dr. Sukenik had arrived in New York and was seeking an interview. Having planned a second visit with the Metropolitan for the afternoon of March 22, I suggested to Dr. Sukenik that we meet in New York that morning at the headquarters of the American Friends of the Hebrew University, where he was staying.

Eager to hear his side of the story, I listened carefully as Dr. Sukenik related his experiences. His statements revealed the clarity and precision of the great scholar that he was. The interview proceeded very pleasantly until he began to make strong claims regarding the disposition of the Syrian scrolls, which he asserted belonged to the State of Israel. With mounting agitation he insisted that the scrolls were a part of Jewish heritage. He was then preparing a document, he revealed, to circulate to all libraries and universities which might consider purchasing the scrolls. In it he was warning them that such a purchase would be illegal and subject to the antiquities laws, which could be invoked to return the scrolls to the country of their origin. Despite the somewhat heated conclusion to our interview, I departed with additional valuable information and proceeded at once to record it in detail. Unraveling the story back of the discovery had become for me a vital concern.

On the New Jersey side of the Hudson River that afternoon, I found Metropolitan Samuel well prepared and eager to discuss his story for the *Biblical Archaeologist*. Much revision of the first draft was necessary; he had given each event considerable thought, he asserted, and found evidence to provide a more accurate picture. Paragraph by paragraph we went over the draft, rewriting much of it, particularly at the beginning and the end. It was then that a number of changes, destined to complicate our problems in the future, were introduced.

Believing it unwise to reveal my interview with Dr. Sukenik that morning, I failed to challenge the Metropolitan's claim that the scrolls were shown to Sukenik late in February, 1948. His evidence—that he offered instead to Sukenik the photographs which I had prepared in the meantime—seemed valid. Thus I agreed to his revision without debate. The article seemed fairly consistent with the facts we had been able to check up to that time.

In the meantime Dr. Carl Kraeling, then president of the A.S.O.R., was moving ahead with arrangements for unrolling the "Fourth Scroll," a fragment of which I had deciphered the previous December. From my transcription of its few incomplete lines, Dr. Albright had concluded that the scroll was related to the apocryphal Book of Enoch. Soon this tentative identification began to appear in news releases.

Arranging to take the month of April, 1949, away from my office, I planned to assist in the unrolling process. With high hopes of success at last in this long-awaited adventure, I drove with my family and all my photographic equipment to New Haven. There the Metropolitan met with us to discuss the procedure. Our plans to do the work at Yale University had, in the meantime, collapsed. Immediately Dr. Kraeling had suggested that we contact authorities at the Metropolitan Museum of Art in New York. Technical experts there agreed to examine the scroll and consider undertaking the task. We persuaded the prelate to take the scroll there the next day.

Arriving on the morning of April 6 at the New York Museum ahead of the Syrian prelate, I discussed with the two technical experts the nature of the problem, on the basis of photographs. When the Metropolitan arrived with the scroll an hour later, the interview therefore took relatively little time. Already the conclusion had been reached that we should seek the services of Dr. Rutherford J. Gettens, who was then associated with the Fogg Museum at Harvard. We were advised, however, that a special box should be prepared to preserve the scroll more adequately.

That afternoon, while we were guests of the priest of the Assyrian Orthodox Church of West New York, the Metropolitan secured the Isaiah Scroll from the bank vault in which it was being kept, in order that I might add a tiny fragment containing portions of five letters which had not been properly located in Jerusalem. It belonged in the gap in Column 6. This meant rephotographing the column, though it was already too late to get it into our publication. At the same time, I rephotographed several of the final columns which had been done in Jerusalem on the poorer sheets of portrait film.[4] Although I should have liked to have done many more, the circumstances permitted only a few exposures.

In view of the delay in the "Fourth Scroll" plans, it was decided that I should take the box of fragments and the "Fourth Scroll" to New Haven for further analysis and study while negotiations were proceeding with the Fogg Museum. Thus, I carried the precious documents to New Haven that night.

To expedite the process, Dr. Kraeling arranged for the use of a laboratory at the Yale Gallery of Fine Arts. On closer examination of the fragments, it became apparent that they offered few obstacles to adequate treatment for photographing. While studying them the previous February, I had cleaned the loose ones and mounted them between lantern-slide cover-glasses for protection. They were thus ready to photograph at once. With my photo equipment mounted on the table nearby, I then began a

Metropolitan Samuel discussing "Genesis Apocryphon" Scroll with author in New Jersey

careful study of the matted mass of leather. Gently unfolding to one side the loose piece on top, I laid a sheet of glass over the whole exposed surface to record its initial appearance on both sides. A check of some Aramaic words on this piece quickly led to Daniel 3:22-25 as its text. New zest was thus added to the delicate task.

Nine layers of leather could be detected along the edges of the total mass, though three were obviously folded pieces, indicating that at least six different fragments from three different scrolls might emerge from the total. The upper edges of the mass showed no signs of adhering, and almost at once the fourth and fifth layers fell from their position. They comprised a small folded piece of thin, light-tan leather ($1\frac{3}{8}$ x $2\frac{1}{4}$ inches). Though already cracked along the line of its fold, the piece opened up easily,

Isaiah "A" Scroll, Column 6, with additional fragment

Khirbet Qumran and Wadi Qumran from cliff to west

Looking southeast across Khirbet Qumran from defense tower

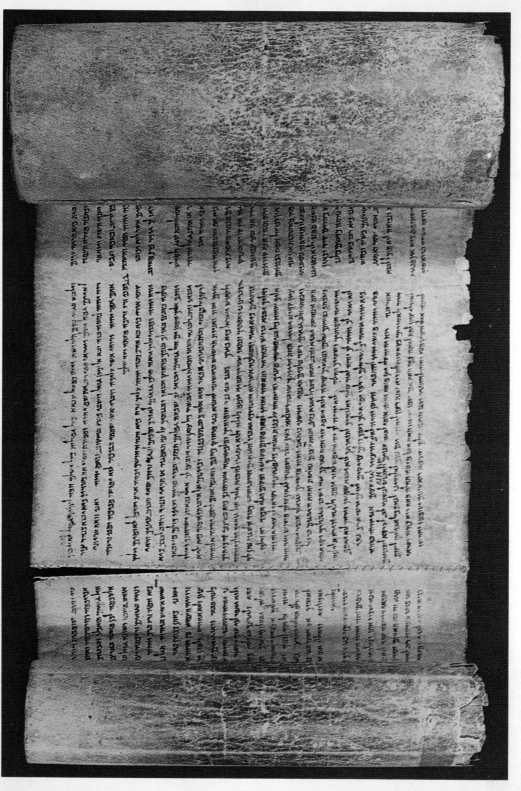

Isaiah "A" Scroll opened to column 49, showing Isaiah 61:1

revealing a script that was the same as that on the fragments beneath which it had lain. Physically, it seemed unrelated to any of the adjacent fragments, but I called it unit "d." Immediately I mounted and photographed it with three other loose fragments.

A fine crack at the lower right of the first layer on the mass indicated on examination that it could be removed quite easily by gently working down from the top. As this fragment separated from the gelatinized area, unfortunately the first two letters of the word for "man" remained with the next level, where they appeared on the subsequent photograph. Just before photographing this first layer, I noticed that one of the already-mounted loose pieces joined perfectly with it, completing three words along an original fold. Thus, the two were joined and mounted together and photographed as unit "a," measuring 1½ x 2 inches.

Another of the loose fragments immediately associated itself with the exposed second layer, producing a sizable fragment (2½ x 2 inches) with seven lines of text (unit "b"). Again a crack separated this layer from the disintegrated leather at the lower corner; its removal was equally simple. With this operation, however, the two letters from layer one still adhering at the lower right crumbled away. As this fragment was removed, a small, narrow, uninscribed fragment, totally unrelated to any of the other fragments in texture and color, fell from beneath; it had been completely hidden from view.

Still another of the loose fragments matched along a fold at its right edge with the third layer on the mass, forming unit "c" (2 x 3¼ inches), which again was immediately photographed. This third layer was already cracked down its middle and showed signs of crumbling in several places. Since it adhered tightly to the back of the fragment which lay beneath, I made no attempt to separate them; the danger of loss to either or both was too great.

The sixth layer (layers four and five had slipped out already, as mentioned above) was of a different kind of leather and seemed to have been folded over in ancient times on top of the seventh layer. Disintegration along the entire lower part of this fragment made separation very difficult; with gentle prodding, however, it finally came loose without any loss. The script on this sixth layer was identical with that on the seventh. The piece was badly blackened with age, but its script was dimly readable. Soon it was identified as a part of the same column of text, containing portions of Daniel 3:27-30. This scroll is now called 1QDan^b.

With the sixth layer removed, the remainder of the largest fragment was revealed. Now parts of Daniel 3:22-31 (3:22–4:1 in English) had appeared on two fragments. Having impressed me at first as revealing a script somewhat similar to the Manual of Discipline (1QS), I tentatively thought of the fragments as belonging to the middle of the first century B.C. Although the text contributed nothing new, its significance among Biblical manuscripts was immediately apparent. *Here was a fragment written barely a hundred years after the original composition of the Book of Daniel!*[5] Since my first study of the fragments, however, I have come to believe that a mid-first-century A.D. date of origin is more likely. Even at that, these fragments may be unique among Old Testament manuscripts in point of proximity to the date of original composition.[6]

Only the folded leather adhering to the back of the large Daniel fragment (layers eight and nine) now remained unopened. At first the two layers appeared to be so firmly pressed against each other that I wondered if they might have been completely fused. After some moments of careful probing of the edges at almost every point, suddenly these layers literally burst apart. Almost immediately I noticed the expression, " . . . and Daniel said unto . . . ," in a beautifully-formed script, as black as though it had been inscribed but a few days before. The appearance of the script reminded me of a printed page, it was so elegantly executed. The fine leather on which it was written had been carefully ruled, probably with a reed, and the letters formed with utmost precision. Although they bore an impression of modernity, closer examination left no doubt that they belonged to the same paleographic tradition as the rest of the scrolls from the cave.[7] This fragment is now designated 1QDan^a.

On the right half of the fragment appeared portions of Daniel 1:10-16 from the upper lefthand corner of a column, while on the left half were parts of Daniel 2:4-6 from the upper righthand corner of the adjacent column. A paragraph indentation appeared on the fourth line of the left portion, and all that followed on the fragment was in Aramaic. It is in the middle of Daniel 2:4 that the Biblical book shifts from Hebrew to Aramaic, the latter continuing through Chapter Seven. Fortunately, this interesting feature of the book has been preserved on such an early fragment.

The main question posed by these two sections from Daniel was whether or not they belonged to the same scroll. The fact that the Songs of Thanksgiving Scroll (1QH) was prepared by two quite different hands argued immediately for a similar phenomenon for the Daniel Scroll. It now seems paleographically probable that both parts come from about A.D. 50.

The nature of these fragments and their relation to each other creates the impression that they were deliberately torn from a scroll in ancient times and crumpled together with destructive intent. Could it have been that this scroll of Daniel came into the hands of some Roman soldier who gave it this treatment, only to have the pieces picked up by a devout member of the community and cast into the cave to avoid further desecration? Only theories can explain the strange form in which these fragments were found. These were not the only scrolls from the cave, however, which indicated such ruthless treatment in the ancient past. Sections of the Hebrew University Songs Scrolls (1QH) appeared to have suffered similar abuse, as well as their scroll of Isaiah (1QIs^b).

Gradually during the subsequent months, as I found time to translate the other fragments from my photographs, the relation of units "a," "b," and "c," with their closely written lines, became apparent. They all belonged together, forming a strip of inscribed leather about 2 inches wide and 8 inches long. They formed sections from two columns of a Hebrew prayer scroll. One prayer ended, " . . . from generation to generation, blessed be our Lord who has caused us to rejoice." Another began, "A prayer for the Day of Atonement: Remember, O Lord . . . ." Another contrasts the fate of the wicked with the blessings of the righteous. But most important in the text are the words, "Thou hast chosen for thyself a people in the time of thy pleasure, for thou hast remembered thy covenant . . . . Thou didst . . . separate them for thyself as holy from all the peoples, and thou didst renew thy covenant for them in a vision of glory . . . ." The writer of this manuscript believed himself to belong to a people of the New Covenant![8] This scroll is now designated 1QPrayers (1Q34).

Other fragments from the cigarette box gradually found their places among these two scrolls, leaving unidentified only the piece of papyrus, a ragged piece of coarse leather with crude writing (it later proved to be a fragment of "The Book of Noah" [1Q19]. See p. 146, and a few uninscribed pieces of disintegrated leather adhering to some cloth. All the fragments were carefully mounted between glass and photographed in both black and white and color films. Although a few letters were lost from one fragment of the prayer scroll during the separation process, they were preserved in the photographs.[9]

The next few days in New Haven were spent on the "Fourth Scroll." Soon a sturdy wooden box replaced the inadequate cardboard one I had made in Jerusalem. Study of the scroll revealed that above and below the place where I had removed the fragment while in Jerusalem, additional loosening of the leather had occurred on the soft side of the scroll. Along the edges of the brittle, badly disintegrated side, slight additional cracking had occurred.[10] Without damage to the rest of the scroll, it was soon apparent that, with patience, considerably more of the softer part could be removed. Most of one day was spent gently probing the edges along the cracks until finally a large fragment, measuring 4¾ x 8½ inches, came loose.[11] Gradually it flattened enough to mount between glass and photograph.

More than half of each of twenty-six lines of Aramaic text from this scroll were now available for study. Since the ink used for this manuscript had apparently been metallic, the lines of script were badly disintegrated. With this large number of lines, however, gradually more and more words could be deciphered.

Some weeks later, Dr. Burrows pointed on my transcription to the combination of letters *lmk*. "Is that the name Lamech?" he asked. I had been trying to read it as a verb. Toward the end of the same line were the letters *bt'nws*, which I thought might mean "daughter of Enosh." Since it all seemed one word, however, the name "Betenosh" seemed also probable. A check in R. H. Charles' huge volumes, *Apocrypha and Pseudepigrapha*, led to Jubilees 4:28, where Betenosh is the name of the wife of Lamech; they were the parents of Noah. Soon the whole line became clear: "Then I, Lamech, hastened and went to Betenosh, my wife. . . ." Since the name Lamech occurred once again with the first-person pronoun, we began to call the document the Book of Lamech, for such a writing was mentioned in an early Greek source.

Dr. Albright's suggestion that the smaller fragment was related to the Enoch literature was now further confirmed. At least this part of the manuscript seemed to be a paraphrase of the story of the birth of Noah, as developed from the Book of Genesis in the Noah portions of the Enoch literature (chapters 106-107). There, however, Enoch speaks in the first person. The possibility that this scroll might have been one of the sources from which the Book of Enoch had developed seemed also to be indicated.[12]

In the midst of all these efforts toward the handling and publication of the scrolls and fragments, our major project was the preparation of the first A.S.O.R. Dead Sea Scroll volume. Edited by Dr. Burrows, with assistance from Dr. Brownlee and myself, it was to contain introductory information along with full-sized facsimile photographs of the Isaiah Scroll and the Habakkuk Commentary. To speed its completion for the scholarly world, the usual critical discussions found in such publications were omitted. Some months previously, I had begun the process of producing the necessary enlarged prints of each column from the negatives made in Jerusalem. The large negatives, however, posed a problem for my equipment. Only one half of each column could be enlarged at a time; the two halves, therefore, had to be spliced together.[13] While in New Haven I imposed upon the kindness of a commercial photographer friend, who permitted me to use his laboratory and equipment to complete the full-sized prints for our publication.

Contacts with the Fogg Museum proved encouraging, and arrangements were soon made for the Metropolitan to meet there with Dr. Gettens. Since the Syrian prelate was then in Rhode Island, it fell to me again to carry the "Lamech Scroll" to Cambridge, Massachusetts on the afternoon of April 13. Arriving at the Fogg Museum well ahead of the Metropolitan the next morning, I discussed the scroll problems privately with Dr. Gettens. Although he exhibited much enthusiasm for the delicate task, his previous commitments unfortunately would not permit undertaking it short of several months.

By the time the Metropolitan arrived, most of the discussion was completed, and there was left merely the formality of obtaining the prelate's permission to leave the document in Dr. Gettens' care. We were confident now that at last the proper procedure had been established and the process of opening the rest of the scroll would be only a matter of scheduling. Our mission concluded with a pleasant fellowship at lunch in a Chinese restaurant on Harvard Square. Gathered on a street corner for our parting expressions of mutual goodwill, I held in my arms our three-year-old boy, who eyed the robed Metropolitan intently. As I reached for his outstretched hand, suddenly Jimmy lunged forward with a gleeful utterance and grabbed the prelate's heavy beard! It was an embarrassed family that headed that day toward Chicago.

The weeks sped by as I tried, in the midst of my other duties, to include the writing of a detailed report on the fragments for the A.S.O.R., while seeing several articles through to publication.

Late in May, 1949, the belated April issue of the *Bulletin of the A.S.O.R.* appeared. In it was an article by Dr. Ovid Sellers, reporting the rediscovery and excavation of the cave by the Dead Sea the previous February. There I read the words: "The operation was complicated by previous clandestine excavators, who last November dug up the surface of the cave to a depth of several inches in vain hopes that the Bedouins had missed some scrolls. . . . The identity of two who conducted the unauthorized excavation is known. . . ."[14] The background of the fragments on which I had been working suddenly took on new light.

Immediately I wrote to the Syrian prelate, outlining Dr. Sellers' report and suggesting that, in view of the circumstances under which these fragments had been secured, he should expect them to be claimed by Jordan. Since Dr. Sellers had seen at least some of them prior to November,[15] I assumed they must have been picked up before the clandestine excavation; but the connection with the latter seemed too close to allow any claim to ownership, I reasoned. In a letter dated June 10, 1949, the Metropolitan replied that the fragments had been secured in 1947 and requested that nothing about them be said or published.[16] Meanwhile, however, the belated May, 1949, issue of the *Biblical Archaeologist*, which included the Metropolitan's own article along with an editorial report about the fragments, had just been mailed. The scholarly world would know about the existence and the nature of the fragments within a matter of days.

Correspondence flew between the A.S.O.R., myself, and Metropolitan Samuel. He telephoned me from Detroit and made a trip to my home in Des Plaines, Illinois, to discuss the issue. Meanwhile I hastened to complete the work of assembling, mounting, photographing and studying the fragments.

It seemed to me that only one procedure was proper—the fragments must be immediately reported and offered for return to Jordan. The prelate requested that I draft for him an appropriate letter to send to the Jordanian Department of Antiquities, which I did on July 16. Copies of a full report, which included my step-by-step photographs, were sent to the A.S.O.R. and to the Jordanian authorities in late July. On December 3 I delivered the mounted fragments to the Metropolitan in New Jersey. The A.S.O.R. meanwhile decided to delay publication until the fragments were returned to Jordan or until Jordan's Department of Antiquities granted permission. The latter was given early in 1950, but the fragments were not returned.

Silence descended upon the matter, as other problems took precedence. The A.S.O.R. understandably continued to hesitate about publication. A transliteration and French translation, made from the photographs sent to Jordan, appeared in 1955 in the official publication of the Cave I materials;[17] but the mystery of the disposition of the fragments continued.

In an interview with Metropolitan Samuel on August 19, 1962, and in subsequent letters dated November 10 and December 19, he again stated that the fragments were secured in 1947 and that he considered them his property.[18]

15

Failure as a Salesman

THOSE of us who lived in the midst of those tragic last months of the British Mandate of Palestine continued to be deeply concerned about Partition's injustice to the native Palestinian Arabs. All of us had written numerous letters and articles describing our personal experiences and insights, in the vain hope of stemming the flood of political propaganda that had engulfed the United States.

To unburden his concerns, Dr. Burrows departed from his usual scholarly pursuits and wrote a little book entitled *Palestine Is Our Business* (Philadelphia, The Westminster Press, 1949). My humble expressions were published in our Methodist periodical *The Christian Advocate* ("Viewing Palestine from the Inside," April 15, 1948, pp. 4-6, 31). More practical, however, were several hundred dollars provided for Syrian Orthodox Christian refugees with profits made from the sale of scroll photographs.

Along with these direct expressions of our concern, we assumed that efforts toward the sale of the scrolls could produce more significant results toward the relief of suffering. Several major obstacles, however, stood in the way of a successful sale.

In the first place, not long after the Metropolitan arrived in the United States, a rumor began to circulate that he was claiming a value of one million dollars for the scrolls. Potential donors, having a distaste for the Oriental bargaining custom, shied away from such a fantastic figure. Only two ancient books, as far as I was able to discover, had brought more than $250,000 — a Gutenberg Bible evaluated at $375,000, and the famed Codex Sinaiticus, which was sold to the British Museum for the equivalent of almost $500,000.[1] Through two widely separated experts in rare books, Dr. W. F. Albright of Johns Hopkins University and I had appraisals made of the Syrian scrolls. The estimates ranged from $150,000 to about $250,000 for the four scrolls, in the light of all the current factors. Both appraisals were communicated to the Metropolitan, who offered no comment other than an expressed desire for our assistance. Repeatedly he called upon me to draft letters and statements.

A second problem arose almost immediately upon the appearance of the first preliminary publications. Our appraisal of the antiquity of the scrolls was vigorously challenged in scholarly circles, as we had expected. Until 1952 the number and influence of negative pens seemed almost to outweigh those which came to our defense. If the scrolls were medieval, as some of these antagonists proposed, their value could barely exceed a few thousand dollars. Would-be purchasers therefore could be expected to await a resolution of this major obstacle. One scholar published a vigorous attack against the Isaiah Scroll, in view of certain technical details which he interpreted as rendering the manuscript virtually worthless to Biblical studies, regardless of its age. Much printer's ink was expended from 1950 to 1952 over these fine points.[2]

Probably the most knotty problem was the tangle which arose in 1949 over the Syrian prelate's ability to deliver a clear title to the scrolls. After Trans-Jordan and the Arab section of Palestine were joined on December 1, 1948, to form the Hashemite Kingdom of the Jordan, jurisdiction of the cave area by the Dead Sea came under that country's Department of Antiquities. Almost immediately, G. L. Harding, Director of Antiquities for Jordan, sought to control not only further cave explorations but also the circulation of already-discovered scrolls and fragments.

Queries were also raised concerning the observance of the antiquities laws in connection with the original find. Early in 1949 Dr. Sellers communicated Mr. Harding's concern to me and I immediately prepared a full report about the dealings the previous spring with the Syrians and the Mandate Department of Antiquities (see pp. 66-67, 78, 82-83). That report, unfortunately, failed to reach Jerusalem. Apparently it was lost in the chaotic postal situation. Without having a proper understanding of the situation, therefore, Mr. Harding published in a leading British archeological journal a harsh condemnation of all those who originally dealt with the scrolls.[3]

Meanwhile Dr. Sukenik's statement about invoking the antiquities laws to force a return of the Syrian scrolls to Palestine (see p. 126) was circulated widely. An aura of possible illegality thus surrounded these documents. Libraries and potential donors were wary.

To complicate the problem of title, several compatriots of the Metropolitan voiced strong claims to partnership with him in the ownership of the scrolls. Having learned that he was asking a million dollars for the documents, both Kando and Isha'ya put forth a claim, based on the fact that they had guided the Bedouins to St. Mark's Monastery and that the Syrian prelate had "promised to remember them with a gift" when the scrolls were sold.[4]

A more serious and persistent claim to partnership was that of Mr. Anton Kiraz (see pp. 109, 112-113), whose connection with the scrolls was first made known through Dr. Sukenik's writings. Having lost most of what he owned as a result of Partition in 1948, Kiraz suffered the plight of many refugees. Early in 1949 a serious illness added to his predicament. Finally he was sent to a sanitarium in Beirut, where the high cost of his convalescence soon reduced him to a state of virtual poverty. In the midst of his despair and illness, he naturally resorted to his hope for assistance from the sale of the scrolls. When he read the Metropolitan's published account about the scrolls, in which Kiraz's claim was categorically denied, he sought the help of an attorney, who advised a lawsuit.

None of these obstacles, it seemed to me, was insurmountable. Having received reliable guidance in the matter of price, I urged Metropolitan Samuel to abandon his Oriental method of bargaining and establish a reasonable price as a basis for negotiation. In numerous discussions with potential purchasers, I always stated the figure of $250,000 as the probable top price, even though the Syrian prelate gave me no specific confirmation of his willingness to sell at that price.

Although on the basis of paleography my confidence in the antiquity of the documents remained unshaken throughout the intense debate which arose among scholars, that problem could only be handled through the ponderous process of scholarly research and publication. At first, paleography was our only reasonably reliable method of dating the scrolls; the early disputes therefore centered mostly around that approach. In February, 1949, however, the rediscovery of the cave produced the long-awaited pottery and other archeological evidence. Significant weight was then added to our arguments, even suggesting that our conclusions were somewhat conservative.[5] Late in 1950 results from the application of the "Carbon-14" age-determination test applied to some of the linen cloth found in the cave provided a "mean date" of A.D. 33 for the cave deposit. The margin of error of plus or minus 200 years, however, left a degree of uncertainty about the value of that evidence.[6] By 1952 only a few scholars had not conceded the substantial accuracy of our initial dating proposals.[7]

The problem of title actually plagued us most. During July, 1949, at the request of the Metropolitan I drafted a letter for him to send to the Director of Antiquities for Jordan, in which the Daniel and other fragments were reported and a request for clearance of his title to the four scrolls was made. Apparently the letter failed to arrive, and a second one was sent in late December. Finally an answer was received by the Metropolitan in late January, 1950, in which certain conditions were articulated for clearance of title. On reading a copy of the reply, I was personally convinced that clearance of title with the Jordanian government could be achieved. The conditions seemed both reasonable and not too difficult to meet. I urged the Metropolitan to begin immediately to carry them out.[8]

The claim to partnership by certain Syrians in Jordan proved elusive and troublesome. That of Kando and Ishaya offered no serious obstacle, but the testimony of Kiraz seemed to carry some evidence to support it. During his serious illness in the summer of 1949, he appealed to me for help. Having no firm basis for judgment, I could only express my sympathy to him and explain the problem that a lawsuit against Metropolitan Samuel would create. To secure aid for himself and other suffering Syrian Orthodox Christians, I pointed out, a sale of the scrolls was imperative; but a lawsuit over title would obstruct any sale. As a gesture of sympathy with him in his plight, some relief assistance was sent to him from funds raised by the Metropolitan. The threatened lawsuit was averted.

Meanwhile a mystery figure, a Czechoslovakian refugee in Jerusalem, entered the picture as a protagonist for Mr. Kiraz. Long, involved, and difficult-to-read letters began to pour in from him; he claimed to have concrete evidence in support of Kiraz and was preparing to publish a book on the whole story. When he sent a photograph of several pages from the book, it was immediately apparent that, if published, it could only serve to hurt the whole cause and do no one any good. After investigation of the circumstances, through those who were close to the man, I refused to cooperate in his endeavor to get the book published and impressed upon him the damage such a publication would bring to all parties concerned. When I sought assistance for him in his own physical plight through other channels, he abandoned his plans, so far as I know.[9]

Confident that all these obstacles could be surmounted in the face of a firm bid from a prospective donor, I continued to press various leads toward a possible sale. Our first hope had been that Yale University would be able to secure a donor, but recent purchases of the Boswell papers and the Bay Psalm Book had tapped their potential resources to the limit. The J. Pierpont Morgan Library in New York expressed keen interest, but the fanfare over the problem of title at that time soon cooled their ardor.

Our thoughts then turned to the Library of Congress, and an exhibit of the scrolls in October, 1949, opened up a new approach. During the exhibit I discussed the prospects with the head librarian, who made it quite clear that the million-dollar claim had closed the door to their potential donors. My assurances that a figure nearer $250,000 would very likely solve the problem brought no change in the picture.

Another exhibit of the scrolls at the Walters Art Gallery in Baltimore the following month opened new contacts; but the same obstacle appeared, and again potential donors lost interest. Additional exhibits followed during 1950 at Duke University and the Oriental Institute of the University of Chicago. Although huge crowds formed long lines to view the famed scrolls at each exhibit, potential donors failed to appear.

All my efforts toward a sale of the scrolls ceased on October 15, 1950, for six months. Through an agreement between the International Council of Religious Education and the A.S.O.R., a leave of absence was generously arranged to enable me to pursue my paleographic studies uninterrupted. For the first three months I attempted to exhaust the University of Chicago libraries of every resource relating to

DATING THE DEAD SEA SCROLLS BY PALEOGRAPHY

This chart illustrates how paleography provided the clue to the dating of the first Dead Sea Scrolls. Six representative letters are shown from each of twelve different manuscripts, including many of the Cave I scrolls. A study of each letter from left to right reveals an evolvement of the basic form in the direction of the stabilized form at the right (second to ninth centuries A.D.).

Columns 1-3 represent papyrus documents from Egypt, dated respectively 408 B.C. (Elephantine Papyrus), third century (Edfu Papyri), and second century B.C. (Nash Papyrus).

Columns 4-10 represent the Syrian manuscripts and fragments, whose letter forms are more evolved than the previous ones. Column 11 represents the Murabba'at Exodus Fragment. Though not discovered until 1952, it is now one of the best illustrations of the second century A.D., when the forms became stabilized. Column 12, the Cairo Codex of the Prophets, which can be dated to A.D. 895 from its colophon, reveals little change in basic forms from the second century.

This chart was prepared by cutting the letters directly from photographs of these documents and pasting them in position. The paste-up was then rephotographed with high contrast film to provide the print used by the engraver. Each letter, therefore, is a separate photograph of the original scribe's work.

Note that the special "M" form for word endings is not found on the fifth-third century documents, thus no forms are shown. This final form seems to have appeared about 200 B.C.

Examples of the samekh ("S") are lacking on these fragments, unfortunately.

early Hebrew inscriptions and manuscripts, as well as those in Aramaic and other closely related languages. Much time also was spent at home, developing a new technique for preparing paleographic charts by means of photographs to avoid "the human element" which some scholars were claiming was falsifying our evidence. Using unretouched photographs from which selected letters were clipped and pasted to the chart, all freehand drawing of letter forms was eliminated. When rephotographed with a high-contrast copy film, a perfect chart resulted.[10]

Fellowship stipends from the A.S.O.R. and the American Philosophical Society enabled me to spend the last three months of my leave in England scouring the libraries of the British Museum and of Oxford and Cambridge Universities. Several thousand Hebrew and Aramaic manuscript fragments were examined, primarily to see if any could be found which might show similarity of script to that on the Dead Sea Scrolls and thereby challenge my former conclusions. At Cambridge University Library alone, more than two thousand fragments from the famed Cairo Genizah[11] collection were systematically examined. There, also, I spent several days examining under a magnifying glass every letter of the Nash Papyrus and took copious notes on my observations. Special photographs were secured of many of the documents for use in a master chart already being developed.

Everywhere my wife and I went, we were most cordially received. Visits with dozens of Hebrew scholars produced immeasurable values in both information and friendships. Several days spent in the home of the eminent Hebraist, Dr. Paul Kahle, in Charlbury, near Oxford, proved an education in itself, despite his skepticism regarding paleography as a means of dating Hebrew manuscripts. The gracious assistance of Dr. David Diringer at Cambridge proved equally helpful. Another highlight of the experience was an interlude of several days in Paris at the Louvre Museum, where I examined a number of ancient Hebrew inscriptions. Dr. André Parrot, Director of the Near Eastern Section, graciously arranged a reception one evening, where we met many of the leading savants of Paris. Their cordial hospitality warmed our hearts, as did an evening in the home of Dr. A. Dupont-Sommer, who was even then becoming a controversial figure in the interpretation of the scrolls. With a satchel loaded with photographs and abundant notes, and more convinced than ever about the validity of paleography as a means of dating ancient Hebrew manuscripts (as well as the accuracy of my dating of the Dead Sea Scrolls), we sailed for home in April, 1951, aboard the H.M.S.*Queen Elizabeth.*

Metropolitan Samuel was growing impatient. The long delay over the sale of the scrolls, together with the complexities involved in attempting to clear the problem of title and negotiate the arrangements for the opening of the "Lamech Scroll," gradually brought our relations with the prelate to a breaking point. Suddenly he withdrew the "Lamech Scroll" (1QApoc) from the Fogg Museum and refused any further cooperation, declaring that his agreement with the A.S.O.R. had expired. Technically the agreement had expired, if figured from April 3, 1948, when we had worked out the details.

Dr. Burrows, during an exhibit of the scrolls at the Art Museum in Worcester, Massachusetts (October, 1951), attempted to ameliorate the situation. While on a trip to New York two months later, I spent an evening with the Metropolitan to discuss the whole problem, and we seemed to part with a much better understanding. A letter received a few weeks later, however, indicated that the situation had not improved, as I had hoped. A break with the Metropolitan seemed inevitable for both the A.S.O.R. and myself.

Fortunately, the first A.S.O.R. volume, *The Dead Sea Scrolls of St. Mark's Monastery*, Vol. I, which included full-sized reproductions of the Isaiah and Habakkuk Scrolls, had appeared in March, 1950. A similar publication of the Manual of Discipline had been pressed to completion by Dr. Burrows early in 1951. The scholarly world therefore had access to the three main documents.

Meanwhile, on November 30, 1951, the Metropolitan placed the scrolls under a trust agreement, leaving financial matters relating to them in the hands of the chairman of the trustees. This move impressed me as a good one to inspire confidence in his intentions with regard to the disposition of funds which might accrue from the sale of the scrolls.[12]

Continuing to believe that a successful sale of the scrolls would relieve all the tensions, I eagerly seized every opportunity to discuss the documents with potential donors. Dozens of detailed letters were written. The nature of my lecturing schedules throughout the United States provided numerous contacts with interested persons; given the slightest opening, I related the story in detail. Invariably the problems of price and title plagued the discussions, but always I emphasized my conviction that both could be solved once a sizable sum was assured.

On one occasion, when I visited Midland, Michigan, the Dow Chemical Company generously arranged for a discussion with some of their technical experts on the problem of preservation of the scrolls. New channels of interest there at first seemed promising. This contact, too, proved fruitless.

In March, 1953, an invitation to lecture in Dallas, Texas, before a large group of prominent businessmen appeared to open a most promising door toward success. Carefully planned by a number of influential and keenly interested religious leaders, educators, and businessmen, the stage seemed to be set for some real progress. One enthusiastic officer of a large company generously provided my round-trip plane fare to support the program. An illustrated address, designed to arouse enthusiasm for the scrolls, was presented in a large home to the select audience. Private conversations with several key leaders followed, and I returned to Chicago full of hope.

Not many days later, Mr. Norman M. Yonan arrived in Dallas with what has been claimed to be a fourth- or fifth-century A.D. Syriac New Testament. Having the document with him, he was able to arouse interest in it immediately; but in the course of those negotiations he learned about the interest in the Dead Sea Scrolls. Yonan, apparently influenced strongly by Dr. Sukenik's circulated statement, injected serious doubt about title into the minds of those interested. On learning of this unfortunate turn of events, I outlined in detail how the problem of title could be solved, but to no avail. The hope vanished.

A considerable prospect list had been gradually compiled, and I wrote copiously to every name on it. Much interest was expressed at every contact, but each trail disappeared into a hazy blur. Periodic attempts to learn what progress the Metropolitan was making brought only silence, so I continued hopeful that a sale might be made that would solve all the problems shrouding the story of the Syrians' scrolls.

During the fall of 1953 an idea was born that appeared to offer the finest possible disposition of the four scrolls. It was a by-product of a project on which I was working

Dr. Yigael Yadin views exhibit of Isaiah "A" Scroll and two Cave I jars at Hebrew University, Jerusalem, Israel

for the Religious Activities Committee of the United States Junior Chamber of Commerce.

A book entitled *Cradle of Our Faith* was being planned to enunciate the new religious emphasis added to the "Jaycee" Creed—"We believe that faith in God gives meaning and purpose to human life." Two men who were keenly interested in the book piloted me in their war-surplus, remodeled "Twin Cessna" plane to Baltimore one day for an interview with Dr. W. F. Albright concerning the project. Passing over the first range of the Shenandoah Mountains in western Virginia, we entered a heavy bank of clouds. Dropping beneath the overcast, the pilot followed a valley northeast, seeking a break over the next ridge. None appeared. He climbed above the overcast, hoping to get into Harrisburg—again only clouds. Minutes seemed like hours. Suddenly, through a hole in the clouds, some green fields appeared below. The pilot plunged the plane earthward as the co-pilot spotted a yellow airport wind-sock beside a large grassy meadow. Circling the unidentified landing strip, our pilot skillfully set the plane down lightly on the grassy field and taxied toward the deserted fieldhouse and hangar. Not a soul appeared, but beside a gateway to the field a large sign said, "Welcome to Gettysburg." With his location known, the pilot wanted to take off again and head on into Baltimore on instruments. Firmly I said, "We are staying in Gettysburg tonight."

With our appointment postponed by telephone, we relaxed in a small hotel room while I shared the story of the Dead Sea Scrolls with my two pilots. Their enthusiasm mounted with each episode. An idea began to emerge that night that could tie our project to the sale of the scrolls. By the time the book was ready for release the next fall, therefore, we had agreed upon a plan to present to the International Junior Chamber of Commerce, which would be meeting for its Ninth Congress in Mexico City the last week in October, 1954.

The book was interfaith and international in scope, and the International Jaycees embraced almost every country of the world. We proposed to the Congress that the book be accepted as an international project with the understanding that all profits from sales would be used to build a fund to purchase the four Dead Sea Scrolls, which in turn would become an international project. Title to the scrolls would be placed in the Palestine Archaeological Museum and arrangements made through the International Jaycees to conduct exhibits of the scrolls around the world, after which the documents would continue to reside in Jerusalem, Jordan. The money paid for the scrolls, we suggested, would go to rebuild the Syrian Orthodox Monastery in Jerusalem and to support other educational and rehabilitation projects there. Thus we hoped a double benefit could accrue from the project.

For almost a week we discussed our idea with the international leaders in caucus rooms, lobbies, and halls of the Del Prado Hotel in Mexico City. It was only exploratory, we knew, but the interest and enthusiasm exhibited by men from many corners of the world gave us assurance that the project could succeed.

With renewed confidence I returned home ready to lay the plan before the trustees of the scrolls. Lying on my office desk[13] was a letter from Dr. Burrows; its words hit me like a dash of cold water—the scrolls had been sold!

Mystery surrounded the sale, but the fact of it seemed certain. A letter to the Metropolitan seeking confirmation brought no reply. Again I wrote, outlining the plan we had so carefully prepared—again silence. On February 13, 1955, the details were finally revealed by the Prime Minister of Israel at a news conference in Jerusalem. Dr. Yigael Yadin, son of the late Eliezer Sukenik, had secretly purchased the scrolls for the State of Israel and had sent them to the Hebrew University in Jerusalem.[14] The sale had been consummated on July 1, 1954, at a price of $250,000, the highest estimate our advisors had claimed could be expected.[15] Another battle of the scrolls was ended. Dr. Sukenik had won, posthumously. I had lost.

16

The Adventure of Discovery

THUS far the discoveries in Cave I, which the Bedouin shepherd boy first entered during the winter of 1946-1947, have dominated these chapters. By 1952, however, other adventures in the Judean desert—which were destined to dwarf those related to that first cave—occupied the attention of scholars and public alike. For the reader who has not followed closely these oft-repeated stories, a brief summary of these later adventures seems warranted here. Furthermore, before any attempt is made to evaluate what has been discovered, more of the evidence needs to be reviewed.

With the rediscovery of the first cave early in 1949, a meticulous excavation of the debris left by the Bedouins and the Syrians was carried out by a group of archeologists from February 15 to March 5. Fragments of some fifty tall, cylindrical jars, and almost an equal number of bowl covers, were recovered. It took several months of tedious work in the Palestine Archaeological Museum to reconstruct a few of them to their original shapes. Four small oil lamps, three bowls, a cooking pot, a pitcher, two forehead phylacteries,[1] parts of four arm phylacteries, a wooden comb, some pieces of wood, and an abundance of linen cloth constituted the artifacts recovered. Hundreds of fragments of inscribed leather, indicating the presence of at least seventy manuscripts at one time in the cave, were sifted from the debris. Several pieces belonging to five of the scrolls and larger fragments previously found by the Bedouins and Syrians clearly related the cave to the original discovery.[2]

From among many tiny bits of leather, scholars were gradually able to identify portions of Biblical scrolls of Genesis, Exodus, Leviticus (written in archaic Hebrew script), Deuteronomy (two different scrolls), Judges, Samuel, Psalms (three scrolls), and Ezekiel. Adding these to the two already-described scrolls of Isaiah and Daniel (possibly two scrolls), a total of fifteen different Biblical manuscripts were represented in the first cave.

At least fifty-five non-Biblical scrolls are therefore indicated by the rest of the leather (and some papyrus) fragments. Among these, "commentaries"[3] of Micah, Zephaniah, and the Psalms were also identified. Adding the famed Habakkuk Commentary, four manuscripts of this type are known from that cave. Other documents represented among the fragments included phylactery scrolls (one containing the Decalogue in Deuteronomy 5:1-22), the Book of Jubilees (six fragments), the "Book of Noah" (Enoch 6-10, 106 — twenty-one fragments), the "Testament of Levi," "Sayings of Moses," a book of "Mysteries," some hymns and other liturgical scrolls, and several unknown apocryphal works. From all these it is clear that the cave once contained a considerable library of varied religious literature.

During the spring of 1949, Yusif Saad, the indefatigable secretary of the Palestine Archaeological Museum,[4] was hard on the trail of the Bedouins and their Bethlehem agent, Khalil Eskander, who had kept discreetly in the background. Saad's chance meeting one day with a woman who lived across the street from St. Mark's Monastery uncovered the fact that her husband, Jabra, had participated in the Syrian clandestine excavation during November 1948.[5] Jabra, when shown the materials secured during the official excavation, and with the help of some generous "bachshish," identified the cave beyond any question of a doubt. (He recovered his cigarette roller from among the ancient finds spread on tables in the Museum!) Finally he revealed the name of the Bethlehem cobbler, Kando; and Saad set off for Bethlehem by donkey via the tortuous and circuitous road through the Judean wilderness. The story of Saad's efforts to make the acquaintance of Kando, and finally (in 1950) to secure the mass of fragments which the cobbler and his associates had dug from the cave, reads like a Sherlock Holmes detective adventure.[6] It was then that fragments of the Hebrew University Isaiah Scroll (1QIs[b]), some from the "Genesis Apocryphon" (1Q20, now 1QApoc), several large pieces (including two almost-complete columns) from the Manual of Discipline (1QS)[7] and some fragments of a scroll of Deuteronomy (1QDeut[b]) were secured for the Department of Antiquities, but only after payment of the large sum of £P1,000 ($2,800).[8]

During the long period while Saad was seeking out Kando, this Bethlehem merchant (according to John Allegro) seems to have become fearful and buried a number of large pieces of scrolls on his Bethlehem property. When he went to retrieve them later, the moisture of the soil had reduced them to lumps of worthless glue.[9] How many manuscripts and fragments were lost through this fatal error can only be surmised. Probably it was the remainder of the materials secured during the November 1948 clandestine "excavation."

G. L. Harding and Father R. de Vaux at work
in Cave I (courtesy Dr. Ovid Sellers)

During the official excavation of Cave I, the small ruin called Khirbet Qumran, lying on a prominence of the marly plateau barely half a mile to the south where it ends abruptly at the Wadi Qumran, was examined briefly. Some nearby tombs also were excavated, but the archeologists drew the tentative conclusion that the *khirbeh* ("ruin" in Arabic) had no relation to the cave. The ruin appeared to be the remains of a Roman military outpost abandoned about the end of the first century A.D. Further excavation there seemed unwarranted. For more than two years, therefore, the focus of attention was turned on the scholarly battle which raged in the United States and Europe over the authenticity and antiquity of the scrolls.

Mounting pressure from scholars who sought further archeological evidence finally refocused interest on the *khirbeh*. Late in 1951 (November 24 to December 12), the first of six seasons of meticulous examination of the area of occupation was undertaken by G. L. Harding and Father R. de Vaux. Their excavation had not proceeded very far into the southwest corner of the main building when coins and pottery began to link the site to the same period of history and events represented by the cave. One jar in particular, found sunk in the floor of one room, was of the same shape and size as those found in the cave. Some indications pointed toward a sectarian religious center, perhaps of the Essenes, who had already been suggested as related to the scrolls. Archeological enthusiasm mounted.

In the meantime, however, the Ta'amireh Bedouins had been actively searching for new caves, and during October, 1951, appeared in Jerusalem with some fragments from a new source. Mystery surrounded the discovery, though authorities were led to a cave out in the Judean wilderness. Twice the area was visited, but prospects of more scrolls and a fruitful excavation seemed dim; excavation was not deemed advisable.

Hardly had the excavation at the *khirbeh* begun, when Kando offered Father de Vaux a sizable group of leather and papyrus fragments for purchase. With patience and adroitness, de Vaux pursued negotiations directly with the Bedouins until finally, on January 21, 1952, an expedition was begun among the precipitous cliffs of the Wadi Murabba'at, almost twelve miles south of Khirbet Qumran.[10] Four huge caves produced a vast amount of valuable manuscript and archeological data related not to Qumran, however, but mostly to the second Jewish revolt of A.D. 132-135, under Bar Kokhba ("Son of a Star"). A new door to manuscript discoveries in the Holy Land had been opened.[11]

With the scholars momentarily absent from the Qumran area, the indefatigable

Reconstructed jars and other remains recovered from Cave I in February, 1949, on exhibit in Palestine Archaeological Museum, Jerusalem, Jordan.

Bedouins resumed their search for caves there. During February another cave (Cave II, 2Q) close by the first cave produced 187 manuscript fragments. Parts of seventeen Biblical scrolls were recovered, plus numerous non-Biblical pieces. It was now apparent that Cave I (1Q) was no isolated cache from ancient times.

An expedition was needed to stem the clandestine Bedouin diggings. From March 10 to 29 teams of scholars and several Ta'amireh Bedouins, who were pressed into their employ, scoured some 200 caves and crevices for a distance of five miles north and south of Wadi Qumran in search of the precious bits of inscribed leather. Twenty-six caves produced characteristic Qumran pottery sherds, but only one contained manuscript fragments. This one, Cave III (3Q), discovered on March 14, turned up the strangest manuscript yet known—a copper scroll (in two sections) which added mystery and a treasure hunt to the already fantastic story. A few other fragments on leather were also recovered from the cave, but their importance was minor.

The approaching heat of summer brought peace and silence once more to the Judean desert. July, 1952, however, found the Bedouins again in Jerusalem with more manuscript fragments, the source of which remained undisclosed (see pp. 151-154). Apparently from somewhere south of Wadi Murabba'at, these documents were also related to the second Jewish revolt and not to the Qumran materials.

Shortly thereafter other manuscripts were brought in by the Ta'amirehs. This time they included Greek New Testament papyri and some early Arabic documents. Already some scholars had begun to link early Christianity to the Qumran community, and the first reports of the finding of New Testament manuscripts near Qumran added confusion to the story. It was soon apparent, however, that these manuscripts had no relation to the Qumran materials, for they dated from the fifth to the eighth centuries A.D. They were from the ruins of a Byzantine (Christian) monastery at Khirbet Mird, the site of the ancient Maccabean fortress of Hyrcania, five miles west of Qumran. (For an earlier similar discovery, see Appendix II, "1937.")

A new wave of excitement began in August, 1952, when the Bedouins came upon Cave IV (4Q), a few hundred feet southwest of Khirbet Qumran and separated from it by a deep ravine which cuts north into the terrace from Wadi Qumran. On a prominence overlooking Wadi Qumran, Cave IV was dug in ancient times into the face of the eroded terrace. From a deep hole to one side of the cave, thousands of leather and papyrus fragments were exhumed. Fortunately, the archeologists discovered the new dig before all the fabulous cache had been emptied by clandestine diggers; fragments from a hundred manuscripts were thus recovered under controlled conditions during a systematic excavation there from September 22 to 29. Thousands of dollars had to be raised, however, and several years were to elapse before scholars would be able to recover the great number of fragments looted by the Bedouins.[12]

It is estimated that some 40,000 fragments came from Cave IV alone. An international team of scholars—two from America, two from England, two from France, one from Poland, and one from Germany—was selected to tackle the arduous task of cleaning, assembling, and analyzing them. The work of assembling the myriad fragments was not completed until the summer of 1960.[13] Almost 400 different manuscripts were found to be represented, about 100 of which were Biblical. The scroll story thus took on gargantuan proportions, and another new chapter began. Publication of this vast assembly of manuscript fragments will occupy many years and many volumes. Only a few representative fragments have so far been published in scattered articles.[14]

During the excavation of Cave IV, another cave a few yards to the north was noticed and proved to contain some badly decomposed fragments. Cave V (5Q), like Cave IV, had been cut into the side of the marly terrace in ancient times and, like most of the other caves, may have been used as living quarters by members of the community. One suggestion is that the caves cut into the terrace were originally made for use as tombs, perhaps in the eighth or seventh century B.C. Another possibility is that they were cut by community members as an additional source for clay used in the manufacture of pottery, large quantities of which were made in the community's pottery-manu-facturing center.

About the same time, the Bedouins located Cave VI (6Q), this time in the face of the rocky cliff close by the Wadi Qumran. Only fifty-seven fragments of leather were recovered from it, but 718 papyrus pieces were gathered—a most unusual proportion of papyrus for a Qumran cave. Although at lease six Biblical books are represented among these finds, the most interesting feature of this cave was a group of first-century A.D. leather fragments (6Q15) related to a manuscript known as the "Damascus Document," which was first known from the famous Cairo Genizah discovery in 1897. Somewhat similar in contents to the "Manual of Discipline" (1QS), this manuscript, however, refers to a sojourn in Damascus, the meaning of which continues to arouse considerable debate.

After all the excitement of 1952, with its five Qumran cave discoveries (plus the excavation of four Wadi Murabba'at caves and another somewhere farther south), the scholars returned to the meticulous task of excavating what was now clearly the community center from which the Qumran scrolls had come. The long second and third seasons of work (February 9—April 24, 1953, and February 13—April 14, 1954) confirmed beyond any doubt the nature of the community center. The general outlines of the main building (100' x 120') and its adjacent assembly room (15' x 73') with a pantry to the south, the pottery-manufacturing center to the southeast, the east wall, and the elaborate water system of cisterns and channels were exposed. Most significant during the second season was the discovery of the remains of a "scriptorium," a second-floor room in which a long, plaster-covered table and bench, a wash basin, and three inkwells indicated that manuscripts had been copied there. The only inscribed evidence was a potsherd (ostracon) from a nearby first-century B.C. "dump." On the ostracon the Hebrew alphabet had been copied in a hand that suggested a schoolboy practicing his lesson. Its value to paleography was immediately apparent.

Numerous coins made possible a reconstruction of the history of the community, which was established about 125 B.C. (Period Ia), was expanded about 100 B.C. (Period Ib), and was abandoned in 31 B.C. after severe destruction, apparently caused by an earthquake. It was restored about 4 B.C. (Period II) along lines similar to those of Period Ib, and continued to flourish until its violent overthrow by the Romans, about A.D. 68, during the first Jewish revolt. (See Appendix II for an outline of the community's history.)

A fourth season of excavation (February 2 to April 6, 1955) concentrated on the western quarter of the community center and revealed the complex beginning of the water conduit and cistern system with its sluice gates at the northwest corner of a large courtyard northwest of the main building. Further evidences of the daily activities of the community center were also uncovered in this area. In the midst of this season, a new series of caves was discovered by the excavators along the edges of the Qumran terrace on which the *khirbeh* lay. Caves VII-X (7Q-10Q), though mostly collapsed and eroded away along with the many manuscripts they probably once contained, produced only a handful of manuscript fragments.[15] Meanwhile the Bedouins discovered another obscure cave in Wadi Murabba'at, not far from those excavated in 1952. There they came upon an almost-complete, but badly disintegrated Hebrew scroll of the Minor Prophets from the second century A.D. It was the only manuscript found in that cave.

During the fifth season of excavation at Qumran (February 18 to March 28, 1956) the final clearing of the entire community center was accomplished, revealing all that could be recovered from the ancient ruins. In addition, eighteen of the more than one thousand tombs in the cemetery directly east of the center, beyond its outer wall, were excavated. Each grave was identical to the others, dug in an "L" shape (a vertical shaft with projection at the bottom, in which the body was laid and sealed off with stones), always oriented north and south. They were humble burials, without artifacts. Two other cemeteries were located, one farther north and another farther south from the center. Some evidences of what appeared to be related buildings near 'Ain Feshkha, two miles to the south, were also uncovered.

During February, 1956, once again the Bedouins came upon a cave, this time about a mile north of the community center, not far from Cave III. This one (Cave XI, 11Q) took ingenuity to locate and superhuman effort to open, for the entire front had collapsed. Apparently it was discovered from its very small opening out of which bats were seen to emerge; tons of rock had to be removed to expose the cave. Once opened, however, the discovery was amazing: two complete manuscripts and five large portions of others made this discovery as significant as that of Cave I. For a long time lack of funds stood between these scrolls and the scholarly world avidly waiting to study them. Endowment funds of the Palestine Archaeological Museum were sacrificed to recover the scrolls from the Bedouins, until finally all the documents were safely locked in the Museum vault.

In the meantime, only tempting, sketchy descriptions of a few of the manuscripts were released. A scroll of Leviticus in archaic Hebrew, an extensive, well-preserved Psalms scroll (11QPss), a fragmentary scroll of Ezekiel, an Aramaic translation (or interpretation?) of the Book of Job, and an apocryphal scroll about the "New Jerusalem" were announced as being among these significant finds. During the summer of 1956 curiosity heightened with the opening of two copper scrolls from Cave III, and the discovery that they contained lists of fabulous treasures stored in remote and vaguely identified places.[16]

A sixth and final season of digging in the Qumran area was conducted from January 25 to March 21, 1958, in the area just north of 'Ain Feshkha, where soundings in 1956 had indicated related buildings were to be found. A significant irrigation system was traced, and farm buildings were exposed. Here stables, toolsheds, and what appeared to be rooms for preparing leather for its various uses completed the story of the daily life of the Qumran community.[17]

But adventures with manuscripts in the Holy Land were not yet ended. From a rumor that Bedouins had found manuscript fragments in a cave in the Nahal Tse'elim area north of Masada in Israel, the Israelis were spurred into a systematic search of that treacherous mountain and desert region which lies by the Dead Sea, from En Gedi south to Masada. For two weeks beginning March 23, 1960, teams of scholars and

1. Sluice gates of water conduit
2. Bath?
3. Settling basin for water
4. Water channel
5. Round cistern (8th Cent. B.C.)
6. Large water cisterns
7. Defense tower
8. Kitchen
9. Council chambers?
10. Scriptorium
11. Courtyard
12. Laundry
13. Pottery kilns
14. Assembly room
15. Pantry
16. Storage rooms
17. Stables?
18. Cemetery
19. East wall

Air view of Qumran community center after completion of excavation (courtesy Palestine Archaeological Museum) students explored the rugged terrain which provided refuge for the Jews' last determined stand against the Romans in A.D. 135. In the Nahal Heber, about three miles south of En Gedi, the team under Dr. Yigael Yadin met with amazing success. There, in a cave high up on the sheer cliff, fifteen papyrus letters in a goatskin bag were unearthed, along with several baskets of skeletal remains (which punctuated the grim end of the Bar Kokhba revolt).

Further explorations in the same cave during March, 1961, uncovered a still larger collection of papyrus documents, some thirty-five dated business documents (A.D. 88-132) relating to the affairs of families in and near En Gedi. These were written in Aramaic, Nabataean, and Greek. Another leather bag contained five manuscripts, of which three were in Hebrew and relate to Bar Kokhba's lease of some property in En Gedi.[18] It is believed likely that the Greek text of the Minor Prophets—secured by the Ta'amireh Bedouins in July, 1952, from an "unidentified cave"—came from this same cave. The silence of the Bedouins regarding the source—which was not far from the border of Jordan, but in Israel—would thus be readily understood.

Meanwhile negotiations continued in order to release the scrolls from Cave XI for study and publication. A generous gift received by the A.S.O.R. was used to secure the rights to publish the Psalms Scroll. During November 10-20, 1961, Dr. J. A. Sanders of Colgate-Rochester Divinity School, to whom the scroll was entrusted, opened and began to study this well-preserved scroll. In his preliminary report,[19] Dr. Sanders indicates that the document is more than half the length of the famed Isaiah Scroll, or about thirteen feet long. It contains some thirty-seven Psalms, plus seven "non-canonical compositions" which can be expected to provoke much discussion. The fact that Psalm 151, previously found only in Greek (the Septuagint), Old Latin, and Syriac versions of the Psalms, appears in Hebrew in this manuscript, is of itself most significant.

Attempts about the same time to open the badly disintegrated Ezekiel Scroll from the same cave unfortunately proved disappointing to Dr. W. H. Brownlee, who had been assigned to study it. Only a few lines of text could be obtained from the entire document.[20]

Despite the diligence of authorities and the search by scholars, the Judean wilderness west of the Dead Sea may not yet have yielded up all its manuscript secrets from the ancient past. One of the problems now is to sift rumor from fact, and forgery from authentic document. During 1960 it was reported that the Ta'amireh Bedouins had discovered still another cave (Cave XII?) in the Qumran area; mystery still surrounds that story. When I interviewed some of these Bedouins during the summer of 1962, they hinted broadly about a new cave discovery recently made near Nablus; but they produced no sound evidence of it, as they had promised. Many manuscript fragments were shown to me, but they all proved to be either forgeries or modern Hebrew manuscripts which had been treated to appear ancient.

Indeed the Bedouins had discovered another cave, as was revealed a few months later, but it was unrelated to Khirbet Qumran. While their flocks were grazing near Nablus, they happened upon a tremendous cave complex in the Wadi ed-Daliyeh, nine miles north of modern Jericho in a most rugged and treacherous terrain. There, in a huge cave called Mugharet 'Abu Shinjeh, fragments of some forty Samaritan papyrus business documents were recovered from among hundreds of human skeletons and personal artifacts, all clearly dating from the fourth century B.C.! It soon became apparent that the cave had been the refuge of the Samaritan leaders when Alexander the Great attacked Samaria on his return trip from Egypt in 331 B.C. The grim evidence revealed that the Samaritans had been trapped and massacred, or had suffocated.[21]

Just as the final editing of this book is being done, still another manuscript discovery is reported. During the winter of 1963-1964 Professor Yigael Yadin's excavation of Herod's fortress near the southern end of the Dead Sea at Masada yielded ninety ostraca, a fragmentary scroll of Psalms (81-85), five chapters of a first-century B.C. Hebrew scroll of Ecclesiasticus, and a sectarian liturgical scroll, plus some other papyrus fragments. Most of them appeared in a stratum which represents the Jewish Zealots' suicidal last stand against the Roman legions in A.D. 73. The sectarian scroll contains "The Song of the Sabbath Sacrifice," identical to a Qumran Cave IV document; it is the first Qumran document found outside the Khirbet Qumran area.[22]

Thus, as the momentous task of translating, publishing, and interpreting the vast amount of newly discovered ancient documents from the Holy Land proceeds unabated, the prospects of further additions to these monumental finds continue to keep scholars and Jordanian as well as Israeli authorities alert and expectant. So continue the amazing adventures with manuscripts.

17

A Way in the
Wilderness

Hixi up on the precipitous cliff that dominates the Qumran plateau to the west, I climbed to a rocky ledge one Sunday afternoon (May 4, 1958) to gain a panoramic perspective of the Essene community center. At last, the dream of many years had been fulfilled; before me lay the scene of the drama of the Dead Sea Scrolls, the source of my own adventures.

Like a great cathedral, the scene provided an appropriate setting for a unique experience of worship. My rocky ledge was the back "pew" of the balcony. Below, perhaps 100 feet and stretching some 300 yards to the east, the marly plateau formed the great nave. Deep undulations cut into the plateau from the Wadi Qumran at the right, simulating the pews of the imaginary nave. Remains of an ancient water conduit followed the sloping plateau at the left, like an aisle beside the pews. The terrace, where ruins of the ancient community center lay exposed by the spades of the excavators, formed a natural sanctuary dominated by the altar, the focal point of most Christian churches. Symbolizing commitment and sacrifice, the excavated remains of the Qumran community fulfilled the function of the altar in the church of my imagination. The deep azure of the Dead Sea, and the purple-tinted cliffs of ancient Moab beyond, provided the reredos and dossal curtain to complete the ecclesiastical setting.

It was a service of silence. Not a cricket could be heard, nor the song of a bird or the whir of its wings; not a breeze stirred among the crags. The sun's glare bore down with irritating intensity upon the placid scene, having already blighted the few tufts of grass which had managed to emerge from the sparse soil in rocky crevices during the brief rainy season just past. Here was consummate desert isolation in Palestine's "Great Rift," the lowest point on the surface of the earth—a veritable inferno of heat nine months of the year. Frequented for centuries only by Bedouins, until one of them accidentally happened upon that certain cave a half mile to the north of where I sat, this barren waste was now the focal point of world attention.

The sermon was a deep, silent meditation with the usual three or four emphases. The first, as might be expected, was a personal reminiscence. Fifteen miles to the west, across the rugged wilderness of Judea, the Israelis were celebrating the tenth anniversary of the formation of their state. Now I was enjoying my own tenth anniversary in peaceful solitude. Exactly ten years ago I had traveled across Europe clutching a satchel full of photographs and negatives that would make possible the publication of three of the now-famed Dead Sea Scrolls. The thrill of those weeks immediately preceding that homeward journey flashed momentarily through my mind. It had been a privilege to be the first American to examine, evaluate, and photograph these oldest Biblical documents yet discovered, and to bring them to the attention of the world. The whole panorama of events which the Qumran site had unfolded during those ten years crowded together to dominate my thinking.

A second phase of meditation soon overshadowed the joy of pure reminiscence, as provocative academic and religious questions arose. Has anything really important been discovered here? Or is it all merely the excitement of adventure within the ordinarily sterile structure of pure historical academics? Is it possible to evaluate the meaning of such a discovery, when only a small fraction of the materials has yet been published? Ultimate meaning and values, to be sure, must await more definitive information; but certain values are already apparent from that which has been published.

From a purely academic standpoint the values of the Dead Sea Scrolls have already proved to be tremendous. The fact that Biblical Hebrew manuscripts copied before the tenth century A.D. have at last been discovered in the Holy Land is of itself of monumental importance. It is estimated that more than 125 Old Testament manuscripts, including every book except Esther (many of them very fragmentary, to be sure), have now been recovered from the Qumran caves. They range in date from about 250 B.C. (a blackened fragment of Exodus from Cave IV, 4QEx^f) to about A.D. 70. Some, therefore, are more than a thousand years older than previously-known documents in Biblical Hebrew. In addition, there are the several second-century A.D. fragments found at Wadi Murabba'at and Nahal Heber, not to mention the later Khirbet Mird documents. A whole new horizon for Biblical textual studies has thus been provided.

No startling alterations in the Old Testament text will be necessary from what has been discovered so far, nor are any expected. The textual contributions, in fact, will seem insignificant from the layman's point of view, but to the scholar every minor point is an important step toward his dream of the ultimate recovery of the original Biblical text. The scholar cannot assume, however, that the greater age of these documents guarantees their textual superiority. Each point must be weighed carefully, and many variant readings in them may be rejected on sound grounds. Others will be disputed. It may be asserted, nevertheless, that the Qumran scrolls have provided scholars with a major breakthrough into the complex prehistory of the standard (Masoretic) Hebrew text of the Old Testament. For the layman, on the other hand, the very fact that these many documents testify to the *substantial* accuracy of the traditional text of the Old Testament will seem of prime importance.

An important part of the "major breakthrough" for scholars is the contribution of the scrolls to Septuagint (Greek Old Testament) studies. Already it has been shown, from the extensive Hebrew Samuel fragments from Cave IV (4QSam^a), that at Qumran some manuscripts were in use that were similar to those used by the Greek translators. Another Hebrew recension, therefore, has been discovered, and it differs considerably from the traditional text. Other similar values are certain to be forthcoming from many other Biblical fragments. Unpublished first-century B.C. Septuagint Greek fragments of Leviticus and Numbers, reported from Cave IV, will doubtless provide more light. Prior to this discovery only a few pre-Christian fragments of a Greek Deuteronomy scroll had been available. Furthermore, the Greek text of the Minor Prophets (probably from Nahal Heber), though from the second century A.D., is of great importance, since it is Jewish in origin. Previously only Christian papyri from that early date have been available, in the already highly-prized Chester Beatty Old Testament papyri.[1]

What appear to have been pre-Samaritan scrolls have also been discovered. At least two scrolls from Cave IV (4QEx^a and 4QNum^b) promise to shed light on the history of the Samaritan Pentateuch. Thus, still another pre-Masoretic recension of the Old Testament text has been recovered, to add to the pre-Septuagint Hebrew text revealed in the Samuel fragments and the sectarian (or pre-Masoretic?) recension of Isaiah in the large Isaiah Scroll. What ultimate values may come from these materials cannot yet be predicted, to be sure. That more than one text-type of the Old Testament Hebrew is now available to Biblical scholarship is indeed of paramount importance. One thing is clear: there was no fixed textual tradition at Qumran, despite the sect's zealous devotion to Scripture.[2]

For the paleographer, who needs evidences of many scribal hands to date documents of unknown date, these discoveries have been of phenomenal importance. Suspected by many scholars in 1948 because of its lack of sufficient evidence, Hebrew-Aramaic paleography has now been promoted to the level of a respectable science. What were thin threads of inscriptional and manuscript materials in 1948 have now been woven into a sizable fabric by the thousands of fragments spread over such a broad, yet crucial, historic period, about 375 B.C. to A.D. 135. Many types of script used by the scribes of that period have been recovered (more than 500 have been identified from the Qumran Cave materials alone), some datable within narrow limits, even to the very year, as in the Bar Kokhba and Wadi ed-Daliyeh documents.

The fact that Aramaic manuscripts, some of them quite extensive (such as the "Genesis Apocryphon" from 1Q, and the Job Scroll from 11Q), have been gathered from this great horde is especially significant for the background of New Testament studies. It is a happy coincidence that at least some of these documents can be dated paleographically to the very lifetime of Jesus, whose native language they represent. What values may be forthcoming from their study can now only be surmised. The scholarly battle which raged during the early part of the twentieth century over the influence of Aramaic on the New Testament seems destined to be reopened with much more academic acumen, as a result of these manuscripts.

Although the textual, paleographic, and philological values are significant, the literary values have already proved to be more so. Here a whole new field of research has appeared. Nearly 500 Qumran manuscripts out of a total of about 600 belong to the categories of Apocryphal (Ecclesiasticus fragments from 2Q, and Tobit fragments from 4Q) and Pseudepigraphical literature; that is, writings which were religious but not accepted as authoritative in Judaism. Some of the latter have been previously known in later translations, but most of these are now represented in Hebrew fragments for the first time. These include the Book of Jubilees, the Testaments of Levi and Naphthali, the Book of Enoch, the Damascus Document, and several other closely related works.

The great bulk of this literature, however, is entirely new and casts a flood of light upon sectarian Judaism in the last two centuries B.C. and the first century A.D. Manuscripts in which Biblical writings are interpreted (such as the Habakkuk Commentary, 1QpHab), provide a valuable insight into sectarian methods of handling the Biblical text. At the same time, they reveal bits of information about history (often couched in veiled language, to be sure) and the nature of sectarian thought. These many new manuscripts will become a part of the pseudepigraphical literature, which has grown rapidly during recent years through discoveries. Having been rejected by early Judaism because they were of sectarian origin, such manuscripts can hardly be expected to gain canonical status now.

Out of the whole discovery, manuscript and archeological materials alike, have come details to broaden our knowledge of that very period which saw the birth of Christianity. Introductions to the New Testament and textbooks on early Christian history are already undergoing revision to incorporate this vast new storehouse of information, particularly on the nature of Jewish sectarianism in the midst of which Christianity emerged. No study of the background of Christianity is now complete without a perusal of what has already been revealed by the Dead Sea Scrolls. The milieu of thought which surrounded the origin of these scrolls is the same as that within which John the Baptist, Jesus, and the early Apostles moved. They were living contemporaries of the Qumran sect.

It is right at this point—the relationship between Christianity and the Qumran-Essene sect—that another battle of the Dead Sea Scrolls has been raging since 1955[3] in church, synagogue, and even secular circles. The "fallout" of controversial theories from this archeological explosion has become phenomenal; publishers, both popular and scholarly, have been prematurely flooded with articles and books presenting a confusing array of claims based on similarities between what is found in the New Testament and tentative (not always accurate) translations of what is found in the Dead Sea Scrolls.[4]

It needs to be remembered that nothing has been found in the Qumran caves or at Khirbet Qumran itself that can be called genuinely Christian. Though the whole historic lives of both John the Baptist and Jesus, it is now clearly established, were contemporary with the second period of the occupation at Khirbet Qumran, no artifact nor any manuscript so far discovered and reported reveals any direct contact between these religious movements. What have been claimed as evidences of contact are merely literary and ideological parallels and similarities. Furthermore, the fallacy of *argumentum ad ignorantiam* (arguing from the absence of information to the contrary) has loomed large in many of the published theories, such as the one which claims that Jesus must have spent His early life at Qumran, or that John the Baptist had been a member of the community. Attractive as such theories may seem, on the basis of possible historical associations, they still remain unproved theories based on circumstantial evidence. Since they cannot be proved untrue, these theorists imply that one should assume that they are true. In the realm of history such specious reasoning is particularly hazardous.

From my rocky "pew" high above Khirbet Qumran, the final questions seemed most important: What is this drama recovered from the past trying to tell us? What does it mean for our faith?

Into that barren wilderness about 125 B.C. and inspired by a devout, dedicated teacher, went a sincere group of religious enthusiasts who believed that they were the "Sons of Light" chosen by God to prepare in the wilderness "the way of the Lord" (Isaiah 40:3). Descendants of the Hasidim, a pietistic movement of the early second century, they were eschatologically oriented; that is, concerned with the end of the age. The drama of history was nearing its dénouement, they sincerely believed; time was running out. The "Sons of Darkness," who were believed to be under the demonic power of Belial, were destined to destruction. The final battle between truth and falsehood, right and wrong, purity and perversity, light and darkness, was drawing near. The chosen ones therefore went into the wilderness to fulfill Scripture, but also to avoid contamination with the "Sons of Darkness" and to retain their "purity" through the perfect manifestation of the commands of God in their lives—as though they were already in the new age. In their "Manual of Discipline" appear the words:

And when these things occur for the community in Israel, by these ordinances they shall be separated from the midst of the habitation of unrighteous men in order to go to the wilderness, there to prepare the way of the LORD, according as it is written, "In the wilderness prepare the way of the LORD. Make straight in the desert a highway for our God" [Isaiah 40:3]. That [refers] to the study of the Torah [the Law or teachings] which he [God] commanded by the hand of Moses to do according to all that has been revealed from time to time and according to that which the prophets revealed through his holy spirit [1QS VIII:12-16].

There on the Qumran wilderness plateau, they led austere, disciplined, dedicated lives under a most rigorous, semi-monastic organization. Frequent lustrations, sacred meals, and solemn assemblies marked their daily routine; nor did they shy away from hard work and menial tasks to meet their daily needs in their isolated community center. Apparently they spent the nights in tents and caves. Reading, copying, and meditation upon Scripture also occupied much of their time. Those who sought to join the community were placed under the most severe testing and disciplined preparation for at least two years.[5] It is difficult in the pages of history to find better examples of men who strove more diligently for perfection of moral character and religious devotion. From the standpoint of man's limited ethical perspective, at Qumran, it would seem, were men upon whom God might look with utmost favor.

If devotion to the law, a particular interpretation of Scripture, purity in thought and deed, piety, personal denial, and rigid discipline were prerequisites for salvation and immortality, certainly such men might be judged as having achieved it. But grim evidence from archeology is that in the summer of A.D. 68, the Qumran community was ruthlessly destroyed at the hand of pagan Romans who were supposedly the "Sons of Darkness" destined for eternal destruction. Here is a supreme example of "Truth forever on the scaffold, Wrong forever on the throne." God's justice in dealing with men is brought under acute scrutiny. It out-Habakkuk's Habakkuk, the proper interpretation of which only the Qumran teacher was believed to understand (1QpHab VII:1-5). It out-Jobs the Book of Job, whose inimitable dialogue became canonized in the Bible and has thus survived the centuries without interruption; its turbulent drama and its theophany (Job 42) thus continue to be shared with many who have found comfort in its words.

The Qumran community died; its voice was silenced, its manuscripts were hidden in caves, gradually to disintegrate with the passing centuries and the ravages of animals and insects. Not until a stone casually tossed into a hole in the side of a cliff aroused a Bedouin shepherd's curiosity were the remnants of their manuscript treasures brought to light after being lost for nineteen centuries. Except for a few allusions by some early Greek and Latin historians to the Essenes, whom this community seems to represent, the idealism and hopes of these people were swept from the stage of history. Not even an "immortality" like that of Job's preserved words was accorded the devout ponderings of the dedicated men of Qumran. To the religiously sensitive observer, the natural question is, Why?

Anyone who may be concerned about the possibility that this discovery may undermine the foundations of Christianity needs only to remember these simple facts:

the Qumran community died; Christianity lives. A more important question is, Why did the Qumran community die, while Christianity lives? The answer seems to be found in the narrow focus of that ancient community's faith, with its intensely eschatological orientation: it was not broad enough to embrace the possibility of suffering and defeat. It is not the similarities between the Qumran sect and Christianity, therefore, upon which one should dwell, but rather the differences, if he would gain the lessons this discovery teaches.[6] Despite the hazard of oversimplification, the following contrasts might be pointed out by way of elucidation:

1. The Qumran community was an intensely separatistic sect; they rigidly avoided the "Sons of Darkness," contact with whom meant defilement and impurity. In the "Manual of Discipline" the expression "to be separated from all unrighteous men" (or "men of error") appears repeatedly (1QS V:1, 2, 10; VIII:13, etc.).

Jesus, however, is reported to have moved deliberately among those whom Jews, in derision, termed "tax collectors and sinners." When criticized, His reply was, "Those who are well have no need of a physician, but those who are sick; I came not to call the righteous, but sinners" (Mark 2:17; Matthew 9:12-13; Luke 5:31-32). Jesus and the Apostles considered association with others essential to preaching the gospel, the "good news."

Both the Qumran sect and Christianity may be said to have drawn inspiration from the fortieth chapter of Isaiah—but from different verses. For the men of Qumran it was verse 3: "In the wilderness prepare the way of the Lord, make straight in the desert a highway for our God"; thus they moved away from other men. For Jesus, verse 9 provided His emphasis: "Get you up to a high mountain, O Zion, herald of good tidings; lift up your voice with strength, O Jerusalem, herald of good tidings. . . ." Christians carried the "good tidings" to men.

2. The Qumran community was esoteric. Its members were sworn to secrecy about its teachings. Many of its documents were written in obscure and cryptic language, for only the initiated were intended to know the hidden meaning. Translation of many of the documents is exceedingly difficult because of this deliberate use of veiled language. Several manuscripts from Cave IV are reported to contain a completely cryptic, esoteric language. Some, however, have been deciphered. In the "Manual of Discipline" the member is admonished "to conceal [keep secret] the counsel of the Torah among unrighteous men" (1QS IX:17).

What a contrast their attitude was to that of Jesus, who "called to him the twelve, and began to send them out two by two, and gave them authority over the unclean spirits. . . . So they went out and preached that men should repent" (Mark 6:7, 12)!

3. The Qumran community lived its isolated life in the wilderness, waiting for God to act—the Kingdom was yet to come. It was almost fanatically apocalyptic in outlook, as many of the scrolls reveal. The "War Scroll" (1QM) portrays with vivid abandon the community's preparation for the anticipated destruction of the "Sons of Darkness." As the "chosen ones of God," the community members believed they would be instruments of that destruction when God so chose. Commenting on Habakkuk 1:12-13, a Qumran writer says, "The word means that God will not destroy his people by the hand of the

nations, but into the hand of his elect God will deliver the judgment of all nations and by their chastisement all the wicked among his people will be punished" (1QpHab V:3-5).

Jesus and the early Christians firmly believed that God was already acting to redeem; the Kingdom was already beginning to be felt. Jesus came preaching that "The time is fulfilled, and the kingdom of God is at hand; repent, and believe in the gospel" (Mark 1:15). To the Pharisees He said, ". . . behold, the kingdom of God is in the midst of you" (Luke 17:21). Although Christianity, too, began with an apocalyptic emphasis very similar to that of the Qumran sect, it contained the spiritual basis for a gradual shift to an ongoing fellowship (compare the Book of Revelation with the Gospel of John).

4. The Qumran community lived an ascetic life, rigidly disciplined to fulfill literally the commands of the Torah. Emphasis was placed on the preservation of their purity and avoidance of anything which might make them ceremonially unclean. Thus they focused their spirit inwardly, keeping themselves constantly under critical self-examination in the light of their careful observance of Torah. Repeated admonitions to perfection appear in the manuscripts, such as:

. . . to cleanse their minds by the truth of the statutes of God, and to direct their energy according to the integrity of his ways . . . not to deviate at all from any of the words of God in their times [of worship?]; not to advance or delay the times of any of their appointed festivals; nor to swerve from his true statutes, to go either right or left (1QS I:12-15).

Christians shared the spirit outwardly, giving purity a qualitative rather than ceremonial emphasis. Jesus said, "Hear and understand: not what goes into the mouth defiles a man, but what comes out of the mouth, this defiles a man. . . . For out of the heart come evil thoughts, murder, adultery, fornication, theft, false witness, slander" (Matthew 15:10-11, 19). To Jesus, God's commandments dealt with those qualities which bind man to man in brotherhood. In a similar vein is the important Christian thought: ". . . whoever loses his life for my sake and the gospel's will save it" (Mark 8:35).

5. The Qumran community was priest-centered. The head priest and the "Sons of Aaron" held the positions of highest authority, even above that of the "Messiah of Israel"! In the "Rule of the Congregation" occurs the statement:

This is the session of the men of renown [literally, "the Name"] invited to the feast for the council of the community, when God begets the Messiah [to be] with them. The priest shall come at the head of the whole congregation of Israel, and all the fathers of the Sons of Aaron, the priests, invited [?] to the feast of the men of renown. They shall sit before him, each according to his rank. Next shall come the Messiah of Israel [the Davidic Messiah?], and before him shall sit the heads of the thousands of Israel, each according to his rank. . . . And when they meet for the common table or to drink the wine . . . no one shall put forth his hand on the first [portion] of the bread or the wine before the priest . . . [1QSa II:11-15, 17-19].

Christianity began as a lay movement without any formal organization; neither Jesus nor His disciples had any priestly background. The only prerequisite for joining the fellowship was a common spirit. Organization came only with expansion and as problems of the spiritual fellowship demanded it.

6. The Qumran community was rigidly organized, with a strict hierarchy of position for each member. In the "Manual of Discipline," for instance, the order is clearly elucidated:

First in order to pass over shall be the priests, according to their spirits, one after the other. Then the Levites shall pass over after them. Third in order to pass over shall be all the people, each after the other by thousands and hundreds and fifties and tens. Thus every man of Israel will know his position in the community of God for the eternal council. And none shall be lowered from his position and none shall be raised above his alloted place; for all of them shall be in true community [1QS II:19-24].

In the passage quoted from the "Rule of the Congregation" (in "5" above), the rigidity of the order seems to be projected even into the Messianic age.

Christianity began as a fellowship (*koinonía*) of believers. Jesus was opposed to hierarchy, as the Gospels articulate so forcefully:

And they came to Capernaum; and when he was in the house he asked them, "What were you discussing on the way?" But they were silent; for on the way they had discussed with one another who was the greatest. And he sat down and called the twelve; and he said to them, "If any one would be first, he must be last of all and servant of all" (Mark 9:33-35).

After the Resurrection the fellowship was loosely organized around the leadership of the Apostles; only later and very gradually did a hierarchy develop. Certain parallels in structure have been pointed out between the Qumran order and that of primitive Christianity, to be sure; but the Spirit and teachings of Jesus were clearly foreign to a rigid hierarchy.

7. To the Qumran community Scripture was central, and the accuracy of its inspired teacher's interpretation of it was unquestioned. The vast manuscript horde, with many *pesharim* or interpretations, and frequent references therein are testimonies to their belief in the authority of the written Word. In the Habakkuk (*Pesher*) Commentary, the source of their faith in interpreted Scripture is made clear:

Now God told Habakkuk to write what would happen to the last generation, but the consummation of the end he did not make known to him. And when it says "In order that he who runs may read it" [Hab. 2:2] that refers to the Right Teacher, to whom God made known all the secrets of the words of his servants the prophets [1QpHab VII:1-5].

Jesus, though thoroughly familiar with Scripture and strongly influenced by it, emphasized its spirit rather than its words. His was no esoteric interpretation of hidden meanings; it was the obvious intent of the message of Scripture that He made transparent. His "You have heard that it was said. . . .But I say to you" (Matthew 5:21-44) implied not so much a new teaching as a shift from the stress on written words to the spirit of the message of Scripture as a whole. In the writings of Paul this contrast becomes striking: ". . . the written code kills, but the Spirit gives life" (II Corinthians 3:6).

8. The Qumran community divided the world into light and darkness, and saw the two in mortal conflict. Each member was instructed "to love all the sons of light, each according to his lot in the counsel of God, and to hate all the sons of darkness, each according to his guilt under the vengeance of God" (1QS I:9-11[7]; see also the doctrine of the two spirits described in 1QS III:17-IV:26).

Christians, however, were admonished to carry light into the dark world, proclaiming God's redeeming love to the sons of darkness. In its prologue, John's Gospel announces, "The light shines in the darkness, and the darkness has not overcome it . . . . The true light that enlightens every man was coming into the world" (John 1:5, 9). The words of Jesus were unequivocal: "But I say to you, Love your enemies and pray for those who persecute you . . . " (Matthew 5:44).

The vitality of the Qumran organization and faith, though sufficient to perpetuate the community for almost 200 years, was apparently inadequate to survive the final cataclysmic destruction meted out by the "Sons of Darkness," the Romans. Such a reversal of their belief concerning the end of the age was too severe a blow to their neatly ordered faith, and it was shattered.[8] The vitality of Christians, on the other hand, sustained by a dynamic faith focused on God (whom they found revealed in the living presence of the resurrected Christ), could not be destroyed by the most heinous connivings of Roman persecutors. Instead of an order of prescribed rules, Christians possessed a faith which brought the very Spirit of God into their daily lives.

One is reminded of the response of Jesus to those Pharisees who engaged Him in a dialogue concerning purity: "Well did Isaiah prophesy of you hypocrites, as it is written, 'This people honors me with their lips, but their heart is far from me; in vain do they worship me, teaching as doctrines the precepts of men'" (Mark 7:6-7)[9]. "You leave the commandment of God," He said, "and hold fast the tradition of men" (Mark 7:8).

A faith centered in the "traditions of men" will die, but a faith that unleashes in man the Spirit of God cannot be destroyed.

Historic Christianity was clearly not "a child of the Qumran sect" and certainly was no mere "episode in the history of Judaism," as some interpreters of the scrolls have claimed. That Christianity stood closer in its origin to the Qumran sect—in its structure, outlook, ideology, and even its spirit—than it did to normative Judaism of the first century, is apparent. Sectarian Judaism offered the kind of environment—with its enthusiasm, its dedication, its prophetic zeal, its sense of urgency concerning the end of the age, its devotion to the prophetic as well as the legal literature of the past—in the midst of which a movement such as that of the Galilean Carpenter would more naturally be nurtured. Thus one would expect to find literary, ideological, even some ecclesiastical similarities between Christianity and the Qumran sect. But these are not the essentials which have made Christianity the dynamic religion that it is.[10]

When one is confronted by the rediscovered Qumran community (even the virtuous and probably inspired "Right Teacher") he is impressed with their devotion to the order; he admires their discipline; he is amazed at the rigors of their environment in the wilderness where they went to prepare the way of the Lord; he may even share some of the apocalyptic hopes that underlay their chosen way and their love for each other. He does not, however, feel moved to dedication; he is not endowed with a new spirit, nor is he transformed. He is conscious of a story out of history, an hour that was spent, a community that died. It seems remote, detached, a narrowly focused temporal faith—not a living reality that surges with contemporary relevance. He is not moved to join its austere fellowship, its hierarchy of priests and laymen; it is "back there." In that ancient community, dynamic faith that unites man to God and to his fellow man was secondary to the authority of rightly interpreted Scripture and the strict disciplines of the order.

On the other hand, when one is confronted by Jesus and the Christian gospel, even today, he is moved and probably condemned; his faith is inspired, and if not spiritually transformed, he is at least deeply challenged. Thus Jesus has continued to live, ever renewed, ever renewing. It is the Person, not Scriptures nor an order, who has continued to unleash the Spirit in the world and sustain vitality within the Christian movement. Thus Christians continue to proclaim that Jesus Christ is Lord.[11]

APPENDICES

APPENDIX I

Interview With Ta 'Amireh Bedouins

During the fall of 1961, Anton Kiraz, with the help of 'Ayub Musallam, the Mayor of Bethlehem, arranged for a lengthy interview with Muhammed edh-Dhib and Jum'a Muhammed, his older cousin, two of the three Bedouins who happened upon the first scroll cave. Sixty-three questions were sent to Mr. Kiraz to address to the Bedouins, and he arranged with great difficulty to tape-record the entire interview. Mr. J. F. Docmac, Headmaster of the Lutheran Elementary School in Bethlehem, kindly translated the answers of the Bedouins. The tape is now in my possession, and its contents have been analyzed and incorporated, with other interview results, in Chapter Twelve. I am indebted to Drs. B. E. Clarity and S. D. Goitein for their careful checking of the recorded answers of the Bedouins.

The evening before they tape-recorded the interview (November 24, 1961), Mr. Kiraz and Mr. Docmac composed the following account from stories related by the two Bedouins under oath according to oriental custom (of necessity, I have edited their English a little to remove some of the more obvious infelicities):

While Muhammed edh-Dhib and Jum'a Muhammed, his cousin, were tending their sheep on the hills of Khirbet Qumran near the Dead Sea one day during November, 1946,[1] Jum'a noticed a hole among the rocks. It was hardly big enough for a cat to enter. Jum'a threw a stone in to see how deep the hole was, and to his astonishment a peculiar sound was heard within. He also noticed a larger hole a little higher above the other one, and it was large enough for a man to enter. He told his cousin edh-Dhib about the holes; but neither of them dared to enter the larger·hole, for it was late in the afternoon. The sun was setting and darkness came. So they postponed their adventure until later.

Three days later, shortly after sunrise, edh-Dhib ventured into the hole and fell into a cave. There he saw about ten jars around him on both sides of the cave. Some of them had covers on top and some were without covers. Some ruins in the center of the cave, consisting of stones and earth which had fallen from the ceiling, showed broken jars beneath.

From one of the jars he removed the cover and found in it three scrolls, two of which were covered with cloth. The third had no covering. The scrolls presented a greenish appearance. He also noticed a wooden pole in the cave, about three inches in diameter. Removing the scrolls, he took them to his cousin Jum'a, who was tending the sheep about 100 meters away.

Together they went back to the cave, where they searched again and broke a jar full of red earth. They removed two complete jars with covers from the cave. Each jar and each cover had three handles. The three manuscripts and two jars remained with them in the wilderness for about eight days.

When Jum'a's son came to his father, Jum'a left him with the sheep and went back home to the Ta'amireh camp, taking the scrolls and jars with him. There he hung the scrolls on a tent pole. About a month later he took them to Bethlehem to try to sell them to some merchant.

First he took them to a merchant by the name of Ibrahim 'Ijha, an oriental carpenter who also dealt in antiquities. They agreed to leave the scrolls and jars with 'Ijha for some time so he could find out what value they might have. They remained with 'Ijha for about a month, after which Jum'a returned to inquire what had happened. 'Ijha told Jum'a that no one would buy such things. Jum'a therefore took the scrolls again, but left the jars with 'Ijha.

By chance Jum'a met George Isha'ya, a peddler who sold cloaks to the Ta'amireh Bedouins. Isha'ya saw the scrolls which Jum'a, had and asked him to leave them with him to show to some antiquity merchants to find out their true value. Jum'a, however, did not trust George, but rather decided to go to a relative named Sheikh 'Ali Subh in Bethlehem.

'Ali Subh took Jum'a to Kando, who guaranteed to look after the scrolls, and in case they were of any value and were sold, he promised two-thirds of the price to Jum'a. Jum'a agreed and left the scrolls with Kando and George Isha'ya but they did not sell them. When, about a month later, Jum'a inquired again, he was advised to take the scrolls to St. Mark's Monastery to show them to the Metropolitan.

Together with a relative named Khalil Musa, and George Isha'ya, Jum'a started with the scrolls for Jerusalem. Isha'ya took the two men first to his home in the Katamon Quarter of Jerusalem, where he offered them lunch. Afterwards he took them to see the Metropolitan at St. Mark's.

In the Monastery they were received by Bulos Gilf, a monk, who would not let them in, but sent them away, telling them that the scrolls they had brought were of no value whatever.

They all returned to Bethlehem to Kando's shop, where the scrolls were again left with Kando. When Jum'a returned later, he was told by Kando that the sum of £P24 ($97.20) had been offered for them. Jum'a agreed to this and received, according to their previous agreement, £P16 ($64.80).

Sometime later, George Isha'ya requested that Jum'a lead him to the cave where the scrolls had been discovered. Thus, George Isha'ya, Jum'a, and Khalil Musa went together in a taxi from Jerusalem to the crossroad of Jericho-Dead Sea. From there they went on foot for an hour until they reached the cave. As they were leaving, Isha'ya placed some stone markers to help him find his way to the cave again. Later Jum'a met Isha'ya and Khalil Musa in Bethlehem, and they had two more scrolls. They had left these scrolls with Da'ud Musallam for a time, but Jum'a told them to show the two scrolls to Faidi Salahi, another antiquity dealer in Bethlehem. Faidi Salahi bought these two scrolls for £P 7 ($28.35).

Although there are some details given in the taped interview by Muhammed edh-Dhib and

Jum'a Muhammed which are not in the above statement (and likewise there are some details in the above statement which are not in the taped interview), nevertheless there are no discrepancies between the two.

After completing the interview and the sworn statement with the Bedouins, Mr. Kiraz visited Ibrahim 'Ijha, a carpenter in Bethlehem. From his statements Kiraz compiled the following account and sent it to me in a letter dated December 10, 1961:

Jum'a Muhammed and Khalil Musa, some fourteen years before, brought three scrolls and two jars with conical covers to him. They remained in his shop for about twenty days, during which time he showed them to Faidi Salahi. Salahi suspected that the scrolls might not be ancient but were stolen from a Jewish synagogue. He claimed they had no archeological value. Thus 'Ijha was not encouraged to buy the scrolls and thus gave them back to Jum'a when he returned.

These accounts have the merit that they tally in several important points with the official statement prepared by G. L. Harding in 1953 (published in 1955), but they seemed irreconcilable at several points with the first accounts given in 1949 and 1952. The earlier accounts had also been based on direct contacts with the same Bedouins and had the advantage of being nearer the actual events. Numerous questions were therefore sent to Mr. Kiraz, who continued to seek answers from subsequent interviews and report them to me. He found several other persons who could confirm much of the story from personal contacts.

On July 29, 1962, and again on August 10, 1962, I met the Bedouins and these other persons and double-checked their stories, with Mr. Kiraz and Mr. Docmac acting as interpreters. The following persons were thus interviewed: Muhammed edh-Dhib, Jum'a Muhammed, Khalil Musa (the three Bedouins who happened upon Cave I), Ibrahim 'Ijha, Sheikh 'Ali Subh, Sheikh 'Abu Salim (leader of the Ta'amirehs), Jalil Elias 'Abu Sabha (neighbor of Da'ud Musallam), and Mrs. Roginah Marzurqa (witness to Faidi Salahi's dealings with Dr. E. L. Sukenik). These interviews have enabled me to construct in Chapter 12 what is very probably the correct story of the discovery.

APPENDIX II

Outline of the Dead Sea Scroll Story

I. HISTORY OF QUMRAN COMMUNITY CENTER

c. 875 – 750 B.C.

Jehoshaphat and/or Uzziah establish military outpost, apparently called 'Ir Hammelach ("City of Salt"), with round cistern (Joshua 15:62; II Chronicles 17:12; 26:10).

587 B.C.

'Ir Hammelach destroyed by Babylonians.

c. 125 B.C.

Community center established on site of 'Ir Hammelach by group of pious, sectarian Jews, probably Essenes (Period Ia).

c. 100 B.C.

Community center greatly enlarged to accommodate more members (Period Ib). Main building about 124 feet square.

c. 40 – 31 B.C.

Community center abandoned. Evidence of burning (by Parthians?) and earthquake (in 31 B.C.?) found in excavation. *(33 B.C. 14 NISAN)*

c. 4 B.C.

Community center restored much as before (Period II).

A.D. 68

Final destruction of community center by Romans during first Jewish revolt.

c. A.D. 70–90	Roman military outpost established on remains of community center, using mostly main building area.
c. A.D. 132–135	Brief occupation of center during second Jewish revolt under Bar Kokhba; no formal building.

II. MANUSCRIPT DISCOVERIES IN THE HOLY LAND

c. A.D. 220	Origen refers to some manuscripts discovered "at Jericho in a jar" which he used for his "Hexapla" text. (Also mentioned by Eusebius and Jerome in the fourth century.)
c. A.D. 800	Timotheus, Nestorian Patriarch of Seleucia, inquires about manuscripts found "in a cave near Jericho" which apparently formed basis of Karaite Jewish reform movement.
A.D. 900–1000	Al-Qirqisani, a Karaite Jewish historian, refers to a sect of "Magharians" (based on the Arabic word for "cave"), so called "because their books were found in a cave."

*   *   *   *   *

1937	Discovery of papyrus documents by American Colt Expedition at 'Auja el-Hafir (Byzantine Monastery of Nessana) in the Negeb. They included two fragmentary codices of John's Gospel and one of the letters of Paul from the seventh or eighth century. (Compare Khirbet Mird papyri.)
1946, November–December (or possibly January–February, 1947)	Ta'amireh Bedouins (Muhammed edh-Dhib, Jum'a Muhammed and Khalil Musa) happen upon Cave I near Khirbet Qumran and discover three manuscripts in a covered jar. They remove these and two complete jars with covers.
1947, March	Jum'a Muhammed and Khalil Musa offer the three scrolls to Ibrahim 'Ijha, a carpenter and antiquities dealer in Bethlehem. He keeps them for several weeks, but does not offer to buy them.
April	Scrolls taken to Khalil Eskander (Kando) in Bethlehem. George Isha'ya informs St. Mark's Monastery in Jerusalem about them. Metropolitan Samuel seeks to buy them.
May or June	Ta'amireh Bedouins take Isha'ya to cave. Later Isha'ya and Khalil Musa secure four scrolls, three of which they sell to Faidi Salahi, another Bethlehem antiquities dealer. The fourth scroll is kept by Kando.
July 5 (probably)	Four scrolls taken to Syrian Monastery by Jum'a Muhammed, George Isha'ya and Khalil Musa. They were turned away, and returned scrolls to Kando's shop.
July 19 (probably)	Kando purchases scrolls from Bedouins and sells them to St. Mark's Monastery for £P 24 ($97.20).

1947, July (late)	Father Marmardji of École Biblique consulted by Syrians about scrolls. He takes Father van der Ploeg to Monastery to see them. Isaiah Scroll first identified, but considered medieval.
August	Isha'ya takes Father Yusif from Syrian Monastery to visit Cave I. Metropolitan Samuel consults several others about scrolls, including two librarians sent from Hebrew University.
September	Anton Kiraz takes Metropolitan Samuel to Homs, Syria, where scrolls are shown to Syrian Patriarch.
October 1–3	Metropolitan Samuel and Anton Kiraz agree to become partners to the scrolls in return for Kiraz's financial assistance.
October	Tovia Wechsler examines scrolls and considers them to be late and of little value, because he believed he saw a Haftarot scroll among them.
November 23	Armenian antiquities dealer in Jerusalem contacts Dr. E. L. Sukenik at Hebrew University about scrolls in hands of Faidi Salahi.
November 29	Sukenik buys two scrolls (and some fragments—1QM and 1QH) from Faidi Salahi in Bethlehem.
December 22	Sukenik secures another scroll (1QIs^b?) and two jars from Faidi Salahi.
1948, February 4–6	Sukenik borrows St. Mark's scrolls for examination and offers to buy them.
February 18	Father Butrus Sowmy, monk at St. Mark's, calls the A.S.O.R to get information about scrolls.
February 19	Syrian scrolls examined by J. C. Trever at A.S.O.R. He is told they had been in the Monastery for forty years. Antiquity of scrolls suspected.
February 20	Trever visits St. Mark's Monastery to pursue examination of the scrolls and to secure permission to photograph them. Antiquity confirmed.
February 21	Isaiah (1QIs^a) and Habakkuk (1QpHab) Scrolls repaired and photographed at A.S.O.R.
February 22	Manual of Discipline (1QS) assembled from two scrolls, repaired and photographed.
1948, February 27	Trever consults Director of Antiquities about scrolls, seeking film for further photographing. Dr. William Brownlee identifies the "Habakkuk Commentary" (1QpHab).
February 28	Dr. Millar Burrows, Director of A.S.O.R., returns from Baghdad and learns about scrolls.

March 5	Syrians reveal true story about their purchase of the scrolls in 1947.
March 6–11	Isaiah and Habakkuk Scrolls rephotographed for publication.
March 12 (?)	Arrangements made with Department of Antiquities to visit Cave I with Syrians.
March 15	Dr. Albright's letter confirming antiquity of scrolls arrives in Jerusalem.
March 18	Importance of scrolls revealed by A.S.O.R. to Metropolitan Samuel through prepared news release.
March 20	Discussion at Haram esh-Sharif with sheikh from Nebi Musa about plans to visit cave.
March 23	Plans to visit cave abandoned after discovery that Jewish Haganah controlled region near cave.
March 25	Father Sowmy takes Syrian scrolls to Beirut for safekeeping.
April 3	Agreement worked out between Trever and Syrians for A.S.O.R. publication of their scrolls.
April 11	First news release appears in newspapers around the world.
April 26	Sukenik releases news about manuscripts at the Hebrew University.
May 15	End of British Mandate of Palestine and beginning of battle for the Old City of Jerusalem. Father Sowmy killed during battle.
August (?)	Apparently during second truce Isha'ya visits cave again and secures Daniel and Prayer Scroll fragments and a few others, which are turned over to St. Mark's.
1948, September	First published articles on scrolls, with photographs, appear from A.S.O.R. and Hebrew University.
November	Isha'ya, Kando, and others "excavate" cave and secure many more fragments.
1949, January	Dr. O. R. Sellers and Yusif Saad seek to locate cave. Isha'ya demands payment, and negotiations cease.
January 24	Captain Philippe Lippens elicits aid from Arab Legion to relocate cave.
January 28	Captain Akkash el-Zebn rediscovers cave near Khirbet Qumran.
January 29	Syrian Metropolitan arrives in the United States with four scrolls and fragments.

February 4	Trever meets Metropolitan in New Jersey to begin arrangements for unrolling "Fourth Scroll" (1QApoc) and examine newly discovered fragments.
February 15 – March 5	Cave I (1Q) excavated. Fragments of about seventy scrolls recovered, and pieces of fifty pottery jars and covers.
April 7 – 9	Syrian fragments separated, mounted, photographed, and identified as parts of Daniel and, later, a Scroll of Prayers.
April 10	Large fragment removed from "Fourth Scroll" and later tentatively identified as "Lamech Document" (1QApoc).
April 14	"Lamech Scroll" taken to Fogg Museum at Harvard to prepare for opening.
Summer	Hebrew University Isaiah Scroll (1QIs^b) unrolled and identified.
October	St. Mark's scrolls exhibited at Library of Congress.
November	St. Mark's scrolls exhibited at Walters Art Gallery, Baltimore.
1950, February	St. Mark's scrolls exhibited at Duke University.
1950, March	First A.S.O.R. volume containing facsimiles of 1QIs^a and 1QpHab appears.
Spring	Yusif Saad succeeds in purchasing the remainder of the Cave I fragments (1QSa, 1QSb) from Kando for Palestine Archaeological Museum.
Fall	"Carbon-14" Age-Determination test applied to some cloth from Cave I. Date of A.D. 33 ± 200 years determined. Published in January, 1951.
November	St. Mark's scrolls exhibited at Oriental Institute of University of Chicago.
1951, Spring	"Manual of Discipline" (1QS) published by A.S.O.R.
Summer	Metropolitan Samuel withdraws "Lamech Scroll" from Fogg Museum and refuses to allow further work on it.
October	St. Mark's scrolls exhibited at Art Museum, Worcester, Massachusetts.
October	Ta'amireh Bedouins discover manuscripts in caves at Wadi Murabba'at. Two fragments of inscribed leather offered for sale in Jerusalem.
November 3	Dr. Awni Dajani, Inspector of Antiquities, and members of A.S.O.R. explore new caves claimed to be source of new fragments. Results uncertain.
November 24 – December 12	First season of excavation at Khirbet Qumran in which connections with Cave I begin to appear.

November (late)	Many manuscripts from Wadi Murabba'at offered by Kando to École Biblique in Jerusalem.
1952, January 21 – March 3	Four Wadi Murabba'at caves located and excavated under direction of Harding and de Vaux.
February	Ta'amireh Bedouins discover Qumran Cave II (2Q) close by 1Q.
1952, March 10 – 29	Systematic exploration of the Qumran area; about 225 caves and crevices explored by A.S.O.R. teams.
March 14	Cave III (3Q), with "Copper Scroll" and a few dozen leather scroll fragments, discovered by expedition.
July – August	Manuscripts from unidentified cave (Nahal Heber?) brought by Ta'amireh Bedouins to Jerusalem. Greek text of Minor Prophets from second century A.D. among them.
Summer	Byzantine and early Arabic manuscripts (including some Greek New Testament manuscripts) discovered by Bedouins at Khirbet Mird, five miles west of Qumran.
August	Ta'amireh Bedouins discover Cave IV (4Q) in terrace adjacent to Khirbet Qumran.
September 22 – 29	Excavation of 4Q in which fragments of about 100 manuscripts were recovered. About 40,000 fragments ultimately recovered from this cave, including parts of almost 400 different manuscripts, over 100 of which are Biblical. International team of eight scholars chosen to assemble and study the fragments for publication.
September	Cave V (5Q) discovered a short distance to north of 4Q by excavators working on 4Q.
September	Bedouins discover Cave VI (6Q) on cliff by Wadi Qumran. Mostly papyrus fragments recovered, including "Damascus Document" fragments.
1953, February 9 – April 4	Second season of excavation at Khirbet Qumran. Further light shed on structure of main building. Site clearly related to scroll caves and recognized as esoteric religious center.
February – May	Belgian scholars excavate Khirbet Mird.
1954, February 15 – April 15	Third campaign at Khirbet Qumran. Community meeting room, pantry, and pottery workshop cleared.
1954, July 1	St. Mark's scrolls purchased in New York by Y. Yadin for State of Israel for $250,000 and sent to the Hebrew University in Jerusalem.
1955, February 2 – April 6	Fourth campaign at Khirbet Qumran; western quarter opened and water storage system uncovered. Caves VII-X (7Q, 8Q, 9Q, 10Q) discovered by archeologists in terrace

	around Khirbet Qumran. Very few manuscript fragments recovered.
March	Hebrew scroll of Minor Prophets (from second century A.D.) discovered by Ta'amireh Bedouins in fifth Wadi Murabba'at cave.
Spring	Publication of materials from Cave I in D. Barthélemy and J. T. Milik, *Discoveries in the Judaean Desert I: Qumran Cave I*.
	Publication of *The Dead Sea Scrolls of the Hebrew University* by E. L. Sukenik (posthumously completed by N. Avigad and others).
1956, February 7	Announcement of unrolling and decipherment of "Fourth Scroll," named "Genesis Apocryphon" (1QApoc).
February 18 – March 28	Fifth and final season of excavation at Khirbet Qumran. Eighteen more tombs in nearby cemetery explored. Another cemetery to south, one to north, and remains of buildings near 'Ain Feshkha explored.
February	Ta'amireh Bedouins discover and "excavate" Cave XI (11Q), one mile north of Khirbet Qumran—at least seven extensive manuscripts recovered.
June 1	Contents of "Copper Scroll" from 3Q revealed to be a list of deposits of fabulous treasure. Scroll cut into strips at Manchester University, England.
1958, January 25 – March 21	Sixth season of excavation in Qumran area. Farm installation north of 'Ain Feshkha excavated. Rooms for treating leather believed found.
Spring	Scroll fragments from cave near En Gedi in Israel discovered by Bedouins and brought to attention of Israelis.
1960, Spring	John Allegro conducts soundings at various sites in Jordan to attempt to uncover treasure deposits mentioned in "Copper Scroll." His transcription of that scroll appears in *The Treasure of the Copper Scroll* (New York, Doubleday).
March 23 – April 6	Israeli expedition to En Gedi region. Cave in Nahal Heber, with remains from Bar Kokhba revolt, discovered. Fragments of Psalms and fifteen papyrus letters in Hebrew, Aramaic, and Greek recovered.
Summer	Assembling of 4Q fragments completed by international team of scholars working in the Palestine Archaeological Museum.
1961, March	Nahal Heber cave excavated farther. About forty more papyrus business documents recovered, dated A.D. 88-132, in Hebrew, Aramaic, Nabatean, and Greek.

Spring	Publication of Wadi Murabba'at manuscripts and artifacts in *Discoveries in the Judaean Desert II: Les Grottes De Murabba'at.*
November 10–20	Psalms Scroll (11Q Pss) opened, and work of analysis begun by Dr. J. A. Sanders. Twenty-eight partial columns of the text are preserved, and three more among additional fragments. Thirty-seven Psalms and seven noncanonical compositions included.
1962, March	Fragments recovered from scroll of Ezekiel (11QEzek) studied by Dr. W. H. Brownlee.
Spring	Ta'amireh Bedouins discover about forty Samaritan papyrus documents in large cave in Wadi ed-Daliyeh, nine miles north of Jericho.
Fall	Publication of fragments and artifacts from Caves II, III, V-X in *Discoveries in the Judaean Desert III: Les 'Petites Grottes' De Qumran.*
1964, January	Three fragmentary papyrus manuscripts discovered by Israelis in excavation of Masada. They include Psalms 81-85, a scroll of "Songs of Sabbath Sacrifice," and five chapters from a first-century B.C. scroll of Ecclesiasticus.

List of Abbreviations

BA	*Biblical Archaeologist*
BASOR	*Bulletin of the American Schools of Oriental Research*
DJD	*Discoveries in the Judaean Desert*, Oxford, The Clarendon Press
JBL	*Journal of Biblical Literature*
JNES	*Journal of Near Eastern Studies*
JQR	*Jewish Quarterly Review*
PEQ	*Palestine Exploration Quarterly*
RB	*Revue Biblique*
RQ	*Revue de Qumran*
RSV	*Revised Standard Version of the Bible*

Notes

CHAPTER 1

1. This branch of the Christian Church is usually called *Assyrian Orthodox* in the United States.

2. Officially he was a monk, secretary of the Monastery, and teacher of the young monks. He did not wish to become a priest, as I was later informed by one of his close friends in Jerusalem.

3. The A.S.O.R., as it is abbreviated, was established at Jerusalem in 1900 (at Baghdad in 1921) to afford opportunities for Biblical study and research in "the lands of the Bible" by graduates of American colleges and universities.

4. Assuming that the call had come for Dr. Burrows, the Director, and that Omar therefore had turned it over to me, I gave the matter no further thought. During the excitement of the following days, I failed to understand the significance of Dr. Brownlee's diplomatic attempts to tell me what he had learned about that call. The servants said nothing more to me about it. Not until the summer of 1950, during a visit with Brownlee in Kansas, did I become fully aware of his relation to that telephone call. He published his understanding of the situation in an article, "My Eight Years of Scroll Research," *The Duke Divinity School Bulletin* 21:3 (November 1956), pp. 68-81.

Father Sowmy actually had asked for Brownlee. Since Omar did not find him in his room, he had called me to the telephone. The Syrians, it seems, had thought it more diplomatic to find out who was at the School. Knowing that Bishop Stewart at St. George's Cathedral lived close to our School, they had called him the previous day to learn the names of those whom they might call. The Bishop informed them that Dr. Burrows had just left and that he did not know who was in charge of the School. He mentioned Dr. Brownlee's name, however, because the latter had come to the Bishop's office the day before to secure a certificate to prove that he was a Christian. When Brownlee returned sometime later, he states, "I . . . was met at the school by a succession of Arab servants informing me that a telephone call had come for me during the day" (*ibid.*, p. 68). He goes on to relate that, arriving in the dining room a little late for dinner, he overheard me speaking to others at the table about the conversation with the Syrian monk and even mentioning the time of the appointment the next day. These details I had completely forgotten, but I see no reason to question the accuracy of Brownlee's memory of them. He gives the time of the appointment, however, as "about 3:30 P.M.," rather than 2:30, which may account for his failure to return in time the next day.

CHAPTER 2

1. The *keffiyeh* is the Arab headdress, consisting of a large cloth held in place by a black goat-hair, ropelike circle, the *'agal*.

2. In my first account of these experiences I gave his name as Karim (*BA, XI:3* [September, 1948], p. 46), but corrected the error in the May, 1949, issue (XII:2, p. 30, n. 7). While visiting in Beirut on April 7, 1948, I met Ibrahim once again, unexpectedly, when I went to see his cousin Karim, as Butrus Sowmy had urged me to do. During this meeting I apparently confused their names.

3. At that time Trans-Jordan and Palestine were separate countries. The Allenby Bridge was the main point of communication between the two, crossing the Jordan River about seven and a half miles north of the Dead Sea.

4. It was the second section of what we later called the "Manual of Discipline" (now designated as IQS). The irregularly broken edge of Column VIII was coiled tightly against the inner turns of leather. See pp. 49-51.

5. A colophon, frequently found at the end of medieval manuscripts, consisted of a symbol or statement about the copyist and often included the circumstances concerning the preparation of the manuscript.

6. Just before leaving for Jerusalem, I had prepared a set of color slides on "What Lies Back of the English Bible?" in which the story of Biblical manuscripts is related. The slide set had been developed for distribution by the Methodist Board of Education and had helped to make my trip to Jerusalem financially possible.

7. Or. 4445.

8. Several Biblical Hebrew manuscripts previously known should have had the distinction of being older. There are some large fragments of scrolls of Jeremiah, Ezekiel, and the Psalms in the Taylor-Schechter collection from the Cairo Genizah in the Cambridge University Library which must be a century, perhaps several centuries, older than the British Museum Codex, as Paul Kahle has shown. Furthermore, it seems quite likely that the Cairo Codex of the Prophets (dated A.D. 895) is as old or older than Or. 4445.

9. Cambridge University Library, Or. 233.

10. "A Biblical Fragment From the Maccabean Age: The Nash Papyrus," (*JBL* LVI [September, 1937], pp. 145-176).

11. I failed to mention this fact in my first article, which was written during the summer of 1948. At that time I was under the impression that it was later when the Syrians mentioned knowing that one of the scrolls was Isaiah. My notes and letters written at the time give no contrary information. Brownlee, however, called my attention to the error in a letter dated December 6, 1950, and has since published his version of the incident (*op. cit.*, p. 70). There he states that the Syrians specified which scroll might be Isaiah and that I indicated this fact to him during our examination of the copied passage. Although I have great respect for Brownlee's memory, I do not believe the Syrians were that specific. That they already knew that the largest scroll was Isaiah, there is no doubt; but they were very cautious about how much they told me at that time, as subsequent events revealed. See pp. 75-76.

12. That evening I summarized all I could remember of the interview on note cards: "Rev. Salmi [misspelled for 'Sowmy'] of the Syrian convent in the Old City in Jerusalem called me yesterday to ask if I would examine some ancient Hebrew MSS. he had and wanted dated. I made an appointment for 2:30 today to see him (and almost forgot it!). He came with his brother

(dressed in army uniform and *keffiyeh*), with the scrolls in a small leather suitcase. Rev. Salmi [Sowmy] was dressed in a garb similar to that of the Greek Orthodox. They both spoke very good English. At first sight the MSS., of which he had five, seemed quite old and in an archaic script of the square Hebrew characters. Immediately I thought to compare the script with the earliest known Hebrew Bible MS. in the British Museum, so I got out my slides on the 'Story of the Bible,' Part I, and examined the page from the British Museum document. There was no resemblance. These were written on leather in unpointed Hebrew by a somewhat careless hand. Vowel letters were used. I tried to pick out familiar words, but certain letters were so strangely written that I could not make out any consecutive words. Comparison with the Nash Papyrus got me excited, for this seemed to show a somewhat similar character. Thus I decided the matter should be investigated. My first thought was to photograph a page or two immediately, but then I remembered all my cameras were at the Museum! Thus I chose a fairly clear section of the largest scroll and started to copy a few lines. Meanwhile Rev. Salmi [Sowmy] told me the story of its origin.

"It seems some Bedouin had found the scrolls in a jar, sealed with potsherds, all in a cave south of Kallia about 7 km. near 'Ain Feshkha by the Dead Sea. One of the scrolls is still in the shape it was as found, and shows all the signs of being very old. The brother of Rev. Salmi [Sowmy] claimed it must date from before 200 A.D., since the practice of mummification ceased about that time! He thought these had been mummified. The one did look like it, to be sure. They claimed that the others had looked the same on the outside, having been wrapped in cloth which had disintegrated. In fact they said the Bedouin had claimed there was a large box of disintegrated fragments from the same cave. This all happened forty years or so ago in the time of another bishop.

"The brother of Salmi [Sowmy] said his theory was that a group of Essenes owned the scrolls and hid them during one of the periods of persecution when they were forced up into the hills into the caves."

On the basis of my record of that first interview, as well as my memory of it, another interview in Beirut two months later, and a statement of an American cousin of Ibrahim's, Aziz Souma, I am inclined to agree with Ibrahim's claim that it was he who convinced Metropolitan Samuel that the scrolls were really ancient. Ibrahim is a student of history, having published a number of writings in Syriac, the sacred language of his people. He is now living in South America, where he recently completed a history of Syriac literature.

13. It contained the first seven columns of the "Manual of Discipline" (1QS), as I learned the following Sunday. See pp. 49-51.

14. This was the "Habakkuk Commentary" (1QpHab). See pp. 67-68. Some months later it was discovered that many of the scrolls had been damaged by white ants and other vermin.

15. This was the "Fourth Scroll," which I later identified tentatively as the "Lamech Scroll," but which we now know is the "Genesis Apocryphon" (1QApoc). See p. 131.

16. Unknown to me, Brownlee had planned to be present at the time of the interview, as he relates in his account (*op. cit.*, p. 69): "Early the next afternoon I decided there would be time to run some errands before the scrolls appeared. By the ever-increasing gunfire, it seemed that our time was running out and I should make every minute count . . . I ran an errand to the American Colony and visited also the Jerusalem Post Office; but I was delayed at various road blocks and carefully interrogated and even searched for weapons by the Arab guards, despite my American passport and a written certificate from Bishop Stewart. . . . Once back at the School, I knocked at the door of the school office to ascertain whether or not Trever was interviewing those bringing the Scrolls. They were not there! I went upstairs to his room, and he was not there! I tidied myself a bit in my own room which was next to his, and soon Trever appeared at my door with the news."

17. Miss Faris was acting secretary for our School and headmistress of an Arab girls' school

in Jerusalem. She was staying in the Annual Professor's apartment at our School because of the troubles in Jerusalem, which cut her off from her home.

18. The paragraph leading up to these words contains another description of that first view of the scrolls: "After lunch I had an appointment with a Rev. Salmi [Sowmy] from the Syrian Christian Convent in the Old City. He brought with him 5 scrolls of Hebrew materials which he wanted me to date. At first I was a bit suspicious, but when he told me the story of their discovery and I had a chance to look at them, I became interested. The writing has all the earmarks of being older than any biblical Hebrew manuscript in existence, so I feel they must be photographed. . . . Though the whole thing may be a fake, there is too much at stake if they are authentic and as old as they appear. The story back of them is another of those romances of Biblical manuscripts. . . . the scroll is apparently the Book of Isaiah, which makes me all the more interested. To me it is quite exciting, and I want to follow it through as soon as possible. Tomorrow I shall go to see him [Sowmy] at the Convent [St. Mark's Monastery], since Abdullah Ramawi is here tonight and wants me to go over there tomorrow morning with him anyway. I am going to try to arrange to have Rev. Salmi [Sowmy] come over here Saturday morning and let me photograph the whole thing with the Recomar [a plate camera which used 9 × 12 cm. cut film] both in color and in black and white. If it is a fake, I will only lose the film, but have a lot of fun in the process."

19. BA, *op. cit.*, p. 50.

20. *Op. cit.*, p. 70. The RSV translation is more probably correct.

CHAPTER 3

1. It was Sowmy's marked reactions to my announcement that the passage was from Isaiah that led me to believe that nothing had been said about Isaiah the previous day (see pp. 25, 184, note 11).

2. The term "metropolitan" has been used since early Christian times in the Eastern Orthodox churches to refer to bishops in large metropolitan centers who exercised some authority over bishops in nearby areas of the same province. The term "archbishop" came to be used in the West for a similar function.

3. *Peshitta* means "simple" in Syriac. It was a translation in the language of these people, begun in the fifth century.

4. Technically, my reference to "Jacobites" was warranted, for it is a common, though misleading, designation for their church. They were apparently disturbed by the implication that their church was no older than the sixth century, when the energetic work of Jacob Baradaeus (d. 578), a Syrian Monophysite bishop and missionary, greatly extended the influence of the Syrian Monophysite Church. These Syrians sincerely believe that their church represents the original orthodox apostolic church founded in the first century, with Antioch as the center, and thus they refer to their patriarch as the "Patriarch of Antioch."

It was after the Fourth Ecumenical Council of Chalcedon in A.D. 451 that the schism occurred when certain Eastern Christian groups could not accept the Western-influenced decision about the nature of Christ. In the orthodox decree of Chalcedon it was asserted that Christ had two natures, human and divine, both of the "same substance" (*homoousion*) with the Father, mystically united in one Person (*prosopon*) or one Substance (*hypostasis*). The Eastern groups, including the Copts of Egypt, the Ethiopians, the Armenians, and these Syro-Jacobites, insisted that Christ was of *one* divine nature; that is, *mono-* ("one") *physis* ("nature"), thus the name "monophysite." Lacking the Platonic philosophic orientation of the West, these Eastern groups had found the decree too much for their Semitic realism.

The term "Jacobite" came to be used by outsiders to distinguish these Syrian Christians from the Nestorians, who were another Eastern "Assyrian" church, formed in the fifth century by followers of Theodore of Mopsuestia and Bishop Nestorius, who had been exiled from Constantinople after the Third Ecumenical Council at Ephesus in A.D. 431. The latter also used the Syriac language for Scriptures and worship.

5. This note appears on a slip of paper along with a number of notations made during that interview.

6. These words are taken from a letter I wrote to my wife on February 21, 1948. Samuel was ordained Metropolitan in Homs, Syria, on December 22, 1946. Apparently the "fourteen months" referred to his services as Metropolitan, for he had been associated with the Monastery for many years before that. He first entered St. Mark's in 1923.

7. See pp. 26-27, 186 (note 18).

8. From an interview (March, 1958) with the librarian of the Jerusalem Y.M.C.A., Malak Tannourji, I learned that he had told the story of the Codex Sinaiticus to Anton Kiraz on February 6, 1948, after Dr. Sukenik had made an offer to buy the scrolls.

9. Jerash was ancient Gerasa of the Decapolis in New Testament times. The objects had been on loan from Trans-Jordan.

10. Ira M. Price, *The Ancestry of the English Bible*, N.Y., Harper & Row, 1934 (rev. ed.).

11. See pp. 23, 184 (note 10).

12. Albright, *op. cit.*, p. 172. Early the next morning I wrote the following to my wife: "I am convinced in my own mind on the matter now, but it may take many months to convince the scholarly world. It is hard for me to believe it possible, but the indications I observed last night point to the Maccabean period for the writing of these manuscripts!! But that dating depends upon the accuracy of Albright's work on the Nash Papyrus. . . . Please keep this confidential, for it might create a premature sensation. If I'm right, it will create a justifiable sensation, but that will have to await further study."

CHAPTER 4

1. This fine-grain film had proved particularly valuable for manuscript copy work.

2. Twenty-four feet and five-sixteenths inch (7.34 meters) proved later to be a more accurate figure.

3. The Assyrians normally refer to their language as Aramaic, but it is more accurate to call it Syriac, which is a dialectical variation of Aramaic.

4. These tiny uninscribed fragments, together with a few others left over from a later repair task (see chapter 14), none of them inscribed, are all I possess from the originals.

CHAPTER 5

1. In Hebrew, this valley is called Ge-hinnom, a name which came to be used in Greek for the place of punishment and is thus translated "hell" in English New Testaments.

2. It now seems probable that another document had been attached, perhaps at this point. Two columns (1QSa) of it were secured many months later by the Palestine Archaeological Museum. See p. 146.

3. A large fragment of the cover to this scroll was later recovered from the cave (see p. 146), though there is still some doubt whether it was attached at this point or before some other columns.

4. The description of the process of joining the two parts of the "Manual of Discipline" (1QS) has been elaborated primarily because of a charge levied by Dr. Solomon Zeitlin ("The Idolatry of the Dead Sea Scrolls," *JQR* XLVIII:3, January, 1958, pp. 243-278). My claim to have joined two scrolls together, he asserts, was an attempt to cover up a deliberate suppression of the so-called "Haftarot Scroll" (see p. 000). He states, "I believe no man had the right to join two scrolls into one without informing the scholarly world that he had done so, otherwise this would constitute a form of scholarly fraud" (p. 244). He presented his paper at the International Congress of Orientalists in Munich on August 30, 1957. Apparently he had failed to read the

published statements about the joining of the two parts of the scroll in *BA* XI:3, p. 53, and *BASOR* 111, p. 11. He based his claim on a footnote in *BA* XII:2, p. 26, where I said, "Two of the five [scrolls] were later joined together to make the 'Sectarian Document.'"

In April, 1958, during a visit to the Hebrew University in Jerusalem, where the scroll is now on exhibit, I noticed that between Columns 7 and 8 the point of joining has pulled away about an eighth of an inch, revealing clearly the backing of adhesive tape. The evidence is also quite clear on several of my color transparencies taken the morning of February 24, 1948.

5. The notching code on each film, which appears on a set of prints in my files (the original negatives are in the files of the A.S.O.R.), clearly shows that it was "Kodak Super-XX Panchromatic" sheet film I used. Since the high speed of this film tends to increase its grain size and thus reduce the definition of enlargements needed for publication, I would normally reject such film for manuscript copying. The range of its "spectogram to tungsten light," however, is identical to that of "Kodak Panatomic-X" sheet film, which accounts for the high-quality negatives obtained, especially since they were developed in a fine-grain developer. It was this set of negatives which was used for the final publication in the *Dead Sea Scrolls of St. Mark's Monastery,* Vol. II, Fascicle 2.

6. In the first edition of his "Pelican Book," *The Dead Sea Scrolls* (1956), Dr. John Allegro, in mentioning this experience of mine, said, "However, he seems to have restrained both his impatience and his tongue, for neither then nor at any other time was any mention of the discovery made to the authorities responsible for the control of antiquities in Palestine. . . ." No "authorities" were present that day, but see pp. 66-67. When I wrote to Allegro about this and other misstatements in his book, he sent me an apology and modified this sentence considerably in a subsequent printing (1957). In the meantime, however, well over 40,000 copies of the book had been distributed.

7. The sheet film had been a gracious and generous contribution to my photographic endeavors by the Ansco Company.

CHAPTER 6

1. In 1950 the I.C.R.E. became the Division of Christian Education of the National Council of the Churches of Christ in the U.S.A.

2. The delay resulted from the broken communication wires which isolated Jerusalem and cut off our electricity.

3. These transparencies were made on 6.5 x 9 centimeter Ansco Color sheet film, using a Kodak Medalist II camera with adapters for ground-glass focusing and plate-holders. The Kodak "Ektar" f/3.5 100 millimeter lens on the camera is particularly valuable for such exacting work.

4. "Ostracon" is the term applied by archeologists to a piece of pottery ("potsherd") containing an inscription.

5. While in Egypt during January, Drs. Beling, Brownlee, and I had the privilege of joining the African Expedition of the University of California, under the leadership of Wendell Phillips, for a week in Sinai. It was from that expedition that Dr. W. F. Albright gathered definitive evidence to show that the Proto-Sinaitic inscriptions found at Serabit el-Khadem must date from the early fifteenth century B.C. and thus were about a century later than the Gezer Ostracon. See *BASOR* 110 (April 1948), pp. 6-13.

6. These third- and fourth-century A.D. papyrus Biblical manuscripts had been purchased in Cairo, Egypt, in 1930 by A. Chester Beatty and beautifully published under the direction of the British Museum.

7. The area is now a ghostly part of the "no man's land" that divides Jerusalem south of Mandelbaum Gate.

8. The Torah comprises the Books of Genesis through Deuteronomy. When prepared for use in the synagogue, it is written by hand on large scrolls, according to very specific rules.

9. I had seen and photographed a similar scroll in the Greek Patriarchal Library a few months before. The prominent use of *tagin,* or "crowns," on the tops of certain letters; the extreme contrast between broad, heavy strokes and fine, connecting ones; the pronounced regularity of the height of the letters; and the greatly exaggerated width of letters to fill some lines at the left margin, all impressed me with the modern character of the manuscript.

Through a series of misunderstandings this manuscript became involved in the controversy over the supposed "suppressed scroll of the Haftarot" (see p. 110). I continue to doubt that it had any relation whatever to that matter. See M. Burrows, "Concerning the Dead Sea Scrolls," *JQR* XLII:2 (October, 1951), pp. 119-125. Dr. Burrows quotes (p. 123) from a letter in which I proposed a specific identification of the scroll. After examining a dozen similar scrolls in the British Museum on March 21, 1951, I realized that my statement was too hasty. That the St. Mark's Torah Scroll is relatively modern, however, there can be no doubt.

10. I am indebted to Dr. Brownlee for helping me reconstruct this incident accurately. Neither of us expected that scroll to become involved in any way in the story of the Dead Sea Scrolls. No one who is a student of Hebrew paleography would claim a chronological relationship between that scroll and the DSS.

11. See p. 183, n. 4.

12. These letters are dated February 25, 1948, but they were written on the twenty-sixth. All the letters I wrote during those three days are dated one day early. Not until Friday the twenty-seventh did I realize my error.

CHAPTER 7

1. *Aleph,* the first letter of the Hebrew alphabet, is a consonant not found in Western alphabets. It was the source of our vowel letter *a*, however. The *taw* is the *t*.

2. The effect of color reproduction on dark manuscripts is similar to but not so great as that of infrared film, which has proved to be so indispensable for recovering many obscure parts of the Dead Sea Scroll fragments. Thus a good color transparency may provide a clearer image of an ancient script.

3. The Edfu Papyri, as they are called, from a Jewish colony in Upper Egypt, were dated largely on the basis of the nature of the names they include. The paleographic consideration was secondary. It was a privilege to examine these papyri carefully in the Bodleian Library, Oxford, in March, 1951.

4. In two letters written the next day, I elaborated this theory. With further study, however, I abandoned it in favor of a date about 100 B.C. for the Isaiah Scroll and have not waivered from this since. It has been interesting to note that several scholars have claimed that same early period of history for the founding of the Qumran community. Even that does not now seem possible on the basis of the accumulated evidence.

5. *Life's* correspondent was very interested in the idea and arranged with his office in New York for me to stop for an interview on my return. Though the article was planned and written, shortly before publication it was rejected and the pictures returned without explanation.

6. See page 36.

7. I have continued to be grateful to the Museum officials for their farewell gift to me—a set of these gallery books.

8. What I did not know then was that very few Biblical scholars and archeologists had any knowledge of Hebrew paleography. That evening after dinner I wrote the following in a letter to my wife: "I . . . went over to the Museum to see Iliffe, only to find that he left suddenly for Baghdad. I did see Hamilton, however, and told him the whole story of the manuscripts, also showing him some of the prints. He was quite thrilled about it all, though he is not a paleographer, so had no judgment to offer. My main purpose was to try to get some help in getting some large-size black and white film to do the Isaiah Scroll over again. . . . The Museum can't help

me on film, but I got some good suggestions where I could get some, so will press the matter tomorrow."

Mr. Hamilton, it needs to be remembered, was facing, with Mr. Iliffe, the stupendous task of planning the protection of that valuable Museum from the inevitable strife that was daily intensifying and destined to explode on May 15 at the end of the British Mandate. Preparing to store the valuable exhibits in bombproof shelters and to internationalize the Museum was occupying every one of their waking moments. The world should be grateful to these men, whose foresight resulted in the saving of all of these priceless records of the past for posterity.

9. In his account (*op. cit.*, page 73) Brownlee errs in saying that "the prints of Isaiah were completed first. . . . " He had persuaded me to interrupt the printing of the Isaiah Scroll on Wednesday evening in order to get Scroll # II (1QpHab) printed sooner. I showed some of the prints of that scroll to Mr. Hamilton on Friday morning. We did not finish making the prints of the Isaiah Scroll and Scroll #I(1QS) until Saturday night. The process of washing and drying the prints made Wednesday night was not completed until Friday afternoon.

10. Whether or not I stopped at the Syrian Monastery that morning to open the issue of permission to photograph the two scrolls again, my records do not show. It could have been that morning, when I was within a short distance of the Monastery in search of film. My memory, however, tends to associate that request with my visit the next Monday. See p. 72.

CHAPTER 8

1. During his stay in Jerusalem, Dr. Burrows assisted Mrs. Vester with her delightful book, *Our Jerusalem,* in which she unfolds the fascinating story of the American Colony.

2. Although there is no question about my having written the preliminary report (I refer to it twice in my letters and twice in my diary), I have no copy of it today. I have only a vague memory of its contents. During an interview with Anton Kiraz in Bethlehem, April 26, 1958, I was told that the Metropolitan had shown Kiraz "a receipt given him [the Metropolitan] by the A.S.O.R. with two signatures on it . . . some time after February 19, 1948." Perhaps that was the "preliminary report." As far as I know, nothing else in writing was given to the Metropolitan by any of us until March 18, when Dr. Burrows presented him with a copy of the first news release (see p. 88).

3. See above (Chapter 7, note 10).

4. Ugaritic is an alphabetic cuneiform language found on clay tablets discovered at Ras esh-Shamrah in Syria in 1928. Dating from the fourteenth century B.C., their language is that used by the Canaanites and later adopted by the Hebrews.

5. A small liturgical document, written on parchment in an unskilled hand, the Dura Fragment was found in the excavation of the synagogue at Dura on the Euphrates and must date prior to A.D.256, when the synagogue was destroyed.

6. On March 3 I wrote in a letter, "I think Dr. Burrows is gradually becoming convinced that these manuscripts date from before the second century A.D." For his own statement see his *Dead Sea Scrolls,* N. Y., The Viking Press, 1955, p. 29.

7. Apparently Mr. Raad's enlarging equipment was partly at fault, for many months later I made some other enlargements from the same negatives on my own equipment and had much better results, but still not what we needed for publication.

8. The Palestinian pound (£P) was worth about $3.65 at that time, though the official rate was $4.05.

9. In my records the expression "two-years outdated" is all that appears, but vaguely I recall that the month indicated was July. One of the two boxes with "1 Sep 47" stamped on it is still in my possession.

10. I had found this formula particularly helpful for manuscript work when maximum contrast was needed in negatives.

11. These are not necessarily Sowmy's exact words, but they are so close to what he actually said that I have given them as direct discourse. For the date of the purchase, see p. 106-107. In my first report (*BA* XI:3, pp. 46-49) I only hinted at this discrepancy in the Syrians' approach, for at the time it seemed wise to avoid undue emphasis upon it. In 1955, Dr. Burrows published a more specific statement (*op. cit.*, p. 14). See also Dr. Sukenik's record of another approach (Y. Yadin, *The Message of the Scrolls*, N. Y., Simon and Schuster, 1957, p. 25). See above p. 184, note 9 for the earliest record and below (Chapter 11, note 4).

12. Dr. E. L. Sukenik had secured the jars from a Bethlehem antiquities dealer on December 22, 1947, it was to be learned later. See p. 111.

CHAPTER 9

1. Having sensed their opposition, I had refrained from revealing to them the fact that I had shared the whole story with Mr. Hamilton, Director of Antiquities, on February 27. This statement contradicts the one found in A. Y. Samuel's "The Purchase of the Jerusalem Scrolls" (*BA* XII:2, p. 31), which I prepared on the basis of interviews with him. The date given there was my error. It was on March 19 when the discussion mentioned there occurred. See pp. 90 and 137.

2. In a letter written to my wife the next night, I said: "Any excavations they [the Syrians] might do at the cave would be illegal, unless they first got permission from the Department of Antiquities. Thus, we decided that Mr. Hamilton should be consulted in the matter to know how to proceed."

3. When developed two weeks later, they proved disappointing but usable. The film had defective color-balance.

4. My estimate was much too conservative, for when opened the scroll gave evidence of having more than 700 lines of text.

5. My confidence was not shared by Dr. Burrows (see his *The Dead Sea Scrolls*, pp. 26-27). No one could anticipate at that time what a difficult problem would be created by the inner lining of thin white leather, which could be seen from one end and in the large break on one surface. See N. Avigad and Y. Yadin, *A Genesis Apocryphon*, Jerusalem, The Magnes Press, 1956, pp. 13-14.

6. It was probably a metallic ink rather than a pure carbon ink, which was used on the other scrolls. Experts claim that this would account for the tendency toward disintegration around the letters, as the manuscript so clearly demonstrates.

7. Ossuaries are rectangular chests cut from soft limestone and used by the Jews for storing the bones of their deceased. They can be dated with considerable confidence to the period from about 40 B.C. to A.D. 70.

8. It was this type of inscription which first convinced Dr. E. L. Sukenik of the antiquity of the other similar scrolls in December, 1947, as we learned later. See pp. 110-111.

9. In his first edition of *The Dead Sea Scrolls*, p. 14, Dr. Burrows wrote, "Soon thereafter this information [the date of the discovery learned on March 5] was passed on to Mr. Hamilton." Immediately on reading this statement, I urged Dr. Burrows to correct the error. My failure to communicate this one point—I knew and I thought he knew—was one of the causes of the misunderstanding that developed later. In March, 1948, I was unaware of the relationship between the date of the discovery and the government antiquities laws. My concern was to get to the cave without acting illegally. Furthermore, at least a week during which I had been under the pressure of rephotographing the scrolls and had suffered several days of illness had intervened since the date was revealed.

10. I have to rely on my memory and indirect evidence for the date of this visit, for I failed to make note of it in either my diary or letters. By then my letters were devoted largely to problems about leaving the country. That the interview must have occurred between March 12 and 20, there is no doubt. The most likely time was on the twelfth, since my first visit to the

Museum after Dr. Burrows and I agreed that I should consult Mr. Hamilton occurred on that day. When I discussed the matter with Mr. Hamilton in Oxford, during late May of 1958, he showed no recollection of the interview. In March, 1948, his mind had been preoccupied with problems concerning the Museum, and it is therefore understandable why this interview made no deep impression on him, especially since he did not know the recent date of the discovery. Our concerns and his instructions to me have remained so indelibly stamped on my mind that there is no question we had the interview. Furthermore, in a letter dated March 20, 1948, I wrote parenthetically: "I have already talked with Hamilton at the Museum about the proper procedure. He has given permission to visit the place to gather up any loose materials left."

From my later correspondence it is evident that during this last interview with Mr. Hamilton I raised the question of the Syrians' right to possession of the scrolls. He assured me that there was no question about their ownership, but warned that if they were to excavate the cave it would be illegal. He made his statement about right of ownership, of course, without the knowledge of the recent date of the discovery.

11. Though it is likely this discussion took place that day, my records leave some uncertainty about the date. The two fragments were returned to the Metropolitan in April, 1949; see pp. 131-132.

12. Unfortunately, it did not occur to me to show this letter to Mr. Hamilton. It would doubtless have made considerable difference in his response. So far as my records reveal, however, I did not see him again after it arrived.

CHAPTER 10

1. Some weeks previously, this family, who lived in a quarter west of the school, had received a threatening letter signed with ominous black dots and warning them to move within twenty-four hours. Dr. Burrows had offered them refuge in the basement of the Director's house. See his *Palestine Is Our Business* (Philadelphia, Westminster Press, 1949), p. 52.

2. It may have been the next day when I made this suggestion, for we discussed the matter on both occasions.

3. The Syrian layman was apparently Anton Kiraz (see p. 113). He attests in an affidavit that he conveyed the Hebrew University request to the Metropolitan but was advised against fulfilling it.

4. Sometime prior to March 5 the Syrians had revealed the fact that some Jews had seen the scrolls "the previous November." No names had been given; but by March 5, as one of my letters indicates, I had assumed that Dr. E. L. Sukenik was one of them. It later became evident that the Jews referred to were the two librarians whom Dr. Magnes sent to the Monastery at the request of Dr. Maurice Brown. See pp. 108-109.

5. At the time the Metropolitan was vague about when Dr. Sukenik had seen the scrolls, and I assumed that it was after I had begun to work on them. It was to be many months before the date was established. See pp. 111-112.

Shortly after I first saw the scrolls, it occurred to me to seek Dr. Sukenik's opinion about their antiquity. I had met him the previous October and had read about his excavation of some tombs on Mr. Kiraz's property. When I tried to make the call, however, I found the telephone circuit broken and did not try again.

6. He was referring to the acacia wood box which had been made by the Hebrews, during their wandering in Sinai, to house the stone tablets of the Ten Commandments (Exodus 25:10-16; 37:1-5; 40:20-21). The mystery of the disppearance of the Ark and its tables of stone has long intrigued Jewish and Christian students of the Bible.

7. While preparing the article "The Purchase of the Jerusalem Scrolls" for Metropolitan Samuel the next spring, I inadvertently gave the date for this discussion as February 27, 1948 (cf. *BA* XII:2, p. 31). It should have been March 19. See pp. 89, 90.

8. Anton Kiraz, in his affidavit, said that he offered Dr. Sukenik, as a substitute for the scrolls, the set of the photographs which the Metropolitan had received from us on March 1. When Kiraz went to the Monastery to get the prints, he says, the Metropolitan refused to let him have them. Mr. Kiraz made no further efforts after that to communicate with Dr. Sukenik. We, of course, knew nothing yet about the scrolls purchased by Dr. Sukenik the previous December. See pp. 110-113.

9. A curious parallel to this bit of the drama of the Dead Sea Scrolls is found in the story of Tischendorf's experiences at St. Catherine's Monastery at Mt. Sinai. In 1853, when he returned to seek more of the pages from the now-famed Codex Sinaiticus, Tischendorf was successful only in securing a small fragment with a few verses from Genesis, which had been used in the Monastery as a bookmark!

10. In my first published account I wrote, "Already jubilant over this newest addition to our valuable finds, I was made even more happy when the Metropolitan informed me that Father Butros had left that morning with all the manuscripts, to take them to a place of safety outside of Palestine" (*BA* XI:3, p. 56). Some scholars took these words to mean that I rejoiced over the fact that the scrolls had been smuggled out of the country, an interpretation which never occurred to me as possible from the context of my words (cf. *PEQ*, July–October, 1949, p. 116). Several scholars continued to perpetuate this unfortunate interpretation in their writings. Finally I felt it necessary to make a special visit to Jordan in 1958 to set the record straight. On my arrival in Jerusalem, I was told by an officer of the Jordan Department of Antiquities, to my utter consternation, that the rumor had grown to such proportions that it was then proclaimed that I had personally smuggled all the Dead Sea Scrolls out of the country and carried them to the United States! In fact, he expressed amazement that I had been admitted to Jordan. When he learned the true story, he graciously arranged for a taped radio interview as a means of helping to correct the false rumors.

I was in no position in 1948 to give legal counsel to the Syrians, who must have known far more about the antiquities laws than I did. (Father Sowmy had studied law for two years, according to a close friend of his, and his brother was a customs official at Allenby Bridge.) It would have been better, of course, had they secured an export license. It needs to be remembered, however, that in the midst of Palestine's virtual state of anarchy, what was legal or illegal was by that time almost purely academic. Furthermore, respect by the natives for foreign-imposed laws in Palestine had for centuries been only partially maintained. Perhaps of greater importance is the fact that the antiquity value of the scrolls had not yet been fully established. As we were soon to discover, the "battle of the scrolls" had not yet begun. (That they were older than the *terminus ad quem* of A.D. 1700, by which the Mandate Law defined an "antiquity," no one was to deny.)

CHAPTER 11

1. Recent archeological evidence has made it clear that this particular tomb could not have been there in the time of Jesus but was cut a century or two later. The surroundings nevertheless provide an ideal place for the tourist to recapture the feeling for the New Testament story. The traditional location under the dome of the Church of the Holy Sepulchre in the Old City of Jerusalem reveals nothing of the original natural environs, and it is thus quite disappointing to the average visitor.

2. Some evidence seems to support this description. See G. L. Harding's statement in *DJD I*, p. 6. Some of the roof and sides of the interior of the cave had fallen. There was no large lower entrance at that time, apparently, but only a second, small opening. See Appendix I.

3. In an interview with Father Yusif on August 5, 1962, he said that he went to the Syrian monastery by the Jordan River that next day, while George Isha'ya stayed longer at the cave.

4. Apparently the source of their opinion was Ibrahim Sowmy (see below—Chapter 12, note

6). When I wrote the first account of these experiences that summer (*BA* XI:3), I deliberately telescoped the story told me on February 19 with items added during these later interviews in order to avoid stressing the inaccurate story told me at first. In fact, most of what appears in the third paragraph on p. 47 of that article was gleaned from these later interviews during March, 1948.

5. See *BA* XII:2 (May, 1949), pp. 35-36. It soon became apparent that any money raised would be needed for refugees. See p. 120 and Chapters 14-15. Unfortunately, the color quality of the Syrian New Testament miniatures proved to be such that I hesitated to attempt to market them. Ultimately the school was established adjacent to the Monastery, where it is functioning today, but the funds had to come largely from other sources.

6. The mystery of the missing export license continued to baffle me. I had paid little heed to the papers given me by Mr. Iliffe at the Museum, but placed them with other papers needed for customs. For years I have assumed that, on the basis of the official's claim, they gave me no export license. Recently, however, in supposedly the same package of papers that accompanied my return trip, I found the license, signed by Mr. Hamilton!

CHAPTER 12

1. The major sources for the earliest accounts are, chronologically: A. Y. Samuel, "The Purchase of the Jerusalem Scrolls," *BA* XII:2 (May, 1949), pp. 26-31; G. Lankester Harding, "A Bible Discovery," *The* (London) *Times,*August 9, 1949 (cf. *The Illustrated London News,* October 1, 1949, pp. 494-495); *DJD I*, p. 5; E. L. Sukenik, *The Dead Sea Scrolls of the Hebrew University,* Jerusalem, The Magnes Press, 1955, pp. 13-17; John M. Allegro, *The Dead Sea Scrolls,* Penguin Books, 1956, pp. 15-19; Yigael Yadin, *The Message of the Scrolls,* New York, Simon and Schuster, 1957, pp. 15-30; W. H. Brownlee, "Muhammad Ed-Deeb's Own Story of His Scroll Discovery," *JNES* XVI:4 (October, 1957), pp. 236-239; J. van der Ploeg, O. P., *The Excavations at Qumran* (tr. by Kevin Smyth, S.J.), London, Longmans Green, 1958, pp. 9-13; J. C. Trever, "When Was Qumran Cave I Discovered?" *RQ* III:1 (February, 1961), pp. 135-141; and W. H. Brownlee, "Edh-Dheeb's Story of His Scroll Discovery," *RQ* III:4 (October, 1962), pp. 483-494, and IV:3 (October, 1963), pp. 417-420.

2. The following account has been gleaned from repeated interviews with Anton D. Kiraz and other members of the Syrian Orthodox communities in Jerusalem and Bethlehem. Considerable documentation (see below) has been gathered for my files to establish the accuracy of the statements.

3. See *Life* Magazine, December 22, 1947, pp. 75-79.

4. Mr. Kiraz presented me with a large photograph taken at the party, and I examined many other related ones which he has in his possession.

5. See B. Couroyer, "Histoire d'une tribe semi-nomade de Palestine," *RB* LVIII:1 (January, 1951), pp. 75-91.

6. Ibrahim Sowmy, customs official in charge of Allenby Bridge from early 1947 to the end of March, 1948, was frequently troubled by the flow of contraband goods which Bedouins carried across the Jordan several miles south of his post. He was aware of the Ta'amireh activities in this regard, as well as those of the Sawahira and Ibn 'Ubeid tribes. This fact accounts for the origin of the association of smuggling with the early reports concerning the discovery. Apparently, however, smuggling was not the reason for the presence of the Bedouins near 'Ain Feshkha at the time of the discovery.

7. This and other information about the Bedouins has been gleaned from repeated interviews with the three Bedouins during the period from November, 1961, to July, 1964. On the evening of November 24, 1961, Anton Kiraz and J. F. Docmac of Bethlehem queried two of them for several hours and composed the account from their statements which appears as Appendix I. The following morning sixty-three questions, which the author had prepared for

the purpose, were addressed to these Bedouins; and the questions as well as their answers were tape-recorded. Several interviews followed during the next six months to secure answers to new questions which arose from an analysis of the recording. On July 29 and again on August 10, 1962, the author personally interviewed these Bedouins and their early associates at length, while Kiraz and Docmac (on July 29) served as interpreters. Still further questions have been put to the three Bedouins by Kiraz and reported in letters between October, 1962, and July, 1964.

8. Khalil Musa was the eldest of the trio and very active in subsequent events. He was interviewed twice by the writer and four times by Mr. Kiraz. He has proved most cooperative in supplying information.

The Bedouins insist that no such person as Ahmed Muhammed was involved, as mentioned in early reports. Since Ahmed is associated with edh-Dhib's name (see below) and another relative, Ahmed Abd el-Qadir (both of whom were with Jum'a when they were interviewed by G. L. Harding in 1949), it is easy to account for this error in reporting their names. Mr. Kiraz examined Jum'a's identity card (#24319, dated at Jericho January 27, 1957) to be certain of his correct name. Cf. *RQ* 15 (October, 1963), p. 418.

9. As a result of the addition of "Hassan" to Edh-Dhib's name in reports from Jerusalem during 1963 (*e.g., BA* XXVI:4 [December, 1963], p. 114, n. 4), I asked Mr. Kiraz to check Muhammed's identity card. On July 21, 1964, Kiraz visited him at his camp near el-'Azariyeh (Bethany) and examined the card, which is numbered 5941/218342 and dated in Bethlehem on October 23, 1956. There his name is clearly given as transliterated here.

10. Khalil Musa, during several interviews, stressed the fact that it was the hope for gold in the cave that motivated their searches.

11. In the November 24-25, 1961, interviews Jum'a and Muhammed mentioned that it was "three days later"; but Khalil Musa, when interviewed separately, asserted it was the next morning. Apparently it was the third day (less than two days later), for in an interview with Jum'a on January 12, 1963, Kiraz was told that the reason they delayed a day was because they had to take all their flocks to 'Ain Feshkha the next day to water them. This was an all-day task which they did every other day, Jum'a explained.

12. He demonstrated the process for me during an interview and in the presence of the other Bedouins on July 29, 1962. Cf. *RQ* 15 (October, 1963), p. 419.

13. The Bedouins' statement (Appendix I) that the covers also had handles was obviously in error, for no such covers have been found.

14. All the Bedouins interviewed, as well as Father Yusif of St. Mark's, insist on the "greenish" appearance of the cloth; but there seems to be no evidence to explain this description.

15. The excellent state of the preservation of these three MSS, in comparison with all the other MSS from Cave I, argues strongly in favor of this conclusion. See *DJD I*, p. 5, where G. L. Harding drew a similar conclusion.

16. All the Bedouins involved, as well as the merchants who have been interviewed (except Kando, see below), have agreed that only three manuscripts were involved in the original find. Yusif Saad first made contact with Muhammed and Jum'a in the spring of 1949, and a few days later Harding also interviewed them. In his first report (*The* [London] *Times*, August 9, 1949) Harding states that the Bedouins withdrew *eight* scrolls from the cave at the time of the discovery and divided them equally. In *DJD I*, p. 5, however, Harding states that the Bedouin shepherds took only three scrolls (he assumes they were 1QIs^a, 1QS and 1QpHab) and never returned to the cave for others. Both of these accounts now need to be modified on the basis of the Bedouins' own testimony (see below).

17. In the November, 1961, interviews they mentioned taking the manuscripts and the jars at that time (see Appendix I), but Jum'a and Khalil Musa stated (July 29, 1962) that they went back for the jars at a later time when they decided to try to sell the materials in Bethlehem.

18. Muhammed edh-Dhib's statement in 1956 to Najib Khouri (*JNES* XVI:4, p. 236) that in 1945 he found "some rolled leather" in a cave and left it hanging in a bag in his "house"

for "more than two years" is obviously inaccurate. See J. C. Trever, "When Was Qumran Cave I Discovered?", *RQ* 9 (February, 1961), pp. 135-141. Edh-Dhib has made no such claim in several recent interviews (see Appendix I). If the scrolls were first discovered in November, 1946, as asserted in the November, 1961, interviews, then they must have remained in the Ta'amireh camp for at least three months. That it was in March, 1947, when the scrolls were first taken to Bethlehem now seems apparent from the evidence (see below).

19. Discussions with the Bedouins about the breaks in the manuscripts proved fruitless, but they did seem confident that the cover of the Isaiah Scroll broke off and was destroyed during their handling of it. The writer possesses six very small uninscribed fragments (altogether they make an area less than a square inch) which the Syrian Metropolitan claimed had been a part of the original cover (see pp. 43-44).

20. When 1QS was broken into two parts seems impossible to determine from the evidence. Kando claimed, in an interview on August 10, 1962, that he delivered four manuscripts to St. Mark's Monastery; but in all the early interviews with the Syrians in 1948-1949 they stated that they had purchased five manuscripts, including the two parts of the 1QS. They seemed much surprised when I told them, on February 24, 1948, that the two parts belonged together (see pp. 49-51, 57). Apparently 1QSa and the 1QSb fragments were still in the cave when the other scrolls were sold. If they had been a part of the original 1QS, therefore, they must have become separated in ancient times. See p. 146.

21. The month of March is established from the combined testimony of the Ta'amirehs, Ibrahim, 'Ijha (see below), and Metropolitan Samuel. The latter stated, as early as 1948, that he first heard about the scrolls during Holy Week in 1947. To allow for the previous events to which both the Ta'amirehs and 'Ijha testify, the month of March is the most likely time for the first appearance of the scrolls in Bethlehem.

22. The fine state of preservation of the three scrolls then being peddled may account for Salahi's skepticism. The "Fourth Scroll" (1QApoc) was not yet with the others, for when I showed 'Ijha a full-sized photograph of it on August 10, 1962, he was confident that he had never seen it.

23. This date is established by the fact that the Bedouins usually went to Bethlehem on Saturday, their market day, and that it was the following week when Metropolitan Samuel first heard about the scrolls (see below).

24. During interviews with the Syrians in 1948 it was indicated that the Bedouins went first to the Bethlehem Muslim Sheikh (see *BA* XI:3, p. 47) and were told that the scrolls were probably Syriac and thus they should go to the Syrians. Apparently the "sheikh" was none other than 'Ali Subh, as Jum'a has now revealed. 'Ali Subh was interviewed by Kiraz and Docmac on May 16, 1962; being a very old man, he remembered very little about the incident. Mr. Kiraz says of the interview, "He only said that Jum'a brought to him 3 scrolls which he called 'books', one larger than the other two. They were the color of earth and not wrapped in anything when he brought them. But Jum'a had told him that originally they were wrapped in cloth and put in jars." (Quoted from letter dated May 17, 1962.)

25. In an interview with Jum'a on January 12, 1963, Mr. Kiraz learned that Khalil Musa joined the others later at Kando's shop.

26. These details were established by Metropolitan Samuel in 1949. See *BA* XII:2, pp. 26-27.

27. The interview occurred on August 10, 1962, in Bethlehem, with Mr. Kiraz serving as interpreter.

28. Although in the interviews of November 24-25, 1961, Jum'a indicated that this and a subsequent visit to the cave took place *after* the sale of the first scrolls to St. Mark's Monastery (*i.e.* after July 19, 1947), Khalil Musa and Kando (during interviews on August 10, 1962) maintained that these visits to the cave were made *prior to* the sale to St. Mark's. The fact that 1QApoc was included with the scrolls which Kando delivered to St. Mark's is a strong argument in favor of the chronology presented here, for that scroll definitely came from one of these later visits to the

cave (see note 31). When Kiraz checked this specific point with Jum'a on January 12, 1963 (his letter to me was sent that same day), Jum'a agreed that Khalil's scrolls were sold to Faidi Salahi several weeks *before* the first scrolls were sold to St. Mark's (see what follows).

29. This interview took place in Kando's shop on August 10, 1962, with Mr. Kiraz as interpreter.

30. Both Kando and Khalil Musa, during separate interviews (August 10, 1962), agreed on this statement.

31. In order to check this assumption, I showed a full-sized photograph of 1QApoc to Muhammed edh-Dhib and Jum'a (July 29, 1962), and neither could remember it. When it was shown later to Khalil Musa, he agreed that it looked like one of the manuscripts he and Isha'ya had secured on their second trip to the cave. When I showed the same picture to Kando, he was quite certain that it was one of the scrolls which he delivered to Metropolitan Samuel. He seemed to think, however, that it was one of the scrolls which Jum'a had brought on his first visit. This and other points in Kando's statements, however, indicated that he was somewhat confused about the order of the securing of those first scrolls. In view of the large number of scrolls and fragments he has handled, it is understandable that he should be vague about the earliest contacts. Since the Bedouins whom I interviewed had dealt with only a few scrolls, it seems reasonable to suppose that their memories would be more accurate in this matter. The testimonies of Jum'a, Khalil, and Kando, during separate interviews, all agreed that the first group of scrolls had not yet been sold to St. Mark's when Isha'ya made these two trips to Cave I.

32. This statement was secured from Jalil Elias 'Abu Sabha, who was a neighbor of Da'ud Musallam in 1947 and who is also a good friend of Khalil Musa. Jalil claims to have seen the scrolls when Da'ud had them. Mr. Kiraz interviewed Jalil and reported to me in a letter dated March 3, 1962. Jalil confirmed the essentials of Jum'a's story but claimed there were at least five scrolls brought to Da'ud. Two of them, he said, were destroyed when the Bedouins tried to soften them with water to open them. Mr. Kiraz and I interviewed Jalil in his summer hut on some property he owns north of Bethlehem (15 dunums with 170 fruit trees) on August 10, 1962. His description of the scrolls he saw fitted those which Dr. Sukenik secured. When I showed him the photograph of 1QApoc, he seemed certain that it was not one of those which he had seen.

33. See below, pp. 110-113. Faidi Salahi died in 1955, but Mr. Kiraz arranged for me to visit his home on August 10, 1962. There I was introduced to Mrs. Roginah Marzurqa, who had witnessed the transaction between Salahi and Sukenik. She is the widow of an orphan whom Salahi had raised, and she lived with her husband in Salahi's home at that time. She assured me that Salahi received that first group of scrolls from the Ta'amireh Bedouins during the summer of 1947. She added that Sukenik had been a frequent visitor to discuss antiquities with Salahi. She also said that she had recently sold two jars similar to those Sukenik had purchased, except they had no covers. Salahi had secured them from the Ta'amireh Bedouins, but she offered no other information about them. Allegro (*op. cit.*, p. 77; 1964 ed., p. 86) says he purchased a similar complete jar from Salahi in 1953.

34. This date was firmly established during my interviews with the St. Mark's Syrians in 1948 and 1949. See *BA* XII:2 (May, 1949), p. 27, where the Metropolitan's reference to the "first Saturday of Tammuz" would be July 5, 1947.

35. The Syrians mentioned "three Bedouins" in connection with this part of the story (see *ibid.*, p. 27), but in all recent interviews the Bedouins have maintained that there were just the two who accompanied Isha'ya to Jerusalem.

36. According to A. Y. Samuel's account (*BA* XII:2, p. 27), the Bedouins must have arrived at the Monastery *before* lunch. If so, to equate the story with Jum'a's testimony, Isha'ya must have given the Bedouins an early lunch in order for them to have arrived at St. Mark's before the Metropolitan's lunch. Though difficult to equate the two stories at this point, it is not impossible.

37. During an interview with Father Yusif on August 5, 1962, the aged priest told me that

Isha'ya talked to him about the scrolls at first, for they were close friends. It was he whom Isha'ya was seeking, he claimed, when he brought the Bedouins to the Monastery. Father Yusif was absent from the Monastery at the time, and thus Isha'ya met Father Bulos. It is difficult to evaluate this conflicting testimony, but it is included here for the record. I interviewed Father Bulos on August 6, 1962; he asserted that he did not see the Bedouins but only Isha'ya, who brought the bag of scrolls into the Monastery.

38. This encounter with a Jewish merchant has been a persistent part of the Syrian story, but it is now denied by the Bedouins. Perhaps the Arab-Israel tension might account for the reluctance of the Bedouins to mention the matter now, if it actually did occur.

39. From the early accounts it has been assumed that there was a division of the scrolls at this time and that one Bedouin did not leave his share with Kando. The Metropolitan maintained in all the early interviews that Father Bulos had been certain that there were more scrolls shown to him at the Monastery gate than the prelate finally secured (see *ibid.*, p. 27). Perhaps the Metropolitan learned about the scrolls sold to Faidi Salahi and somehow connected them with this part of the story.

40. Metropolitan Samuel was very confident (in interviews during February and March, 1949) that two weeks elapsed before he finally secured the scrolls (see *ibid.*, p. 27).

41. Father Sowmy, in the presence of the Metropolitan late in March, 1948 (according to notes I made at the time), told me that Kando delivered the scrolls after paying the Bedouins their share. Both Jum'a and Kando now have testified that this is the way it happened. (Cf. *ibid.*, pp. 27-28.)

42. See J. van der Ploeg, *op. cit.*, p. 13. The Metropolitan stated that it was the last week of August (see *BA* XII:2, p. 28); but on the basis of the photographs he took at St. Mark's, van der Ploeg was able to establish the fact that his visit was in late July.

43. He published a book (in 1942) about ancient Syrian monastic life.

44. The 1QApoc Scroll was not included. See van der Ploeg, *op. cit.*, p. 11.

45. He died December 30, 1960.

46. *Ibid.*, pp. 9-13. Personal letters from van der Ploeg, which I received in late 1948, further confirm his story.

47. The evidence from reports of the Hebrew University and an affidavit prepared by Mr. Kiraz establishes this date for Dr. Brown's visit. A. Y. Samuel thought (*BA* XII:2, p. 30) it might have occurred in October.

48. Yigael Yadin, *op. cit.*, p. 25.

49. About October 1, according to evidence presented to me by Mr. Kiraz, the Metropolitan referred to this offer as they discussed another problem (see below). On several occasions during 1948 and 1949 the Metropolitan mentioned to me that Mr. Sassun had made ever-increasing offers, but the amounts were never indicated.

50. The title reference to "Antioch" is still retained, despite his residence in Homs. He died in 1957. More recently the Patriarchate was moved to Damascus.

51. I have checked the passports of both the Metropolitan and Mr. Kiraz (in February, 1949, and April, 1958, respectively) to determine the accuracy of these terminal dates.

52. This account of Anton Kiraz's claim to partnership with the Metropolitan, through a typically Near Eastern gentleman's agreement, is greatly condensed here to provide only details which I deem essential to the history of the Dead Sea Scrolls. The entire account, however, has been carefully documented and thoroughly checked from evidences in Mr. Kiraz's possession, which I have fully examined during many hours of cross-examination. It is recorded in detail in an affidavit, sworn to, signed, and notarized in my presence in Jerusalem, Jordan, on May 12, 1958. The original copy of the notarized affidavit is in my possession. See pp. 137-138.

53. Mr. Stephan died in May, 1949.

54. The *Haftarot* are selections from the Prophets, organized for reading following the Torah readings each sabbath.

55. T. Wechsler, "The Revealed Genizah and the Hidden Genizah," *Ha'olam,* December, 1949 (in Hebrew). I am grateful to Drs. Carl Kraeling and Millar Burrows for providing me with an English translation of this article. Anyone who has worked intimately with 1QIs^a and 1QS soon becomes aware, while reading his statements, that what Wechsler describes as a *Haftarot* scroll is none other than 1QIs^a itself, which his memory, dimmed by passing time and the troubles he experienced in 1948, confused with some features of 1QS. Numerous blank lines, used to indicate paragraph or chapter divisions, as well as many marginal markings, are found on 1QIs^a. What he calls "the scroll of Isaiah" in his article, on the other hand, clearly describes 1QS. See J. C. Trever, "The 'Suppressed' Scroll of the Haftarot," *JQR* XLI (July, 1950), pp. 71-81.

56. See his son's excellent account: Yigael Yadin, *The Message of the Scrolls*, New York, Simon and Schuster, 1957, Part I. Dr. Sukenik died in 1952.

57. The Palestine Archaeological Advisory Board was established in 1920/21 as a provision of the Antiquities Ordinance of the Mandate Government.

58. See G. L. Harding, "The Dead Sea Scrolls," *PEQ*, July—October, 1949, p. 115.

59. Section 6 of the 1929 Antiquities Ordinance reads: "Any person who discovers an antiquity without being furnished with a license to excavate in accordance with Section 9 of this Ordinance shall forthwith give notice of his discovery to the nearest officer of the Department, or to the nearest District Officer or Assistant District Officer, and shall take any other action that may be prescribed by Regulation under this Ordinance."

60. They were the Isaiah Scroll (1QIs^a), the Habakkuk Pesher (1QpHab) and one of the two pieces of the Manual of Discipline (1QS).

61. Mr. Kiraz is not quite certain whether this offer was made then or at the beginning of the next meeting. According to Sukenik's various reports, he never did make an offer.

62. This information was checked with Mr. Tannourji in March, 1958, in the same office, which is now in Israel. On April 26 I heard the same story from Mr. Kiraz in his home in Bethlehem, Jordan. The independent testimony of the two Syrians agreed in almost every detail. Mr. Tannourji also testified to Kiraz's references to "his partner." A. Y. Samuel gives a quite different account of these matters in *BA* XII:2, p. 31.

63. When I prepared the article for the May, 1949, *BA* for Metropolitan Samuel, he assured me that it was "late February" when these events occurred. He offered as evidence the claim that I had already given him a set of photographs, which he offered to Sukenik instead. At the time this seemed adequate evidence, and therefore I did not challenge him, despite the fact that Dr. Sukenik had insisted on the dates February 4-6 that same morning in New York, where I interviewed him. That the Metropolitan's chronology was in error, there is now no doubt. See pp. 125, 126.

64. On March 19, 1948, the Metropolitan mentioned to me, according to my notes, that Father Sowmy had been "quite upset" over the negotiations with Dr. Sukenik (cf. pp. 89-90).

CHAPTER 13

1. He became the Patriarch in 1957, following the death of Aphram I.

2. The basic text of the Old Testament, used for centuries in schools and synagogues, is called "Masoretic," after the Masoretes, a school of rabbis who were the preservers of the textual tradition. Originating with the efforts of Rabbi Akiba in the early second century, the work reached its zenith in the school of Ben Asher in the ninth and tenth centuries A.D.

3. The Committee for the Revised Standard Version of the Bible adopted fourteen minor readings, attested by this scroll, during their meetings in 1949 to 1951. These readings can be identified by the expression "One ancient MS" in the RSV footnotes to Isaiah.

4. He died before the full appreciation of the antiquity of the scrolls had been felt in England.

5. My article and the first installment of Dr. Burrows' collation appeared in the October issue of *BASOR*. Dr. Brownlee's translation was in the December issue. My article on dating the scrolls through paleography and the second installment of Dr. Burrows' collation appeared in the February, 1949, issue.

6. M*e*gilloth G*e*nuzoth I, Jerusalem, Bialik Foundation, 1948.

7. His copying must have been done in haste, for there were at least twenty-seven errors in his published transcription, most of them omissions of features peculiar to the ancient scroll.

8. This story has been skillfully elaborated in Dr. Burrows' splendid book, *The Dead Sea Scrolls*, New York, Viking Press, 1955.

9. He left Jerusalem early in November to go to Beirut, where the scrolls had been in a bank vault since March 25. See p. 94.

CHAPTER 14

1. On July 27, 1948, the Metropolitan wrote: "I am glad to let you know that after you left Palestine I was able to get in my possession some other manuscripts, but their date is not so far old as the first ones." In his letter sent from Homs, Syria, on September 14, he mentioned meeting Dr. Sellers in Amman, and added: "The other manuscripts that I bought lately are in the same language but are not as old as the others and they are written on parchments, from the old testament." On December 22 he wrote: " . . . I expect to come to the States at the beginning of January, probably around the 9th of it. I will bring with me the old and the newly discovered manuscripts. . . . "

2. At the time I assumed that it was one of the Monastery people, but see footnote 16.

3. At the time, he mentioned November as the date of this visit to the cave; but Dr. Sellers had already seen at least some of the fragments on September 1 (see p. 121). During an interview on July 29, 1949, Metropolitan Samuel agreed that it could have been a little earlier than November when the fragments were secured. He mentioned his "poor memory for dates." According to Dr. Sellers, moreover, the Metropolitan had told him that Bedouins had brought the fragments as samples of two other manuscripts they were offering to sell. A study of the fragments makes it very clear that they had not been recently separated from other manuscripts. The fragments represent a complete unit which apparently had existed from ancient times in about the form in which I first saw them. There were no modern breaks anywhere. If the Bedouins had other parts of the same manuscripts, therefore, they would already have been separated at the time they were found. It is very doubtful, furthermore, that the Bedouins would have recognized these as parts of other scrolls which they might have found. That story, therefore, does not appear to be accurate. No such manuscripts have since appeared. What the Metropolitan told me in February, 1949, adequately fits all the evidence.

4. Columns 50-53 were rephotographed at that time. Their higher contrast can be observed in *The Dead Sea Scrolls of St. Mark's Monastery,* edited by Dr. M. Burrows for the A.S.O.R. in 1950.

5. Most scholars date the composition of Daniel in the early half of the second century B.C., sometime before 165 B.C., on the basis of internal evidence.

6. In 1952 a fragment of Ecclesiastes was discovered in Cave IV and probably could claim this distinction with more certainty.

7. This fragment was published in color in *The Interpreter's Bible*, Vol. XII (Nashville, Abingdon, 1957), p. 635, with the permission of the Jordan Department of Antiquities. The reproduction failed, for some reason, to preserve the rich black quality of the script on the original.

8. For a translation of the entire piece, see M. Burrows, *More Light on the Dead Sea Scrolls*, New York, The Viking Press, 1958, p. 399; also a French translation by J. T. Milik in *DJD I*, pp. 152-155. Jean Carmignac has recently suggested (*RQ* 14 [4:2], pp. 271-276) that unit "d" belongs to the lower right of unit "c" (he considers the first line of "d" to be the beginning of line 5 of

unit "c"), thus providing parts of the right half of the first column. Although I considered this possibility while assembling the fragments, I have continued to entertain some doubts because a spacing problem exists on the lower lines of the two pieces. It has not been possible to check the original fragments for this point.

9. Proof that all these fragments came from the same scroll cave is established by the fact that one fragment (1Q34) found by the excavators during February, 1949, fits perfectly into a break along the upper edge of the folded fragment which formed layers four and five of the matted mass (unit "d"). Obviously written in the same script and kind of leather, the *shin* and *resh* on its bottom line complete the word *'shr* in the Prayer Scroll fragment. See *DJD I*, Plate XXXI:34, and p. 152. See below (Chapter 16, note 2).

10. In their introduction to the preliminary publication of this scroll, Drs. N. Avigad and Y. Yadin say, "The condition of the scroll was certainly not improved by the fact that for seven years it was shifted about from place to place, without any particular care being devoted to it." (*A Genesis Apocryphon*, Jerusalem, The Magnes Press, 1956, p. 12.) On the contrary, the scroll was given great care, at least after February, 1948. Between March, 1948, and April, 1949, there was no evidence of further deterioration, except for the slightly longer cracks which made possible my removal of the larger fragment. After my work on it in April, 1949, it was most carefully preserved in its special, cotton-padded box. A detailed comparison of the photographs I made of the scroll in Jerusalem in February, 1948, with those published in the abovementioned volume reveal only very minor evidences of additional deterioration.

11. This measurement included the previously removed fragment (see pp. 81, 84), which was then returned to its former place.

12. See J. C. Trever, "Identification of the Aramaic Fourth Scroll from 'Ain Feshkha," *BASOR* 115 (October, 1949), pp. 8-10. See now N. Avigad and Y. Yadin, *op. cit.*, pp. 16-18.

13. Thus a straight hairline can be seen across the middle of Columns XIX-XXXIX in the A.S.O.R. publication of 1QIs[a].

14. At least three recent books by scholars who have been close to the Dead Sea Scroll story have telescoped this "excavation" into the 1947 visits to the cave: John M. Allegro, *The Dead Sea Scrolls*, Baltimore, Penguin Books, 1956, p. 18 (cf. also pp. 25-27); F. M. Cross, *The Ancient Library of Qumran*, Doubleday Anchor Books, 1961, p. 7; and J. van der Ploeg, *op. cit.*, p. 15. They have apparently relied on G. L. Harding's statement in *DJD I*, p. 5; but cf. pp. 104-106 and Appendix I. That several visits were made to the cave in 1947 and at least three produced scrolls is, of course, now known to be a fact.

15. He saw them on September 1, 1948, the day the Metropolitan visited the American School in Jerusalem. On seeing a photograph of the matted mass of fragments in the fall of 1949, however, Dr. Sellers did not recall seeing it in the box at that time. His written statement at the time implies it was there (see p. 124).

16. The evidence seems clear that most of these fragments, if not all of them, were secured by Isha'ya during visits to the cave, shortly after the establishment of the second truce on July 18, 1948. According to Syrian testimony, Isha'ya had been gatekeeper and messenger for the Monastery. (In my files is an early 1949 photograph of the Monastery personnel, showing him in the garb of a monk.) In view of the strong statements I made to Metropolitan Samuel before leaving Jerusalem on April 5, 1948, it is likely that he would have cautioned Isha'ya then about "excavating" (see pp. 99, 125). Apparently after the prelate left Jerusalem for the United States in early November, 1948, Isha'ya and Kando pursued a more aggressive approach to the cave by actual "excavation." At that time Isha'ya was living at the Syrian monastery near the Jordan River, within easy reach of the cave, according to Mr. Kiraz, who had also taken refuge there for a few months.

17. *DJD I*, pp. 150-155.

18. The historic fact that the Qumran cave area did not become officially a part of Jordan until December, 1948, lends technical support to his position.

CHAPTER 15

1. A copy of the Bay Psalm Book, which was purchased at auction by Yale University for $151,000, seems to have been the next highest price paid for a book.

2. See Harry M. Orlinsky, "Studies in the St. Mark's Isaiah Scroll," *JBL* LXIX (June, 1950), pp. 149-166; John C. Trever, "Isaiah 43:19 According to the First Isaiah Scroll (DSIa)," *BASOR* 121 (February, 1951), pp. 13-16; and notes in *BASOR* 123 (October, 1951), pp. 33-35; 124 (December, 1951), p. 29; and 126 (April, 1952), pp. 26-27.

3. "The Dead Sea Scrolls," *PEQ,* July—October, 1949, pp. 112-116. See above, Chapter 10, note 10.

4. The Rev. John Malak, prompted by the Metropolitan, on August 31, 1950, sent me a detailed account of his interviews with both Kando and Isha'ya regarding their claims. A "gift" of $4,000 was made to each of them, according to the United States Tax Court decision (36 T.C. 641, p. 5). Kando, in an interview on August 10, 1962, said that Isha'ya, who received the money, absconded with the total amount and has since disappeared.

5. Dating of the deposit on the basis of the pottery, which was considered to be "late Hellenistic," was too early, as subsequent evidence was to prove.

6. A by-product of atomic research, this age-determination process was developed at the University of Chicago by means of sensitive Geiger counters which would measure the radioactive intensity of "Carbon-14" in ancient organic matter. See Donald Collier, "New Radiocarbon Method for Dating the Past," *BA* XIV:I (February, 1951), pp. 25-29.

7. Dr. Solomon Zeitlin of Dropsie College, Philadelphia, remained adamant and vociferous as a spokesman for a medieval dating of all the documents, and he refused to accept the evidence relating the scrolls to the cave. In England Dr. G. R. Driver of Oxford and Dr. J. L. Teicher of Cambridge also resisted a pre-Christian dating, but less vigorously.

8. The two main requirements were: (1) that the Daniel (and other) fragments be returned to Jerusalem ("adequate compensation" for them was promised); and (2) that the removal of the four major scrolls from the country be legalized by means of obtaining the proper export license from the Jordan government.

From a strictly legal standpoint, the Jordan government could not press a claim for expropriation of the four scrolls (as Lebanon had successfully done in one case some years before), for the following reasons: (1) the scrolls had been purchased when Palestine was under the British Mandate and were sent to Beirut on March 25, 1948; (2) even though the Mandate Government's antiquities laws had been technically violated at that time, by March, 1948, the administration of many Mandate laws was in a state of chaos, and anarchy existed in Palestine; (3) not until December 1, 1948, when that portion of Palestine was joined with Trans-Jordan to form the "Hashemite Kingdom of the Jordan," was effective government established which could administer the antiquities laws which had continued to be operative in Trans-Jordan; and (4) G. L. Harding, Director of Antiquities for Jordan, in his letter of January 23, 1950, categorically denied any claim of the Jordan government to rights to the four scrolls in the Metropolitan's possession.

9. Apparently the man died, about 1959, and the manuscript is believed to have been destroyed.

10. See J. C. Trever, "Studies in the Problem of Dating the Dead Sea Scrolls," *Proceedings of the American Philosophical Society* 97:2 (April 30, 1953), pp. 184-193; and the revision of the same article, "The Problem of Dating the Dead Sea Scrolls," *Annual Report of the Smithsonian Institution,*1953, pp. 425-435.

11. Dr. Solomon Schechter in 1897 secured some 100,000 fragments, codices, and scrolls from this vast forgotten storeroom in the synagogue of Old Cairo. About 2,000 of the oldest and best fragments have been mounted in glass and carefully filed for easy access.

12. I personally examined the document during a visit (see p. 141) with the Metropolitan early in December, 1951 (see p. 141), and queried him about some of its statements.

13. I was then teaching at Morris Harvey College in Charleston, West Virginia.

14. For a detailed account of the negotiations, see Y. Yadin, *The Message of the Scrolls,* New York, Simon and Schuster, 1957, chap. 3.

15. It is interesting to compare this amount with the price paid in 1949 by the Jordan Department of Antiquities when negotiating with Kando for the remainder of the Cave I fragments—one dinar ($2.80) per square centimeter of inscribed surface. The Isaiah Scroll contains almost 15,100 square centimeters, the "Manual of Discipline" about 3,700, and the "Habakkuk Commentary" a few more than 1,250—a total of 20,050 square centimeters of inscribed surface. Figuring the then-unopened "Fourth Scroll" at $50,000, the three scrolls thus brought the Metropolitan almost $10 per square centimeter, or about three and one-half times as much as the highest price paid for all the other cave scrolls. In the light of the prelate's original payment of $97.20 in 1947, his capital gain was astronomical. In August, 1962, Metropolitan Samuel told me he had paid federal income taxes of about $87,000 on the amount received.

According to the tax decision filed by the Tax Court of the United States on June 30, 1961 (36 T.C. 641), Metropolitan Samuel had amended his trust agreement on October 7, 1952, to provide himself $30,000 cash and $10,000 per year for life. The judge pointed out that, on the basis of life insurance actuarial figures, the total amount received for the scrolls would be exhausted during the Metropolitan's lifetime. The amount received, therefore, was declared personal income and subject to tax. Despite the fact that the trust had been further amended (date not given) to eliminate the annual payments to the Metropolitan, the decision, when appealed by him, was upheld by the Federal Court of Appeals on June 21, 1962 (306 *Federal Reporter,* 2nd Series, pp. 682-689).

CHAPTER 16

1. Phylacteries (called *tephillin* by the Jews) were small leather boxes which were attached to the forehead and arms while morning prayers were recited. They contained minute scrolls inscribed with quotations from the Torah. See Deuteronomy 6:8.

2. The excavators recovered fragments of 1QM and 1QH, which had been among the 1947 finds. They also found small pieces of the larger Deuteronomy fragment, part of which was reported to have come from Isha'ya and part from Kando. Also found by the excavators was a small fragment of the Prayer Scroll (1Q34), larger fragments of which had apparently been secured by Isha'ya during the summer of 1948. A small piece of 1QSb (Col. II) also was sifted from the debris. Larger fragments of this latter document had been secured by Yusif Saad from Kando, along with fragments from 1QIs[b] and some from the "Genesis Apocryphon" (1QApoc). Thus the discovery of all these fragments in the excavation confirmed the fact that the scrolls dug up in 1947, the fragments secured by Isha'ya during the summer of 1948, and those purchased by Yusif Saad from Kando in 1950 all came from Cave I. Lacking only were fragments from 1QIs[a], 1QpHab, and 1QS to confirm positively the entire original discovery. The circumstances of the discovery of these three (see Appendix I) seem to account for the absence of fragments from them. There is no longer any reason to doubt the relationship of these three to the others, however, especially in view of the fact that 1QS, 1QSa, and 1QSb were all written by the same scribe on the same kind of leather. It is reasonable to believe that these are all part of a single scroll. How to account for the separation of 1QSa and 1QSb from 1QS, however, remains a mystery.

3. Technically they are called *pesharim,* from the frequent occurrence of the word *pesher,* meaning "interpretation."

4. He is now the curator in charge of the Museum.

5. This excavation seems to have been organized by Isha'ya and Kando almost immediately after Metropolitan Samuel left Jerusalem (ultimately for the United States) early in November, 1948.

6. It is graphically described by John Allegro in *The Dead Sea Scrolls,* Baltimore, Penguin Books, Inc., 1956, pp. 25-34 (second edition, 1964, pp. 27-36).

7. These parts are now labeled 1QSa and 1QSb, since their contents do not seem to relate directly to the eleven original columns of that scroll. The script on all of these is identical. These parts may have been attached at one time to the larger scroll at one end or the other, where sewing holes clearly indicate that there had been additional sheets of leather.

8. All these and the artifacts from the cave have been published in D. Barthélemy and J. T. Milik, *Discoveries in the Judaean Desert I,* Oxford, The Clarendon Press, 1955.

9. Allegro (*op. cit.,* p. 19; 1964 ed., p. 21) relates this part of the story in connection with his account of Sukenik's purchase of scrolls late in 1947. It seems apparent that Allegro is in error in placing this event so early. There is no conceivable reason for Kando to have become frightened at that time; it was to be many months before the authorities began their inquiries about the scrolls. Furthermore, the scrolls' antiquity and value had not yet been established. There is no evidence that Kando had any scrolls in his possession late in 1947. Faidi Salahi seems to have had whatever scrolls and fragments had been secured from the cave about that time, and he was dealing with Dr. Sukenik. In early 1949, after his participation in, and perhaps leadership of, the November, 1948, clandestine excavation, Kando would have had considerable reason to take such fatal "precautions." Allegro also errs on the same page in stating that Sukenik dealt with Kando.

10. For details of his adventure, see F. M. Cross, *The Ancient Library of Qumran,* Doubleday Anchor Book, 1961, pp. 15-19.

11. Results of these discoveries have now been published in French in *Discoveries in the Judaean Desert II,* Oxford, The Clarendon Press, 1961.

12. As late as July, 1956, the Bedouins brought in and attempted to sell fragments from this cave.

13. For the story, see F. M. Cross, *op. cit.,* pp. 26-47.

14. One of the best summary lists of the published fragments from this and the other caves is found in G. Vermes, *Discovery in the Judean Desert,* New York, Desclée Company, 1956, pp. 24-28. See also M. Burrows, *More Light on the Dead Sea Scrolls,* pp. 407-409.

15. Results of the discoveries in Caves II, III, V-X have now been published in *Discoveries in the Judaean Desert of Jordan III,* Oxford, The Clarendon Press, 1962.

16. See John Allegro, *The Treasure of the Copper Scroll,* Garden City, Doubleday & Co., 1960. He is convinced that the scroll represents genuine treasure, but other scholars are equally convinced that it represents mere folklore.

17. For a vivid reconstruction of that community life, see A. D. Tushingham, "The Men Who Hid the Dead Sea Scrolls," *The National Geographic Magazine,* December, 1958, pp. 785-808. The archeological discoveries at Khirbet Qumran have been well summarized and evaluated by R. de Vaux in his Schweich lectures before the British Academy (1959): *L'Archeologie et les Manuscrits de la Mer Morte,* London, Oxford University Press, 1961.

18. See Dr. Yadin's reports in *The Biblical Archaeologist* XXIV:2 (May, 1961), pp. 34-50; and XXIV:3 (September, 1961), pp. 86-95.

19. See J. A. Sanders, "The Scroll of Psalms (11QPss) From Cave 11: A Preliminary Report," *BASOR* 165 (February, 1962), pp. 11-15.

20. See his published results: "The Scroll of Ezekiel From the Eleventh Qumran Cave," *RQ* IV:1 (January, 1963), pp. 11-28.

21. See preliminary report, F. M. Cross, "The Discovery of the Samaria Papyri," *BA* XXVI:4 (December, 1963), pp. 109-121.

22. See Y. Yadin, "Masada: Herod's Fortress-Palace and the Zealots' Last Stand," *Illustrated London News,* October 31, 1964, pp. 693-697.

CHAPTER 17

1. These were a group of papyrus manuscripts which a collector by the name of A. Chester Beatty purchased in Cairo, about 1930, and among which an important Septuagint manuscript of Numbers and Deuteronomy (963) from the second century A.D. was found.

2. For a detailed presentation of these contributions, see F. M. Cross, *The Ancient Library of Qumran,* Doubleday Anchor Book, 1961, chap. 4.

3. It was the publication of Edmund Wilson's article, "The Scrolls From the Dead Sea," in the *New Yorker* Magazine (May, 1955), that catapulted the controversy from sober scholarship to a popular topic of discussion.

4. Two valuable and sober treatments of the subject are: Krister Stendahl (ed.), *The Scrolls and the New Testament* (New York, Harper & Row, 1957), and Millar Burrows, *More Light on the Dead Sea Scrolls,* Part II, New York, The Viking Press, 1958.

5. A detailed description of the community, its organization, beliefs, and customs, is not yet possible; for there are many obscurities yet to be solved in the key manuscripts. One of the best treatments of the subject is Millar Burrows, *Dead Sea Scrolls,* Part IV, and his *More Light on the Dead Sea Scrolls,* Part VII.

6. Dr. Samuel Sandmel, Provost of the Hebrew Union College-Jewish Institute of Religion, articulated this same approach with scintillating acumen in his presidential address to the Society of Biblical Literature, December 27, 1961. Entitled "Parallelomania," it was published in the *Journal of Biblical Literature,* March, 1962, pp. 1-13.

7. Compare, however, 1QS X:17-18, "I will not return to a man the recompense of evil. With good will I pursue a man. For the judgment of every living being is with God, and it is he who will make each man's recompense complete."

8. It was the less rigid and more broadly focused faith of some Pharisees which managed to survive Roman oppression and eventuate in modern Judaism.

9. Jesus quoted here from Isaiah 29:13, which in the Isaiah Scroll (1QIs^a) differs a little from the traditional Masoretic Hebrew. The New Testament, which is followed here, uses a Greek reading that differs from both Hebrew versions as well as the Septuagint Greek usually found in such quotations. Thus four different textual variants are known for this verse and suggest that it was quoted freely. Jesus was using it obviously in criticism of the Pharisees' emphasis upon the traditional interpretations of the Law (*Halakhoth*), to which they gave divine authority.

10. Some of these similarities may have crept into Christianity after the demise of the Qumran community in A.D. 68, for it is quite likely that some of the Essenes would have been attracted to the Christian gospel. Furthermore, much of the New Testament was composed after A.D. 68.

11. The last three paragraphs have been adapted from the author's article, "The Qumran Covenanters and Their Use of Scripture," *The Personalist,* 39 (Spring, 1958), pp. 135-137.

APPENDIX I

1. The evidence from the interviews would allow for a date as late as January or February, 1947.

INDEX

INDEX

Qumran cemetery, 148, 151
Qumran community, 149 ff., 155, 159 ff., 173,
    189
Qumran, Khirbet, 147 ff., 153 f., 156, 159,
    176 ff., 204
Qumran, Wadi, 147 ff., 155

Raad, C., 68, 73, 75 f., 82, 87, 93, 190
Ramawi, Abdullah, 18, 26, 30, 186
Ras Feshkha, 102
Revised Standard Version of Bible, 118, 186,
    199
Romans, 150, 153 f., 173
Rule of the Congregation (1QSa), 163

Saad Yusif, 10, 146, 176 f., 195, 203
St. Mark's Monastery, 10, 14, 21, 29 f., 32, 75,
    83, 87, 90 f., 97 f., 101 f., 106 ff., 118,
    120 f., 123, 137, 143, 146, 170, 174 f.,
    186 f., 196 f.
St. Mark's scrolls
    discovery, 25, 104, 106, 169 f., 174, 195
    exhibited, 138, 140 f., 177
    preservation, 141
    purchase, 25, 75 f., 106 f., 170
    safety of, 58, 67, 88, 90 f., 94
    sale of, 106 f., 112 f., 120, 142 f., 175
    title, problem of, 136 f., 140 ff., 202
    trust agreement, 141, 203
    see also Manual of Discipline, Genesis
        Apocryphon, Habakkuk Commentary,
        Isaiah Scroll "A"
Salahi, Faidi, 105 f., 110 f., 112, 170 f., 174 f.,
    196 ff., 204
Samaritan manuscripts, 154, 180, 204
Samaritan Pentateuch, 157
Samuel, Athanasius Y., 10, 32 f., 40 ff., 57,
    71 f., 74 ff., 80, 87 ff., 92 ff., 98 f., 102,
    106 ff., 112 f., 118 ff., 123 ff., 132 f.,
    135 ff., 140 f., 143, 170, 174 ff., 187,
    190 ff., 196 ff.
Samuel fragments (1Q), 146; (4Q), 157
Sanders, J. A., 153, 180, 204
Sandmel, Samuel, 205
Sassun, 109 f., 198

Sawahira Bedouins, 194 f.
Schechter, Solomon, 140
Sectarian document, see Manual of Discipline
Sellers, Ovid, 120 f., 123 f., 132 f., 136, 176,
    200 f.
Septuagint, 157, 205
Shahin, Khali Eskander, 105 ff., 136, 138, 146,
    148, 170, 174, 176 f., 196 ff., 201 ff.
Shamoun, George Isha'ya, 97, 105 ff., 121, 136,
    138, 170, 174 ff., 193, 197, 201, 203 f.
Songs of Thanksgiving Scroll (1QH), 111, 130,
    203
Song of the Sabbath Sacrifice, 154, 180
Sons of Darkness, 159 ff., 164
Sons of Light, 159, 164
Souma, Aziz, 185
Sowmy, Butrus, 14, 19, 21 f., 32 f., 40, 42, 44 f.,
    57, 59, 74 ff., 80, 88 ff., 94, 98, 113, 116,
    118, 123, 125, 175 f., 183 f., 186, 193
Sowmy, Ibrahim, 21 f., 84, 103, 116, 185, 193 f.
Sowmy, Karim, 116, 184
Stendahl, Krister, 205
Stephan, Stephan Hanna, 107, 110
Stewart, Bishop, 96, 113, 183, 185
Sukenik, Eliezer L., 89 f., 102, 106 f., 110 ff.,
    117 f., 120, 125 f., 141, 143, 171, 175 f.,
    179, 187, 191 ff., 197, 199, 204
Syriac New Testament, 92, 98, 141, 194

Ta'amireh Bedouins, 102 ff., 111, 147 f., 153,
    170, 174, 177 ff., 194 ff.
Tamimi, Anwar, 59, 65, 84, 86, 89, 91 f., 96,
    98
Tannourji, Malak, 112 f., 187, 199
Teacher of community, 159 f., 163, 165
Teicher, J. L., 118, 202
Testament of Levi fragments (1Q), 146, 158
Testament of Naphtali (4Q), 158
Timotheus, 174
Tischendorf, Constantine, 24, 34, 47, 94
Tobit fragments (4Q), 158
Torah codex (Or 4445), 23, 184 f.
Torah scrolls, 58, 123 f., 189
Tushingham, A. D., 204